SPINOFF

**A PERSONAL HISTORY
OF THE INDUSTRY
THAT CHANGED THE WORLD**

SPINOFF

A PERSONAL HISTORY
OF THE INDUSTRY
THAT CHANGED THE WORLD

CHARLES E. SPORCK
WITH RICHARD L. MOLAY

CONTENTS

SO MUCH HAD HAPPENED

"Spinoff" is a word I first heard in California's San Francisco Peninsula when some brave individuals left their well-established employer to form a new company in the same industry. The word is so descriptive of the process that it hardly needs additional explanation. I guess it has some relationship to the cosmic view of galaxies and the formation of new clusters of mass. Back in the middle of the 20th century, almost before there was such a thing as the semiconductor industry, when capital was difficult to obtain and technology seemed to be the exclusive property of a few large corporations, the economic environment that nurtured spin-offs had not developed. And then, suddenly, there was an explosion of new ventures.

New microelectronic devices were not the only result of spinoffs. A whole new way of financing and nurturing new ventures was born, and continues to encourage such developments to this day.

I was part of that exciting era and I think the story is worth telling. And as I contemplate the beginning of the spinoff trend, the first name that comes to mind is that of Dr. Robert N. Noyce.

Bob Noyce, generally credited as the inventor of the integrated circuit, had been my boss and then my friend for more than 30 years. We were both young men when we first met, and through all the decades that followed we still saw each other as we had been when we were in our late 20s and early 30s. The same was true for dozens of other participants in the development of the semiconductor industry. We worked hard, we played hard and, to ourselves, we remained ageless.

And then Bob died on June 4, 1990. There was a memorial service in Austin, Texas, where the industrywide organization Noyce presided over, SEMATECH, was located. I was called upon in my capacity as Sematech chairman to make a few remarks, and as I looked around the room at hundreds of attendees, many of whom I had known for decades, I realized that none of us was getting any younger. The hair was thinner and what there was, was gray. The eyeglass corrections were stronger. The waistlines were thicker. Some were having trouble getting around. A few who might have attended had already passed on.

My body was in Texas but my thoughts were focused on California's *Silicon Valley*. There were so many questions I should have asked Bob Noyce while he was alive. The development of the silicon transistor, and then integrated circuits and computer chips, is a story with mingled elements of science, engineering and human personality factors. The growth of the semiconductor industry was a drama with all the elements of a major sports contest. Unprecedented wealth was created almost overnight in some cases and everyone had a story to tell.

Who would be next? How many of the others would pass on, leaving their perspectives unexpressed and their stories untold? A very rich part of my life had been lived in the semiconductor industry and I had an opportunity to work with exciting people. I want others now in the semiconductor industry to know what it was like at the dawn of the solid state electronics era. This book represents an effort to capture as much of the anecdotal information as I could.

Many journalists, fascinated by the rapid development of semiconductors and the fortunes that were made in the industry, have done their best to tell this story, but few of them were actually there, in the middle of the action. Their accounts tend to focus on benchmark events and familiar names. I felt that important facts were missing from the books and TV specials that dealt with Silicon Valley. I wanted present-day semiconductor engineers and scientists to know more about the history of their specialty.

During the several years leading up to 1999, I contacted many of those who had been instrumental in the genesis and growth of Silicon Valley. I sat down with each person, turned on a tape recorder and did my best to stimulate conversation. The result was a library of more than 50 such interviews on tape, some lasting two hours or more. Those tapes, and my personal experiences, form the basis of this work. I have not made direct reference to everyone I interviewed, but every contribution of fact and anecdote helped make this project come alive.

As this effort evolved, something more than a simple history emerged. There are priceless lessons to be learned about the management of change and the characteristics of rapid technological development. This is a story of money, too. Where it came from, how it was used, what it meant. I've also included a few details of the technology as it developed, because other accounts I've seen tend to ignore that side of the story.

More than anything else, however, this is really a story of unique individuals and their personalities as seen from my own perspective. The interpretations herein are strictly my own. If there are errors of fact, I made the errors; If there are observations of a personal or critical nature, I included them because I feel they are as much a part of history as the technology itself; if something important was left out, I apologize for the omission.

I wish I had started this project while Bob Noyce was still alive. He would have added a lot to the history retold herein. He loomed very large in my life, and more than anyone else he was instrumental in whatever success I managed to achieve. It is no overstatement to say that Bob Noyce made Silicon Valley what it is today.

Here, then, is how it all appeared to me. And it begins back in the mid-1950s when there were no semiconductor companies in Silicon Valley. As a matter of fact, there was no such place name as Silicon Valley.

I hope you find the story as fascinating as it was to me while I was an active participant.

Charlie Sporck

CHARLES E. SPORCK

CHAPTER ONE

THE BEGINNING:
AN ECCENTRIC GENIUS

Dr. William Bradford Shockley and His Laboratory

Second-guessing history is a risky undertaking. There might have been a good mass-production process for double-diffused silicon transistors without the leadership of Dr. William Bradford Shockley, and there might have been the follow-on developments that led to today's computer chips and mass-storage, solid state memories. There even might have been a thriving semi-

Dr. William Shockley

conductor industry in the place we now call Silicon Valley on California's San Francisco Peninsula without the pioneering efforts of Shockley.

Perhaps. But the genesis of all of those enormously important developments can be traced directly to the activities of a brilliant man who invented his own rules as he went along. Shockley started the revolution that led to integrated circuits. Every detail of his career is fascinating. Even the failure of his own semiconductor company is important, because it brought together those who would go on to make history.

William Bradford Shockley, born in London on February 13, 1910 and died August 12, 1989 at his house on the Stanford University campus, was a genius. His father (also named William,) was a mining engineer and his mother Mary, (nee Bradford,) had served as a deputy mineral surveyor in Nevada. He graduated from California Institute of Technology in 1932 and then got his Ph.D. at Massachusetts Institute of Technology in 1936. There didn't seem to be any detail of chemistry, math, engineering or physics that he hadn't mastered.

During World War II, Shockley was director of research for the antisubmarine warfare operations research group of the U.S. Navy. After the war he served as director of transistor physics research at Bell Telephone Laboratories.

He was one of three research scientists (and the group leader,) at Bell Laboratories now given credit for the invention of the transistor, which actually occurred in 1947 and was revealed to the general public in 1948. The others were John Bardeen and Walter Brattain, and the three of them shared a Nobel Prize for their work, awarded in 1956.

There was a semiconductor industry long before the transistor came along. The old "cat's whisker" detector used in crystal radio receivers was a semiconductor device, the selenium rectifiers used in AC/DC radios of the 1930s, '40s and '50s were semiconductor devices, and germanium diodes, rectifiers and regulators started showing up in electronic equipment developed during World War II. But the transistor was a quantum leap ahead in device capability and potential.

Even in its primitive laboratory configuration, the transistor was obviously a very important invention. A transistor could amplify or switch an electrical signal in a way that closely emulated well-established vacuum tube devices, and it could accomplish those functions without a fragile, air-free glass envelope, and without any secondary power source to heat up an electron-emitting cathode. A great many transistors could be crammed into the same amount of space required for a single vacuum tube, transistors consumed a lot less power than tubes, and transistors created much less heat as a byproduct of their operation.

Equally important, there was no inherent wear out or burn out factor in a transistor. In theory, at least, a transistor could reasonably be expected to last forever. The electronic computers of the late 1940s had thousands of vacuum tubes, and tube burnout was a constant headache. With the advent of transistors, most engineers realized, much more powerful computers could be built in smaller packages without concern for constant tube replacement and without nearly as much consideration for equipment cooling.

Bruised Feelings from a Patent Disclosure

Shockley had every right to be proud of his leadership of the Bell Labs transistor project, and for all I know, an equal right to feel hurt that the first patent papers filed by AT&T did not include his name as an inventor. Subsequent publicity mentioned Shockley on an equal footing with Bardeen and Brattain but that earlier perceived slight, when Bell Labs left his name off the very first patent disclosures, may have played a significant role in the strange behavior that Shockley exhibited later in his career.

George Rostky, editor emeritus of the trade newspaper *EE TIMES*, researched the history of the transistor and is convinced that Shockley actually developed a working grown-junction transistor at Bell Labs *before* the alloy junction configuration was revealed to the world.

According to Rostky, Shockley wrote up a patent disclosure, but lawyers at Bell Labs had come across a disclosure filed by Julius Lilienfeld on October 8, 1926, titled *Method and Apparatus for Controlling Electrical Currents*. The drawings and description indicated a junction field effect transistor. Lilienfeld never built a working model, but AT&T lawyers were afraid that he, or his representatives, might file an interference to the Shockley patent. So AT&T waited a short time until Bardeen and Brattain demonstrated the alloy junction transistor and then filed the first disclosure papers that failed to mention Shockley's name.

Rostky said that he telephoned Shockley years after the fact to discuss the issue, and when he brought up the Lilienfeld patent, Shockley became very irate, pointing out the enormous difference between a good idea and a working model.

The Scientist Becomes an Entrepreneur

Bill Shockley left Bell Labs in 1953 or 1954 and was appointed visiting professor of physics at California Institute of Technology, then served another stint for the government as deputy director of the weapons systems evaluation group of the Department of Defense in 1954–1955. Shockley then joined Beckman Instruments, Inc. in Southern California and soon established the Shockley Semiconductor Laboratory in Palo Alto. The major portion (and perhaps the sole source) of Shockley's funding came from Dr. Arnold Beckman, founder and CEO of Beckman Instruments. Then as now, the Beckman company was a highly successful manufacturer of industrial and medical instrumentation.

Shockley's laboratory was the first semiconductor company on the San Francisco Peninsula and the only such organization in the state outside of the greater Los Angeles area. Twelve of Shockley's original 20 employees were men with Ph.D degrees in some area of science or mathematics.

I was unable to resolve the issue of Shockley's goals for his new company. Some of his original employees were convinced that he was determined to make double-diffused silicon transistors in commercial quantities, and others were just as certain that his objective was a device he called the four-layer diode. Jay Last, who was one of Shockley's original employees, told me that double-diffused transistors were pretty well understood before Shockley set up shop in 1955, and he remembered that there was a lot of contact between Dr. Shockley and Bell Labs during the short period of his company's existence.

Last sent me a copy of a clipping from the *Electronic News* issue of March 2, 1958. A story headlined "Semiconductor Trade Thriving in Bay Area" stated, in part,

> The four-layer diode, invented by Shockley (EN 2/24) is being turned out on a limited production basis in temporary quarters at Beckman Instruments' Spinco division in Palo Alto. This transistor-diode, as Dr. Shockley calls it, has its principal application in computer systems, as noted, but is also expected to find use in communications and a wide variety of industrial, commercial and military instruments. A month ago, the firm, which grows its own crystals, was producing about 100 of the diodes a day. Last week, production was scaled up to 200 a day with the selling price listed at $9 to $15 each.

This is where the history of Silicon Valley begins. In Palo Alto, California. In 1955. Under the leadership of Dr. William B. Shockley.

Germanium vs. Silicon

Those first transistors at Bell Labs were made from germanium, a material that had been employed in diodes and rectifiers for many years. Germanium was relatively easy to work with and the "recipes" for creating semiconductor junctions were fairly well established and understood. Unfortunately, germanium was not capable of handling any significant amount of power, and the electronic performance of germanium transistors was not terribly impressive.

It was broadly understood that silicon was a much more stable semiconductor material than germanium, and, because of its higher melting point, (1410 degrees Celsius for silicon vs. 937 degrees Celsius for germanium,) silicon was capable of dissipating much more power.

By 1955 there was a commercial process available for making silicon transistors but everything about it was complicated. The raw silicon had to be refined for absolute purity, then melted, along with a tightly controlled quantity of another ultrapure ingredient (called a *dopant*,) in an air-free chamber. The dopant had to be evenly distributed throughout the melt in order to produce material with uniform electrical characteristics. It was not a simple matter of stirring a pot on a stove, because silicon has such a high melting point and because the molten material had to be oxygen-free.

The next step was to allow the molten silicon to cool and force it to crystallize in a certain controlled pattern. Then the silicon was sliced into thin disks with a diamond saw and cleaned and polished.

Those first semiconductor junctions were created by placing a small amount of some material such as the tip of an aluminum wire, or a pinhead-size ball of aluminum, on the surface of the silicon, and heating the assembly until the material just barely melted into the silicon. This step could be iterated for volume production. A single disk could have dozens or even hundreds of those little wires, or balls, all fused into the disk simultaneously. Then the disk could be broken apart to yield a number of little "dice," as the individual chips were then, and still are, called.

The result was an *alloy junction* and it required a chemical etching step to establish the desired electrical performance.

Even with all of its clumsiness and empirical aspects, the alloy junction process made possible the commercial manufacture of those first transistors. Engineers at Philco Semiconductor had automated the process in the course of developing the product family Philco called the "MADT," and others, too, had achieved varying degrees of factory automation. Now it was obvious to everyone that if *diffused* junction transistors were going to have a future, somebody would have to come up with a way of making a lot of them at once, at a reasonable cost, and achieving far greater uniformity of final results.

This was at least one of Shockley's announced objectives for his new semiconductor company. He was going to refine and manufacture a far better kind of device, which he described at the time as a *double diffused junction silicon transistor*. Bell Labs, according to those who remember the period, had already defined the product category and had manufactured some for internal use by Western Electric. But there were no "outside" sales and Shockley had a chance to become a market leader. Shockley's other pet project, the four-layer diode, was also a topic of discussion from the very beginning of his company.

Looking for Good Minds

As soon as Shockley acquired laboratory space in Palo Alto, he launched a search for staff personnel. He apparently valued intelligence and academic achievement over all other qualifications. One of his first employees, Dr. Victor Grinich, remembered how he became part of the Shockley staff:

"I was at Stanford Research Institute. We started on a project, funded by RCA, to work on applying transistors to television receivers. That's kind of impossible when you think about what we had to work with—transistors capable of dissipating a few milliwatts, and you could swing three volts. So, we struggled with them but we built up some knowledge. We bought some early TI (Texas Instruments) grown-junction transistors. We were able to get something that we could use to drive a color TV; just the video portion—forget about the speakers. This was about the time that the diffused-junction devices were first being announced from AT&T's Bell Labs.

"I saw the handwriting on the wall. I knew that working with diffused devices would be reasonably close to the leading edge. I'd spent three years at SRI but my experience with high performance transistors was delayed because of the fact that there wasn't much available through RCA. They'd made the

decision that germanium transistors were adequate for everything they wanted to accomplish, so there was no push in the
direction of silicon.

"I was getting the *Proceedings of the IRE* at the time, and I
was just looking through the back, where they printed the ads
for job openings. I saw something that looked like it was written in code. It was a very simple code and didn't require much
time to decrypt it, and it was a job opportunity working for
Shockley Labs. Bill Shockley was a great believer in puzzles
because he figured this would screen those people who weren't
interested in solving puzzle-like things. It was one of those simple substitution things. Where you see E, you put M, and things
of that nature. So I called the number and got an appointment
to see Shockley. When we got together, he proceeded to give
me an oral quiz, as if I were a Ph.D. candidate, and I guess he
felt he had to stump me, which he did. No doubt he was a
genius. He had all this stuff in his head. So, I got a job with his
new company, just based on that interview, and then I met
some of the other people.

"That was in 1956, and my initial salary was something
like $700 or $800 a month. I don't remember the exact number at all. At the time, it wasn't that important, as long as it
was enough to pay my mortgage. It was considered a princely
sum.

"Bob [Dr. Robert N. Noyce] was already there. I think Bob
was an early employee. Shockley's first employee was a guy
named Smoot Horsley. You've heard of the Smoot-Hawley
Act—he was a descendant of that Smoot. An unusual first name.
Anyhow, Smoot Horsley had a Ph.D. in physics, but he served
as Shockley's assistant. He was there, and I think Gene Kleiner
. . . I forget. Gene Kleiner and Julie Blank worked together at
Western, and one of them came and then the other one came.
The second one came about the same time I did. Then there

were Jay Last and Sheldon Roberts. The company had been going about a year."

Gordon Moore was another one of the "bright people" Shockley brought in to his new company:

Gordon Moore (1965)

"The beginning for me was one night when I was sitting at home in Silver Spring, Maryland, and Bill Shockley called me on the phone. I had heard him speak (at professional meetings,) and knew who he was, and in his typical manner after I picked up the phone, he said, 'Hello, Shockley here.' He went on to say he was setting up a thing in California and got my name from Lawrence Livermore Lab, where I had previously interviewed and turned down the job they offered. He'd gotten permission to go through the records of people that they'd made offers to, and found my name. He thought he needed a chemist, and I was nominally a chemist.

"I had been at the Johns Hopkins Applied Physics Lab doing research. That was my first job out of school (Cal Tech,) and I'd been there two and a half years and I was interviewing around, looking for another job. Lawrence Livermore was one of the places I'd been interviewing. I wanted to get back out here (to California) if I could; there weren't many technical jobs in California in those days.

"So I came out for the Shockley interview, and it was pretty much what I wanted. First of all it was right in Palo Alto, which was very close to where I grew up, and an area I really liked. Second, I was interested in getting into something a lot more practical. I'd been doing fundamental research and wasn't really sure anyone was even reading the papers we were writing. I thought I ought to get close to something more practical, and Shockley was going to build a silicon transistor. That got me excited. I started in February or March of 1956."

Julius Blank, another Shockley recruit, remembered the novelty of a first meeting with the man:

"Dean Knapic and I used to hang around and had a lot of things in common at work. One day he says to me that a guy he knows at Bell Labs, a fellow by the name of Rudy Molina, said 'Hey, I got a call from a buddy of mine, Bill Shockley, who's starting up a thing in California. He's looking for some mechanical guys to help him with his manufacturing because most of the other guys are Ph.D.s and physicists, and he asked me who I knew so I gave him your name.' That's how it got started. He got interviewed by Shockley, flew out to California, and I think he was in California when Noyce was being interviewed. Bob was working for Philco at the time.

"I think Dean met some of the other guys along the way before they actually came out here. So, he was put on, and then Shockley said 'You have to get a couple of assistants,' so Dean picked me and Gene Kleiner. Kleiner was very reluctant to do this because he was living in an apartment on Central Park West and had a pretty nice life, and he was teaching at Brooklyn Poly. He was always a little skittish about it. I said, 'Well, I have nothing to lose.' It sounded like an interesting deal, and I didn't want to stay in New York any more.

"I was married, our son was 10 months old, and my wife's mother had died a few months before, so it was a kind of fluid period. Anyway, we had to go over to New York to take a test from a consulting firm called McMurry, Hamstra. This was about six hours worth of psychological testing. You wouldn't believe the drill they put you through! You had to write stories and interpret pictures and then you did the math testing and English, and it was a comprehensive thing. At the end of it, they produced a book 'that thick' written by their consultants. All of the senior staff guys went through this. It was very expensive, even in those days. And I said, 'How the hell did this happen?'

"It turns out that Shockley was being funded by Arnold Beckman of Beckman Instruments, and a few years earlier, down in Anaheim I guess, Beckman had one of their vice presidents go berserk with a knife and stab a bunch of people. Since that incident they had to do something, so they found this consulting firm down there that had offices in L.A., Chicago, New York, and God knows where else, and they started to do this testing. I never saw the report on me. Dean had it and he read some parts of it to me, and parts were OK and some of it was off the wall, but everybody went through this. That's how we got hired.

"One day I met Shockley for the first time. We had lunch at the Newarker Restaurant at Newark Airport, and then he wrote me a letter and offered me a job. They offered to pay my moving expenses, and I figured, what the hell, as long as I have money for the round trip back here . . . I think the offer was for $835 a month. I had been making $500 or $600 or something at Western Electric—I don't remember. Plus he was going to pay moving expenses up to a month's pay. But the whole thing was something brand new and different. It was getting out of New York."

Blank's mention of Dean Knapic brings up an interesting footnote to the history of Silicon Valley: Knapic became the very first "spinoff" company in Silicon Valley when he left Shockley to establish a crystal-growing and wafer-slicing company. Some time later, Knapic sold his company to Monsanto, a chemical company with an established position in silicon.

Julie Blank described the first appearance of Bob Noyce, and in his telling of the story he provided one of the few mentions of the human side of Shockley's character that has been recorded:

> "We had a party one Friday night at Estelle and Dick Rudolph's house for the new guys and that was the first time I met Noyce.
>
> "Noyce had driven in from Salt Lake City non-stop. He had a scruffy little 2-door Ford that was a piece of crap. You wouldn't believe this thing! Did you ever see those cartoons with the upholstery springs popping out? That's it! He had a windshield wiper that was sort of vacuous. When you needed it most, it didn't work. He was still a chain-smoker.
>
> "He showed up in the pouring rain about 10 at night. That's when I met this guy for the first time. Here he comes in, you know, hadn't shaved, he looked like he'd been living in his suit for a week—and he was thirsty. There was a big bowl of martinis on the table there, and he picks up the bowl and starts drinking it just like that, and then he passes out! That was funny.
>
> "Shockley missed it; he was too late. Shockley got a little loaded also and he was dancing the tango with a rose in his teeth. He was dancing with Estelle Rudolph. You have to picture that one! It was a wild bunch."

Apparently, Shockley had two sides to his personality. Even though most of his former employees remembered the stricter, pedantic Bill Shockley, Jay Last saw his warmer, more human side. Because he was the youngest of the group, Last remembered that Shockley took him "under his wing." He had occasional dinners with Shockley and his wife, and after Last had been there for about four months, Shockley gave him a generous raise. But true to the other aspect of his personality, Shockley accompanied the good news of the raise with a mini-lecture. "That'll teach you not to sell yourself too cheaply," he advised Last. In a comment he sent me recently, Jay Last said that *"Shockley managed to turn this upbeat meeting into one where I was very irritated with him."*

Pinning Down the Variables

Shockley's approach to silicon transistor fabrication may not have been totally original, but his determination to pin down all of the process variables was important. The "new way" of making silicon transistors was, in essence, to put the polished wafers of silicon into a high temperature furnace and move a stream of gas across the wafers while they were held at an elevated temperature. Some of the molecules in the gas diffused into the surface of the silicon wafers and created a thin surface layer with different electrical qualities than the material immediately below it.

Then a second diffusion process, using a different gas and different combinations of time and temperature, produced a third layer of material on the surface of the wafer with a new set of electrical qualities.

It was a complicated process and the results varied according to time, temperature, gas composition, gas flow rates, wafer diameter, oven configuration, etc. After the wafer had undergone successive diffusion processes, some of the material around a portion of each individual device had to be removed to define the junctions required for a transistor. A chemical etching process removed channels of material from the surface of the wafer, leaving a pattern of high and low segments. If you visualize a nice, regular layout of bottle caps on a tabletop, with open spaces between each cap, you'll have a good idea of the way it was. And if you've been to the desert of the American Southwest with its unique geological formations, you'll understand at once why this came to be called the *mesa* process.

Nowadays this entire body of information is well documented. But Shockley started before the processes themselves were totally understood, and his staff people truly forced their way into a new technology.

One of Shockley's important contributions was the refinement of what are now called *diffusion constants*. His staff experimented with combinations of time, temperature, gas flow rate and gas formulations, and the resulting layers of p-type and n-type material were measured with great precision.

Jean Hoerni: Brilliant and Difficult

Jean Hoerni

Jean Hoerni—we pronounced his name *John Her-neé*—(1924-1997) is another of those pioneering giants who contributed significantly to today's multifunction integrated circuits. His contributions never got the public recognition they deserved. Hoerni had two Ph.D. degrees, one from The University of Geneva in 1950 and the other from Cambridge, in England, in 1952. He had worked directly under Linus Pauling at Cal-Tech. Gordon Moore, himself a Cal-Tech graduate, was dispatched to Pasadena by Shockley to recruit Hoerni. Shockley put him to work as an analytical mathematician.

Hoerni was a brilliant scientist who later struggled to be an entrepreneur and he wasn't particularly successful at it. He had a personality best described as "difficult." Hoerni himself once told a story about a good position that was offered by Batelle in Switzerland. *"They phoned me early in the morning to make the offer, but I didn't answer the phone. I'm not a morning person."*

To keep Hoerni from being distracted by other employees, Shockley installed him in a motel room, away from the main laboratory. His assignment was the painstaking task of reducing experimental data to a series of graphs that may have depicted (or recorded) the first reliable, high-precision silicon diffusion constants. Hoerni's work amounted to the equivalent of a recipe book for silicon diffused junctions, making it possible for factory technicians to produce consistent results. Shockley himself turned up from time to time to discuss progress, but for the most part Hoerni worked in splendid isolation—which was not entirely to his liking.

Toward the end of his life, Hoerni told me that he begged Shockley to free him from the motel room and allow him to work in the laboratory. This got Hoerni started on experimental diffusion work, which he did so well at Fairchild. From that time on, Hoerni worked in both theory and experimental projects.

Finally, Shockley sent him to the main building and gave him four weeks to make a four-layer diode. Jay Last recalled that *"the PNPN device got designed into some Southern California military system. When the customer replaced the PNPN with more conventional devices, Shockley lost their one big chance."*

A Good Teacher and an Exciting Atmosphere

One of the reasons Shockley was able to attract so many highly capable people to his new venture was his excellence as a teacher. Julie Blank was impressed with the way Shockley brought his new employees up to a level of understanding the new technology:

> "He was a very astute guy with a very, very sharp mind. To this day I think he's one of the best people we ever had. I wish to hell they had video recorders then, because Shockley used to give a lecture series to all the guys. In fact I went through it a couple of times. He would start out teaching you solid state physics, assuming you had nothing more than an elementary school education, lecture 1. Lecture 2, you had to have a high school education. Lecture 3—you know, on and on. By the

time you got to lecture 6 or 7, there were only a few guys left who could follow him. But he had such an uncanny ability to go ahead and explain things in simple English. You didn't have to resort to bouncing differential equations all over the world.

"Did you ever read his book? He explained how electrons and holes move in material by using a full parking garage as an example. He says, 'What happens, when you get something here, you have to move this whole stall of cars out there, so this empty spot can go to a place where you can pull it.' And this was something that physicists didn't do. They had to explain everything with all kinds of quantum mechanics."

Julie Blank tried to remember some of the other personnel at Shockley Labs, and came up with a few additional names:

"There were a couple of other guys there, lab technicians, and there were some people with semiconductor experience—a fellow from Bell, a fellow by the name of Leo Valdez who used to work at a place called Pacific Semiconductor. He went from Bell to Pacific and then Shockley brought him up to Palo Alto. There was a fellow by the name of Smoot Horsley. I don't know where he came from. He came from up in the Northwest. And there was a recent Ph.D. from Berkeley called Vic Jones, who was there. Shockley eventually got him a position as a professor at Harvard, formerly held by C. Lester Hogan. It's a funny world."

A funny world indeed! Clarence Lester Hogan left the academic world at Harvard to head up Motorola's semiconductor division and lead it to enormous success. Many of the key people at Shockley would go on to organize Fairchild Semiconductor. And then, years later, Hogan would become CEO of Fairchild Camera and Instrument Corporation and take on (temporarily,) the additional role of general manager of Fairchild

Semiconductor. It was just one of several fascinating circularities in the history of Silicon Valley.

Wafers, Dice and Headers

Because so much of the semiconductor story involves a specialized vocabulary, this is a good place to make two additional comments about the manufacture of transistors: Obviously, the surface area of the silicon wafer determined the number of devices that could be produced from any single process batch. But larger diameter silicon ingots with the desired physical and chemical characteristics were extremely difficult to produce. And when larger diameters came along years later, all of the handling equipment and all of the diffusion ovens had to be scaled up.

Once the individual little "dice" were fabricated, they had to be packaged in some way that a customer could use. The industry standard was a metal "header" with three sturdy wire legs coming out of the bottom through glass insulators. (What we called a "header" could just as easily have been called a "base," but one of the electrical elements of a transistor is called a base, and it would have been confusing to have two things bearing the same name. So the physical platform that held the little silicon transistor chip was called a header.) The chip was soldered onto the metal header, very thin gold wires were used to connect active areas of the chip with the sturdy pins in the header, and a protective metal cap was resistance-welded into place.

Given a stable fabrication process, many tens of thousands of transistor "dice" could be made for the same cost as a few hundred. Whether a wafer contained 500 transistor dice or 10,000 of them, the wafer processing costs were not much affected. But final assembly of transistors was very labor-intensive because, at that stage, we were working device-by-device instead of assembling many at one time. Assembly automation was far in the future.

The Elusive Four-Layer Diode

Transistor work was under way, it appears, when Shockley became interested in a device somewhat similar to a transistor, but optimized for switching performance. Shockley called it a *four layer diode*. The consensus is that Shockley and AT&T had discussed such a device, which would be useful in telephone switching applications. Nobody I interviewed seemed to know much about the business side of the four-layer diode episode, but it was tremendously important to Shockley and there is at least a possibility that AT&T had granted some development money.

Vic Grinich remembered some of the complications of the four layer diode project:

> "Shockley had us working on this 4-layer diode. Not only was he going to make the silicon, but he was also going to work from the other end. He had some ideas about packaging, and he was going to make a diode package whereby the whiskers (attachment leads) were attached by means of something like a welding operation. The idea was, you moved the whisker in toward the diode chip, it arced and it supposedly would make a bond. I think it was called 'percussive welding'.
>
> "It was a metallurgical nightmare! You were trying to control all the variables, and you'd have to turn on the welding power, hold it at a certain point, get the gap narrowed down, and then you'd have to turn off the power so the joint would solidify. Anyhow, he was going to do all that. There were a lot of things going on. Now I remember also there was another guy on the project named Dean Knapic."

Early Times, Exciting Times

By all accounts, the early months at Shockley Labs were exciting times for all of the participants. Accustomed to the way things were done at established corporations, they found the informal atmosphere to be liberating and productive. Julie Blank gave a very good picture of the intellectual environment:

> "Horsley and Valdez were the senior technical guys. When Knapic was there, he was like the general lab manager. See, you couldn't buy any equipment then. You had to design and build everything yourself, or use lab stuff and rework it. We were very busy with that stuff because anything you wanted to do, you had to build something for it. So, we got a machine shop going.
>
> "Noyce used to be flabbergasted. One time we were sitting down at the lunch table and somebody said 'I gotta have something. I want to try something . . . ' He pulls out some contacts and says 'You have a bell jar . . . ' and he wants to expose the contacts. So he drew something on the back of a napkin. That's the way it was done.
>
> "So I go inside the shop and tell the guys what to do, and let them put something together and I get back to Noyce with the sample and I ask, 'Is this what you want?' Noyce said, 'We just got through talking here!' He said 'You know, if we wanted the same thing at Philco, it would have taken six months!'
>
> "Bell Labs was the same way. At Shockley we could make changes on the fly, and so on. Noyce was really in pig heaven when it came to that kind of stuff. Most of the other guys had similar experiences.
>
> "Kleiner used to teach machine shop, so he was a toolmaker, and I used to be a machinist many years ago, so we had a situation where we could design anything and build it ourselves if we had to. We hired local machine shops to do most of that, but it was still inside work on something new. When we were making crystal growers we figured out we had to use graphite, so we machined a helical spring out of graphite. Everybody was wearing masks to keep from breathing that stuff. Kleiner

was our welding expert. They got me involved in crystal growing because I had the only high-temperature experience from my work on boilers. Nobody knew what refractive materials were. They said, 'It's up your alley. You should know all about that!'"

Turning Sand into Gold

Julie Blank's mention of crystal growing brings up a significant aspect of silicon semiconductor manufacture that would challenge the ingenuity of everyone in the industry for at least the next fifteen years.

Ordinary sand is, for the most part, an oxide of silicon. A few of the major chemical companies refined silicon by removing the oxygen from sand, resulting in ultrapure material. It was delivered to the customer in the form of polycrystalline chunks that closely resembled lumps of hard coal. From that point on, the semiconductor producer had to go through a long, complicated process to prepare the material.

First, the raw silicon was washed to remove any lingering surface contaminants. Then the lumps of silicon, along with a very small quantity of dopant material, were loaded into a cylindrical quartz crucible with an open top. The crucible was positioned inside the coils of an induction heater and the whole assembly was contained within a large, airtight furnace enclosure.

After the furnace was sealed, a vacuum pump removed as much of the air as possible, and the heater was energized. As the temperature rose, more air would be released, and the pump had to operate continuously to maintain the vacuum.

A motorized platform within the furnace rotated the crucible of molten material. At the proper moment, a "seed" with the desired crystal structure orientation, rotating in the opposite direction, was lowered to the surface of the melt. Some of the molten material would "freeze" into a crystal pattern that replicated the structure of the seed, and as the seed was gradually elevated, a cylinder of single-crystal silicon would emerge from the melt. This process was called the Czochralski Method, or "CZ," and honored the name of Jan Czochralski, the Polish metallurgist who first demonstrated the technique in 1917.

The variables were critical. Even the slightest temperature change would affect the diameter of the emerging crystal, as would any variation in the rate at which the seed was elevated. Temperature deviations could also bring about unacceptable changes in the crystal structure.

Worse, the distribution of the dopant material within the melt was never perfectly uniform, and the resulting crystal (called an *ingot,*) would exhibit uneven electrical characteristics from end to end. Molecular distribution problems also produced electrical variations from the center axis of the ingot to the circumference.

Ingot preparation required constant attention from a technician who had to monitor and control temperatures, rotation rates, the seed withdrawal rate, etc.

Fred Bialek, who is mentioned throughout this book, read an early draft and added that the first crystal growing machines had a hand crank system to elevate the seed crystal. He remembered that if the withdrawal rate was too fast, there was "no freeze," and if it was too slow, the result was a "big freeze." His note included a mental picture of a technician hunched over and staring through a small window, trying to match the withdrawal rate to the best possible ingot formation.

Those first ingots were less than an inch in diameter and only a few inches long. Often, upon close inspection, the ingot was unsuitable for semiconductor processing because of defects in the crystal structure or electrical imperfections.

The acceptable ingots were sawed (with diamond saws) into thin disks, called wafers, and ground and polished to as near perfect a surface as possible. All successive manufacturing was a matter of replicating many tiny devices across the surface of each wafer. Obviously, larger diameter ingots would make possible higher volume production, but it

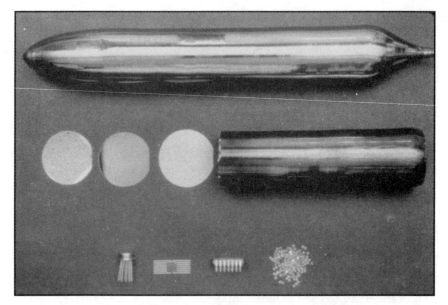

**A silicon ingot, some wafer slices, a pile of dice—
or chips—and some typical packages**

would be many years before anyone could produce large-diameter wafers with the desired characteristics.

Shockley recognized the importance of silicon material production and mounted a major effort to improve the methodology. Julie Blank was involved in that effort and described some of the details:

> "Hewlett-Packard had a lab, a one-man semiconductor lab down in Palo Alto, and we used to go back and forth with ingots like borrowing cups of sugar from one another. The blind leading the blind. HP bought one of those crystal growers from Semi Metals back in New York. And after looking at the HP machine, I knew we could do better than that for half the price
>
> "We decided to design and build our own. We did build it. Those things, you know, lasted a long time
>
> "We had two versions. One was to get something going and the other was for the future, an exotic one which we built but didn't work. Actually we were looking at buying one, but they

wanted a lot of money for it and the damned thing, when I looked at it, was a piece of crap. It looked like it wouldn't stand up at all."

Blank was not the only Shockley employee who remembered a project to build a much-improved crystal growing apparatus. The new machine incorporated a number of automated sensors and controls, and was intended to turn out silicon ingots of uniform quality without a lot of operator intervention. Shockley's custom-designed crystal growing machine kept growing in size. It became so huge that they had to open the ceiling to provide enough vertical space for the thing.

Blank and Grinich both recalled a test run, where one of the motors had not been equipped with a limit switch. The motor kept running, the machine destroyed itself and "made a mess."

Diversions and Distractions

Gene Kleiner told a story about Bill Shockley that I consider a key factor in the company's ultimate failure. It illustrates the conflict between Shockley's academic nature and his desire to be an entrepreneur. It began when Kleiner finished his design drawings for the new crystal growing machine.

Eugene Kleiner

Kleiner showed the plans to Shockley, and Shockley took issue with Kleiner on the size of some bolts. Shockley said that the bolts did not have to be as large as the drawings indicated, and asked Kleiner to change the specification to a smaller size. When Kleiner argued that his spec was suitable for the application and that the bolts were an insignificant detail, Shockley was not content to move on to other issues. He gave Kleiner a lecture on the strength of materials and discussed the specifics of the metallurgy of the bolt material to prove his point. It was a long session and it consumed valuable time, all of which was dedicated to a component that cost very little money and wasn't important in the overall design of the machine.

Kleiner's experience was consistent with Shockley's whole approach to life. It wasn't enough to argue about a bolt; Shockley felt compelled to be a teacher and go into the broader issues of strength of materials. In Shockley's mind, it was more than a simple bolt. It was a question of total understanding of the physics and mechanics of the situation.

The bolt episode illustrates Shockley's mastery of mechanical engineering (among many other disciplines,) and it also underscores the ease with which he was distracted. His tendency to get involved in the smallest details of minor issues was destructive to the structure of the workplace. There was no clear-cut delegation of responsibility.

Disturbing Elements in the Laboratory

Up to a point, Shockley Labs had been a great experience for the professional staff. Ad-hoc teams were formed and re-formed to address the many challenges of mastering the complexities of silicon semiconductor development. In spite of the chaos that Shockley seemed to bring to the party, cooperation was the rule of the day. An atmosphere of invention and innovation kept everyone motivated. And then some disturbing elements began to creep into the workplace. Gordon Moore gave an early example:

> "One thing that really got to me was, he tried to make some sort of a new gadget. He set up one little organization in a little building, and he made this a secret project where the guys working on it could know what it was and the rest of us

couldn't. All he'd tell us was he thought this was potentially as important as the invention of the transistor, which really made *me* feel good, not being able to participate! Everything he did, it seemed, was divisive."

Shockley's behavior gradually became as important to his employees as the work they were doing. Vic Grinich gave a dramatic example of the sort of thing that ate into morale:

"One case I remember was a woman who was handling his travel plans. She made a (supposedly) terrible mistake. In those days TWA and United were flying cross-country from both San Francisco and L.A. In some cases you couldn't get a nonstop flight from San Francisco at certain times of the day, so you'd have to go down to L.A. to get a flight. But if you were clever about it you could use that leg as a separate ticket just on its own and get credit for one of these early frequent flyer deals. Except, in this specific case, the woman forgot to get credit for the additional leg. He canned her on the spot. Everybody got pretty upset about it."

There were many other minor examples of Shockley's increasingly strange behavior, including his habit of firing people within full view of the staff, but there was one pivotal incident that caused the most distress. It was mentioned by every Shockley veteran interviewed for this project, and described most succinctly by Vic Grinich:

"People were getting more and more distressed. There were other things. Not only did Shockley become an egomaniac, but he became paranoid about things. For example, Shockley's secretary suffered a cut finger from a sharp object on the swinging door of her office. Shockley was sure it was a malicious act and

he hired some investigators to find out who was responsible.
There was a general deterioration in the feeling of the people;
they felt something negative was going to happen there. Shockley was just running amok."

The infamous "pin affair" made a deep impression on everyone at the
lab. Jay Last sent me a copy of another version of the same incident, cit-
ing Shockley's hiring of a polygraph testing company, his calls to the
local police to check on the backgrounds of two technicians under suspi-
cion and, finally, his focus on Sheldon Roberts. Apparently Roberts himself did a microscopic analysis of the offending instrument and proved it
was nothing more sinister than a glass-head pin where the glass head had
fallen off.

And then the Nobel Committee, in recognition of the invention of
the transistor back in 1948, made Shockley a co-recipient of the
physics prize, along with his former Bell Labs colleagues, Bardeen and
Brattain. Shockley's reaction to the award was not quite what his
employees expected. Vic Grinich had a particularly vivid memory of
the incident:

"I think the thing that made Shockley become really unbearable
was that he won the Nobel Prize in '56 and that went to his
head. He was an egomaniac before, but he came back from the
award ceremony and he gave a little speech about what happened. I remember him saying that he kind of felt like Churchill
when he got the Nobel Prize. He said, 'It's about time,' or words
to that effect. It's funny now, but at the time it was pretty dis-
tressing."

By the early months of 1957, lots of things were going wrong at
Shockley Labs. Nobody could quite figure out whether the major goal
was silicon transistors or four-layer diodes. Highly educated professional
scientists were assigned routine work on a pilot production line. Small

clusters of researchers were given special projects and ordered to keep their work secret from their colleagues within the company. Shockley would inject himself into simple engineering projects and order changes in the most minor details.

William Shockley, now a Nobel Laureate, began to travel quite a bit. His absences from his company were unexplained to his staff employees and he spent increasing periods away from Palo Alto. Conversation shifted away from the work at hand to Shockley's behavior. There was a growing feeling that the company was disintegrating. Instead of talking about device development, the informal discussions were about concerns for the future and a desire to "*do something.*"

Planting the Seeds of Fairchild Semiconductor

Eight of Shockley's key employees discovered a common bond. They had succeeded in understanding the subtleties of growing silicon ingots. They had worked out the details of producing diffused junctions. They may have even produced small quantities of silicon transistors and they knew that their transistors offered superior electrical performance to the prevailing germanium transistors of the period. In today's environment, any of them could have gone to another semiconductor company. But there were no other semiconductor companies closer than hundreds of miles distant. They had families, mortgages and the beginnings of roots in and around Palo Alto.

Their names were Julius Blank, Victor Grinich, Jean Hoerni, Eugene Kleiner, Jay Last, Gordon Moore, Robert Noyce and Sheldon Roberts. They were about to make their own kind of history.

Gordon Moore remembers it this way:

> "What finally happened (we were getting kind of disgusted with Shockley's lack of management and really kind of screwing things up) was that Arnold Beckman came in one time and

talked to the group. I don't remember what Beckman said, but Shockley got up afterwards and thanked him and then said, if you're not happy with what we're doing up here, I can take this group anyplace else and get funding, or something like that. This was kind of the inspiration he (Shockley) gave us, so we got together and talked and decided to tell Beckman about the problems here.

"I had the questionable privilege of contacting Beckman, and Beckman said 'I get the feeling there are problems up there,' and arranged to come up and have dinner with us."

Jay Last had a vivid memory of Moore's telephone call to Arnold Beckman. The group had assembled at the Black Forest Restaurant in Los Altos and Last described *"the quaking voice of Gordon Moore when he called and asked for "Dr. Beckman."* Moore was extremely uneasy about that first contact with Beckman. Gordon goes on with his narrative . . .

"A group of us went to dinner with Arnold Beckman and came up with the idea of getting Shockley moved aside someplace, to consult or something, or to get a professorship at Stanford. Well, Beckman had three or four dinner meetings with us, and he had a guy he thought would be perfect, a guy named Joe Louis (I'll never forget the name,) who ran a Beckman division. Joe Louis was getting taller and taller every time we talked to Arnold.

"Then, at the last of the dinner meetings we had with Beckman, somebody (from the outside) had evidently gotten to him. The rumor I heard was that the Bell Labs people told him if he did this (replace Shockley) he'd ruin Shockley and so forth. So Beckman all of a sudden changed tone and said 'Shockley's in charge; if you don't like it, tough.'"

Shockley's laboratory organization hadn't really identified any other person as second-in-command, but the wide-ranging capabilities of

Dr. Robert Noyce were obvious to everyone. The Shockley staff included experts in physics, chemistry, mechanical engineering, mathematics and electronics, but Bob Noyce seemed to understand *everything*. He wasn't the oldest member of the company but he was respected by everyone.

As informal talk about dissatisfaction with working conditions grew more widespread, Noyce was seldom a participant. Several of his colleagues have speculated that Noyce was constrained by a strong sense of obligation to his employer, even in the face of obvious organizational problems. Although Noyce was aware of the unrest, he was never a leader in the movement that eventually included Gordon Moore, Sheldon Roberts, Eugene Kleiner, Victor Grinich, Julius Blank, Jean Hoerni and Jay Last. When Noyce finally (and some say, reluctantly,) joined them, they became known as *The Eight*.

Gordon Moore picks up the story here:

> "The original idea was that we'd burnt our bridges so badly we were all going to have to look for jobs. Kleiner wrote to a friend of his father's at Hayden Stone and said 'there are a bunch of us who like working together, and we'd like a company to hire us.' Then Art Rock and Bud Coyle came out (from New York,) and after talking with us for an evening, said 'what you really ought to do is set up your own company, and we'll find the support.' Actually, Noyce was not initially part of that. There were originally seven of us. Sheldon spent a whole evening convincing Bob to even come and meet with Coyle and Rock."

At the time, Bud Coyle was a manager at Hayden Stone, and Art Rock was a young Harvard MBA who worked for Coyle.

> "We took a copy of *The Wall Street Journal* and went down the list of companies, any company you could think of that might reasonably want a semiconductor operation. You know, like electronic component manufacturers or aerospace companies,

or . . . Coyle and Rock went to every one of them and got turned down 100% without anybody even talking to them. They accidentally ran into Sherman Fairchild (founder of Fairchild Camera and Instrument Corporation) . . . or maybe it was John Carter. Carter was chairman and Richard Hodgson was executive vice president. Carter was interested enough to send Hodgson out to talk to us. This was October '57."

The eight men from Shockley Labs were confident that they knew how to make diffused junction silicon transistors, and they convinced the executives at Fairchild that there was enough of a potential market to support a company.

According to Moore, Fairchild put up $1.3 million to support the new venture:

"The deal was that they would support us. First of all, we each put in $500, and $500 was a significant investment for us at that time; it was almost a month's salary. And Fairchild had an option to buy the company from us. There were eight of us that were going to have one share each, plus two shares to Hayden Stone for making the deal, 10 shares in all. They (Fairchild) had the option then to buy the shares after two years for a total of $2.5 million. If they waited until the third year, the price would go up to $3 million."

Fairchild Camera and Instrument then put up $3,000 to fund the initial organization costs. Richard Hodgson provided his copy of Fairchild Camera's original memo of October 2, 1957, addressed to Bob Noyce:

"Attached is a check for $3,000 advance to you to cover necessary expenditures in setting up the semiconductor operation. Until such time as the department is formally organized."

2 October 1957

Mr. Robert Noyce
11645 Lundy Lane
Los Altos, California

Dear Bob,

Attached is a check for $3,000. as advance to you
to cover necessary expenditures in setting up the
semi-conductor operation until such time as the
Corporation is formally organized.

Please keep a record of the expenditures so that
Fairchild Camera can eventually be reimbursed by
the Fairchild Semi-conductor Corporation.

We have a sizeable quantity of surplus shop equipment
which you might be able to use, so let me know your
requirements.

The group will be interested to know that it appears
possible to extend Fairchild's program on group
life and medical insurance to your operation. I'll
let you have the details later.

Best regards.

                          Sincerely,

RH:mtb   Richard Hodgson
enc. ck #9-5003

Copy of the Hodgson letter

Julie Blank added his own perspective to the event:

"Bud Coyle spoke with somebody who told him to go make an appointment and see Sherman Fairchild. So, he calls up, makes an appointment, goes to his townhouse. Coyle was the managing director of Hayden, Stone. So, he gets an appointment to see Sherman Fairchild. He described it. It was funny. He goes to this very fancy townhouse, and Sherman has got some kind of an abscess on his finger, and has his hand dunked in a glass of hot boric acid solution. He's talking to him and explaining this whole thing. Sherman says 'That sounds like a good thing. Why don't you go see John?' Big John Carter. And that's how the thing basically got started. A few weeks later, Carter sends his emissary, Richard Hodgson, who was a young, skinny guy then, and that was the beginning.

"The deal was they were going to fund us. The whole business plan was a page and a half, and I think we needed $1.3 million to get this thing going. They increased it later. Basically, within two years, they had the right to buy us all out, either in cash or in stock. Any time before two years, they had to pay $2.5 million for the whole thing. That was bottom, and after that then there was an add-on. I forget the exact amount.

"The eight guys would get an equal share, and it was split into eight shares, plus two shares for Hayden, Stone, I remember. So, it had 10 pieces, each one of us got 10% and Hayden Stone got 20%. But later they modified it."

It doesn't sound like a lot of money nowadays, but the Fairchild investment was not trivial for the times. $1.3 million represented a significant portion of Fairchild Camera's annual earnings, and the money was going to a group that had never before been involved in an independent entrepreneurial activity. None of The Eight had any business history. They were leaving Dr. William Shockley, the Nobel laureate who was recognized by many as the world's leading authority on semiconductor technology, to prove that they knew more about manufacturing than he did. There was no example of the "product" to examine, there were no commercial sources for much of the equipment that would be needed, and there was no sales history for the product.

In effect, Fairchild Camera was risking more than a million dollars on an idea that was unproved. If it worked out, however, Fairchild would have the right to buy the entire operation at a bargain-basement price. It was one of the first examples of what would come to be called *venture capital*.

A Sad Coda to a Life of Invention

At least a passing mention should be made about Shockley's later activities, after his semiconductor company was only a memory. William Shockley, a brilliant physicist with an equally remarkable mastery of chemistry and mathematics, somehow turned his attention to highly controversial aspects of population demographics.

Super Daddies

At one point, Shockley became convinced that the genetic qualities of Nobel laureates were so precious that they deserved perpetuation. He got involved with a man named Robert Klark Graham, a former optometrist who made a fortune in the early days of shatterproof plastic eyeglass lenses, in the establishment of what they called *The Repository for Germinal Choice*, a sperm bank intended primarily to take deposits from Nobel Prize winners. The idea was, I suppose, that some woman wishing to become the mother of a future genius could apply to the sperm bank for the wherewithal to produce a super child.

According to an Associated Press story dated May 24, 1982, the sperm bank was founded in 1979 as "a means of breeding higher intelligence." Graham was quoted as saying that his intention was "to bring into the world a few more creative, intelligent people who otherwise might not have been born."

Ellen Goodman, the humorist/columnist, wrote a story in July 1982, identifying Shockley as the first of several sperm donors, and saying that a baby girl named Victoria was the first documented result of the project. According to Goodman, the biological father was an "eminent mathematician" in his 30s with an IQ over 200. (That would seem to exclude Shockley, who was about 70 years old at the time of his "deposit.")

Goodman's column picked up parts of an interview originally carried in *The National Enquirer* wherein Victoria's mother, one Joyce Kowalski, was credited with these remarks: "*God, thank you, thank you, I cried. Tears streaked down my eyes as a nurse lifted my newborn baby girl into my arms—a baby who could be the first of a new breed of genius children . . . These are the greatest minds of all time and one of them might be the father of my child, I gasped.*"

As I re-read the *Enquirer* item as cited by Ellen Goodman, I was fascinated with the note of paternal uncertainty in Ms. Kowalski's quoted remark. Goodman's column also included some negative comments about the background of the mother, who, Goodman wrote, had served time in a federal prison on fraud charges and had seen two children by a previous marriage removed from her custody after allegations of child abuse.

If Shockley thought of a way to qualify the prospective mothers, and if he had some ideas about perpetual funding for such an establishment, they have been forgotten by now. The whole concept was hooted down.

Race and Intelligence

Shockley's most controversial undertaking, however, and the one for which he is usually remembered, had nothing whatever to do with physics, semiconductors or sperm banks. He had somehow gotten his hands on a study conducted during World War II regarding test results of draftees. It was Shockley's observation that the average scores of black draftees were lower than those of white draftees. And on the basis of that third-party report, and ignoring all considerations of test methodology or the comparative cultural and educational backgrounds of the subjects, Shockley concluded that black Americans are intellectually inferior to white Americans.

Such a statement, coming from a Nobel laureate, stirred up a huge body of passionate debate. Coming at a time when affirmative action and equal employment opportunity practices were just beginning to be accepted as an ordinary part of American life, the Shockley proposal inspired racists and inflamed proponents of the opposing view. Shockley made himself available for interviews, he appeared on radio talk shows, he gave formal presentations to groups and he fielded questions from the audience. As was the case with his sperm bank idea, his theories on race and intelligence were eventually discredited and finally, ignored.

When the *Atlanta Constitution* ran an article comparing Shockley's genetic theories to those of the Nazis, Shockley sued the paper and its owner, Cox Enterprises, for libel. A federal jury agreed with Shockley's claim, but awarded him only one dollar.

It was a sad ending to a career that had been so brilliant, and that had laid the foundation for so much that was soon to follow.

Maybe We Should Have Called it *Shockley Valley*

I often think about Bill Shockley's short-lived semiconductor company. He could have set up his business in San Diego or Phoenix or Boston or anywhere, for that matter. It was the charismatic genius of Bill Shockley that attracted the likes of Noyce, Moore, Hoerni, Last, Grinich and the others, not the location of his facility. If he hadn't selected Palo Alto as the site for Shockley Laboratories, the industrial complex we now call

Silicon Valley wouldn't have developed, and everything that followed might have been accomplished in an entirely different locale.

With the exception of a few hundred four-layer diodes, Shockley Semiconductor never had any significant sales. It wasn't the products that were important to the history of our industry; it was the people.

Silicon Valley is a testament to Shockley's brilliance and his ability to attract the right people. He was a great scientist and a lousy manager.

CHAPTER TWO

"THE EIGHT" SET UP SHOP

Fairchild Semiconductor Begins

The eight new captains of industry set up shop on Charleston Road in Palo Alto. It was a chilly winter and the building had no heat. More to the point, none of those technical experts had ever done any selling. Fairchild Camera and Instrument Corporation convinced them to take on an experienced marketing specialist. When I spoke with Tom Bay, his memories of forty years earlier were still vivid:

"Early December 1957. Richard Hodgson (of Fairchild Camera and Instrument Corporation) called me at home. I had just decided I was not happy where I was, at Industrial Nucleonics. He called and said that they were talking to six Ph.D.'s and a couple of other guys out in California about starting a company making silicon transistors. I guess they were in the final stages of committing. In fact, when they talked to me originally, he said

41

The founders of Fairchild Semicondutor. From left to right,
Gordon Moore, Sheldon Roberts, Gene Kleiner, Bob Noyce, Vic Grinich
Julie Blank, Jean Hoerni, Jay Last. The photo was taken on February 26, 1960.

they were looking at me in sales or maybe general manager. Even before I talked to the guys I thought sales was where I should go since I didn't know anything about semiconductors.

"I had worked at Fairchild back in New York and left them at the end of 1955 to move to California. I didn't know Hodgson well, but certainly, I knew him, and when they decided to do the semiconductor thing, they really just had the six Ph.D.'s and Julie, and Gene Kleiner and they didn't have anybody else. In fact, I think I was hired before Fairchild Camera officially funded them."

It isn't really critical to the story, but when Jay Last read this manuscript he noted that Fairchild moved into the Charleston Road facility in October and had most of the equipment installed by December 1. He also remembered that "We had hired at least 15 people by the time Tom Bay arrived." Whatever the specific details, Tom Bay's narrative continues.

"I went to work for Fairchild (Semiconductor) on December 8, 1957. We were mopping floors and getting the place ready to move into. They were still working out of Vic Grinich's garage. They had signed a lease at 844 Charleston and we cleaned it up to get it ready for the equipment—although the equipment was basically tables and chairs."

The question of leadership for the new company was, of course, an important one, and in the very beginning there was no rush to volunteer for the job. Tom Bay remembered that his initial conversations with Hodgson touched on the possibility that Bay might serve as the general manager, but Tom Bay was determined to stay in marketing.

Vic Grinich added a few details . . .

"I remember Hodgson brought along several different guys as potential general managers. Although we all thought highly of Bob Noyce, he didn't feel he wanted to be the general manager. So, I remember at least two or three guys. One was Buck Rogers; remember him? He was one, a sales manager. Then Ed Baldwin was interviewed by Hodgson, and he was really impressed when he saw all those diodes being punched out there." [The reference is to the production volume at Hughes Semiconductor, where Baldwin was in charge of diode manufacturing.]

Gordon Moore commented on the search for a general manager . . .

"We ran an ad in The Wall Street Journal in December, asking for a general manager, and every salesman in the country thinks he can be a general manager. I think Ed Baldwin answered the ad. The search got him somehow."

Copy of the Recruiting Ad

Fairchild Semiconductor was barely a month old, and Tom Bay was newly on board as the first addition to the original eight. I asked him what he remembered about the selection of a general manager . . .

"I think the most important influence was the troops at Fairchild [corporate headquarters]: Carter, Hodgson, mostly Carter. They obviously felt that we didn't have anybody in Palo Alto who was old enough, familiar enough with management of a semiconductor facility, to be the general manager. And so, they said, 'We are going to look. But why don't you guys also look for somebody who you think you could work for who also knows the semiconductor business?

"We talked to a few guys who were old friends of Hodgson who were managers of companies. What was the company that made the power tools for Sears? Magna—the guy who was the head of that, if not the head then at least a VP. We talked to him, he was a nice enough guy but I was an engineer by education and the Ph.D.'s were suspicious of a guy who was a business-man with no technical background at all.

"Even though I knew nothing about solid state physics I had taught physics and when they talked to me about these things I understood fast enough. They said they were impressed with how smart I was—but that was probably bullshit. We just felt we needed someone who, if we were all going to report to him, had to be somebody who knew what a semiconductor was all about. I don't know how many guys we talked to, about half a dozen or more.

"I'm not sure where we came across Baldwin or how he got into the equation but he certainly knew semiconductors. He had been at Hughes in what was like product engineering but that isn't what they called it. Ed was the head of that at Hughes. Obviously, he understood all of the processing and everything else so that guys like Gordon and Bob [were OK with him]. I don't think Jean [Hoerni] was as much involved in that decision as Bob, Gordon and I were.

"Anyway, we were impressed with his [Baldwin's] back-ground in terms of what he had done at Hughes because at the time Hughes was the world's biggest producer of silicon diodes. It was all military business. The second largest was TI [Texas Instruments], maybe bigger in dollars, because they did make some silicon transistors that sold for a lot of money, but Hughes was making silicon diodes for everybody."

Baldwin's situation was certainly unusual. He came on the scene as general manager of the new company, but the original eight founders, in effect, owned Fairchild Semiconductor. One way of looking at it is to say that Baldwin was working for the people he was supposed to manage.

The offer to Baldwin included an invitation to participate in the new company's ownership on an equal footing with the original eight. Fairchild Camera would expand the available shares by one, and Baldwin could put up his $500 as the others had done. Apparently, however, Baldwin was not happy with that proposal and thought that he deserved a larger share because of his responsibilities as general manager.

There were continuing negotiations but the issue was never resolved. Baldwin never acquired any equity in Fairchild Semiconductor. According to Jay Last, who knew Baldwin in later years, Baldwin—for obvious reasons—regretted his failure to accept the stock deal that Fairchild offered. Baldwin once said that his rejection of the Fairchild offer was "the dumbest thing I ever did in my life."

In most references that mention Ed Baldwin's short tenure at Fairchild Semiconductor, he is treated as an unimportant footnote to the company's history, and the chronology of events in those earliest months is, to put it kindly, scrambled. Actually, Baldwin's accomplishments were not insignificant. Tom Bay remembers that Baldwin convinced Fairchild Camera and Instrument Corporation to build a new factory building and tool up for high volume production. Bay says that Baldwin's very early insistence on creating a major manufacturing facility was instrumental in the company's almost-immediate success.

Jay Last also had some good words for Ed Baldwin. He told me that

"Thanks to Baldwin, we made the decision to build a 60,000-square-foot building at the end of May, three months before we shipped our first 100 devices to IBM. Baldwin also steadily emphasized the need for quality devices. He arrived early in February of 1958 and his first talk to us about company organization emphasized quality control, life testing, etc."

Ed Baldwin left Fairchild to establish a new semiconductor venture funded by the Rheem company, better known for its climate-control and water-heating products. It wasn't long before Fairchild suspected Rheem of using engineering documents and drawings that had somehow "migrated" from Fairchild to Rheem. There was a legal action and Fairchild won the point.

Before the Factory

There was a lot of work to be done and only a few workers to do it. While just about everyone pitched in with the effort to set up a production facility, Tom Bay and Bob Noyce went after their first sale.

Tom Bay's account of his first Fairchild Semiconductor sales call sounds almost unbelievable now, but his colleagues from that time corroborated every detail. It took place in December 1957, before there was any product. Before there was even a manufacturing capability. Tom's narrative stands on its own as a great business story . . .

> "We hadn't defined a product other than it would be a silicon transistor. And I knew nothing about transistors at the time. IBM Owego, which was their primary military facility, had indicated that they were looking for a silicon device that they couldn't find, so Bob and I went out there about a week after I joined the company.
>
> "Harry Braning was the project guy at IBM. The project was a digital computer to replace the analog computer they used in the B52. That's the job that they were working on. In fact, I had worked selling precision parts to AC Spark Plugs in Milwaukee when I was with Fairchild Camera before I came to California. They made an analog computer that did the same thing that IBM was designing a digital to do.
>
> "What IBM needed was a core driver. And I had no idea at this point what the logic elements in it were, but obviously they were all discrete devices. They needed a core driver that would tolerate the 85 degree (Celsius) operating temperature. The only

transistors that would do the job were germaniums, but obviously they wouldn't take 85 degrees so we met with IBM even though we hadn't even talked about what size and kind of transistor we were going to develop for our first product. But they told us what they needed. They needed to drive at 150 milliamps, 60 volt capability. We said sure, we could do that. I say we, and I mean it was Noyce who said that we could do it.

"Noyce had never made such a device. It was all theoretical. But we all knew that the size of the devices would depend on the current capacity they needed and how much resistance they could stand and how much voltage. The week between Christmas and New Year, they gave us an order for a device that we said could meet the parameters.

"At the time we were working on both NPN and PNP. Gordon [Moore] was working on the NPN and Jean Hoerni was working on the PNP. We said what do you want? They said we don't care, just tell us a month before you deliver whether it's going to be NPN or PNP. IBM's input really decided what the first product was going to be. It was going to be a 60 volt core driver.

"Probably at the same time, or very close together, IBM Kingston was working on another project that needed a core driver. It was obvious to us that there were two groups in the same company interested in the same device and the company was obviously a solid citizen so we weren't worried about getting paid.

"I honestly can't remember how we decided on 150 bucks but that was the price for the first 100 devices. Our thinking was, we're going to develop it for IBM, and we really didn't think we'd sell a million of them at 150 bucks. We thought of it as a development project and they had defined the specs they needed and we agreed to them. And, in fact, we did deliver 100 devices."

I asked Tom why IBM was willing to buy such a vital component from an unknown startup company.

"It's hard to say. I think they knew that the existing silicon devices, which came from Texas Instruments, weren't nearly fast enough to do the core driver job. Part of the spec was the speed. We defined it in those days in terms of frequency capability. It had to be a 50 megacycle [megahertz] device and the things that were out there, and I can't remember the exact numbers, were TI 10 or 15 megacycle devices and that wasn't fast enough to do the job. At that point we were their only choice because they couldn't get a waiver from the Air Force on the temperature requirements and the electrical characteristics requirements were determined by the cores that they were using which were probably state of the art at the time. They literally didn't have a choice. So anyway, that's how the first job got defined."

Jay Last reflected on the question of IBM's willingness to do business with the new semiconductor company and had a much more succinct comment. He said that "Sherman Fairchild was the largest shareholder of IBM, and he went to IBM and put in a good word for us."

Tom Bay continues . . .

"Literally, there was a competition between Gordon Moore and Jean Hoerni that would decide whether the device would be an NPN or a PNP. In all honesty in those days all of the germanium devices were PNPs, so probably there was a leaning towards PNP.

"It's incredible to look back and think how fast this all happened. We took the order at the end of December 1957 and we delivered the first devices in March of '58. And there was an ongoing competition for six weeks as to which it was going to be. Gordon's device got consistently higher yield out of the wafers, which were *huge* half-inch wafers that we were using. (*Yield, or the percentage of good devices on a wafer, was an important consideration.*) And after they were put together in cans we had more problems with high leakage and that sort of thing with the PNPs than we ever did with the NPNs

"IBM was delighted. They immediately said that was the product they were going to use in their system. From that point we started negotiating quantity prices.

"We defined two products—the (2N)696 and the (2N)697. They wanted what we called the 697 because they wanted a minimum gain of 60. We defined the 697 as a minimum gain of 60 hfe, or whatever you want to call it. The 696 was 30 to 60. And in those days getting a gain of 60 was not that easy. We made *a lot more* 696s than we did 697s just because of the impurities and all the limitations on gain characteristics, and we chose Gordon's (Moore's) product."

Those two transistors, the 2N696 and 2N697, were the first successful semiconductor devices manufactured in California's Silicon Valley, long before the region was known as Silicon Valley!

PNP vs. NPN

Tom Bay's mention of the competition between Gordon Moore and Jean Hoerni regarding the very first kind of transistor begs for some elaboration. A reader who is unfamiliar with transistor fabrication can get some vague idea of the situation by thinking about the way simple batteries go into a flashlight. The positive end of one battery touches the negative end of the next battery. The designations of NPN and PNP imply a somewhat similar polarity in transistors. Even then, it was clearly possible to make either kind, and just a short time later it would be necessary to make both kinds.

But for the relatively simple application that IBM had in mind, it really didn't matter, and IBM left the choice to Fairchild. Accordingly, Gordon Moore and Jean Hoerni each embarked upon parallel efforts to develop a fabrication process for their respective choices.

Thirty-five years after the fact, neither Moore nor Hoerni were willing to characterize the process development contest as a divisive one. But others recalled a somewhat higher level of emotion than simple scientific objectivity. Moore's NPN process, at least initially, was easier to control and yielded fewer rejects. Hoerni was sure that his PNP process was potentially the more important one, and given a reasonable amount of development time, he was sure he could match the NPN yields.

Time wasn't available. Fairchild had to deliver on time, and Gordon Moore's NPN transistors went into production. They were well-received by IBM, a much larger follow-on order was issued, and Fairchild was on the way toward being a real company.

True Teamwork

Fairchild's achievement in fulfilling the IBM order was truly remarkable. At the time of that first sales call, Fairchild was, for all practical purposes, an empty factory. Nobody at Fairchild had ever actually manufactured the devices that Noyce and Bay were trying to sell to IBM, and there were no commercial sources for most of the equipment needed to build them. Even so, the new company was able to deliver acceptable devices in respectable quantities less than six months later.

In the absence of any process specifications, the men simply turned to the tasks they were capable of accomplishing.

Bob Noyce and Jay Last worked on the masking process for wafer fabrication. They actually built a step-and-repeat camera and the registration equipment that made possible high-precision optical performance. Device geometry is very much smaller and more complicated these days, but Noyce and Last were breaking new ground in 1958. Last had an optics background and did a lot of the optical and mechanical work. Noyce and Last also developed the photoresist technology that had been used for printed circuit boards, but required much tighter controls for transistor fabrication

Gordon Moore and Jean Hoerni established the diffusion processes. Gordon designed and built diffusion furnaces from scratch and Hoerni applied his experience in diffusion constants to determine temperatures, times and flow rates.

Sheldon Roberts designed and built a crystal-growing machine that turned out the silicon ingots and wafers.

Gene Kleiner and Julie Blank worked tirelessly on machine design, tool fabrication and overall assembly of the factory facilities. They farmed out what they could to local machine shops, and made many of the elements themselves.

Vic Grinich put together a test capability, established electrical specifications for the devices, and figured out how to combine commercially available instruments with those he modified or built himself.

Jay Last was responsible for all operations from mesa etch to final assembly. He handled mesa masking, etching and all subsequent operations through "final seal."

It was a team effort in every sense of the word. Even though most of the participants held doctorate degrees, they rolled up their sleeves, picked up their tools and put together a semiconductor factory. It would have been an impressive achievement even if there had been a pattern to follow, but they were inventing an industry and moving through uncharted territory.

Success was the result of a confluence of several unique factors: The eight men were able to work together; they had all been exposed to the inspiring example of the multidisciplinary Dr. Shockley; they shared a spirit of 'can do.' They were young and energetic, and able to work long hours; they had their own money invested in the venture and they believed in each other. They were ready to meet much bigger challenges.

CHAPTER THREE

AN INVENTION OF STAGGERING IMPORTANCE:

Jean Hoerni's Planar Process

The final step in diffused junction silicon mesa transistor fabrication was a chemical etching process to isolate the active portions of each 'die' on a wafer and to establish the junctions. This was accomplished by masking off the iterated dice on each wafer and exposing the wafer to a strong acid. The acid ate away a pattern of channels between each device.

The junction etching process was a mass-production bottleneck. Jay Last tried a number of methods to speed up the work. A number of acid-resistant materials were tried and the best one was carnuba wax. Initially, after the various diffusions had been completed, Last would put a wafer under a magnifying lens and deposit a drop of wax over each individual die. Imagine a production process where technicians are attempting to do this by the millions!

Constant experiments led to Last's development of a thin metal stencil that was positioned on the surface of each wafer. The holes in the stencil were "registered" to the active areas of each transistor. Then a film of wax was scraped over the stencil, resulting in a pattern of protective wax layers on top of each transistor.

The unprotected portions were dissolved by the acid. When the channels were deep enough, both the acid and the wax were washed away and the wafer contained an array of mesas representing the individual transistors.

Obviously, the placement of the stencil was critical. Registration had to be perfect. And if any wax happened to stray into unwanted places, the wafer had to be sent through a painstaking rewash and recoating operation.

Worse, the etching process itself was empirical. Too much or too little etching would ruin an entire wafer full of devices. And even when the etching was right on target, it was difficult to remove every trace of the acid. Just a few molecules of the acid, left on the wafer, would gradually eat into the transistor, causing it to exhibit long-term degradation.

Finally, assuming that the transistor dice had passed those early electrical tests, they were fastened to metal headers, thin gold wires were connected between 'contact pads' on the chip and the pins of the header, and then a metal cap was welded over everything to protect the little chip.

When the caps were welded, however, small metal particles could be released inside the can. Those particles sometimes moved around and shorted out the exposed junctions. A test fixture was developed that "tapped" each can hard enough to move any stray particles in a way that would reveal the possibility of shorting the junctions.

The fact that the junction was exposed was a fundamental weakness of the mesa transistor process. There had been a number of attempts to isolate individual transistors at the wafer fabrication stage, and a lot of thought had been applied to the problem of those exposed junctions. In the vocabulary of the time, device isolation and junction passivation were key challenges in improving the mesa process.

The Invention that Paved the Way for Integrated Circuits

While he was working on an improved method to fabricate PNP transistors, Jean Hoerni came up with a far better way of accomplishing device isolation without the inherent clumsiness of the mesa process, and without leaving the junctions exposed. Hoerni's inspiration was an additional diffusion step that "passivated" the material surrounding each transistor junction.

Now, instead of etching the fabricated wafer to establish the mesas, an additional diffusion step accomplished the same result within the crystal structure of the wafer itself. The whole messy business of stencils, wax and acid was a thing of the past. Another reliable link in the mass-production chain had been achieved, and yields increased dramatically. More important, it paved the way for the future invention of the integrated circuit.

Fairchild called this *The Planar Process* and applied for a patent. It caused an immediate flurry of excitement when this process was revealed at a series of professional meetings but no corresponding chorus of praise from the Fairchild factory engineers. We didn't realize the importance right away. To us it meant an additional diffusion operation and that meant more process development work.

Phil Ferguson, who would become head of device development at Fairchild and later CEO of a spinoff called General Microelectronics (Gme,) was working at Texas Instruments when Fairchild announced the Planar Process, and he remembered a meeting during which somebody asked the TI general manager, Mark Shepherd, about the development. According to Ferguson, Shepherd's response was, *"It isn't significant."* Ferguson and his colleagues, however, understood the importance of the process, and that comment inspired Ferguson to leave TI and join Fairchild.

The Planar Process produced transistors that were more reliable and easier to make than mesas. Even so, mesa transistors were the best transistors Fairchild had prior to Hoerni's brainstorm. They sold well, they

were incorporated into many
end products that performed
well, and they started
Fairchild Semiconductor on
the road to success.

It is an interesting footnote to history that Ed Baldwin's establishment of
Rheem Semiconductor, after
he left Fairchild, was based
on a replication of the original Fairchild mesa process.
While Baldwin was working
to set up a production line
for mesa transistors, Fairchild
was developing an entirely
new and better way to make
transistors and, in the

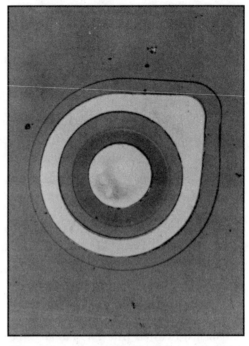

Photomicrograph of the first Planar transistor

process, render mesa devices obsolete. As a matter of fact, it was exactly
two weeks after Baldwin left to set up Rheem as a mesa transistor company that the validity of the new Planar Process was established!

And in yet another branch of this sidebar, the semiconductor division
of Hoffman Electronics, a company in Southern California, with a history of making silicon diodes and solar cells, was also struggling to get
into the mesa transistor business, based on a process that Fairchild had
made obsolete with Hoerni's invention.

CHAPTER FOUR

MY JOURNEY FROM SARANAC LAKE, NEW YORK TO MOUNTAIN VIEW, CALIFORNIA

The Planar Process was just beginning to be a topic of conversation at Fairchild when I arrived in the fall of 1959. This is probably as good a place as any to say a few words about my own background and the events leading up to my affiliation with Fairchild.

I was born November 15, 1927, at Saranac Lake (New York) General Hospital. My father and mother, Christian and Caroline Sporck, were first generation German-Americans, born in Greenpoint, New York. They went to school through the 8th grade. My father was a machinist and my mother, who said she liked the job, worked in a sweatshop making straw hats.

In 1918, while my mother was pregnant with her first child (my brother,) my father came down with tuberculosis. At the time my grandmother was working as a maid for a wealthy family in New York City, and her employers suggested that my father should go to Saranac Lake to take the "rest cure." Saranac Lake was then known as the *Miracle Mountain of the United States* and it was thought that the pure mountain air, combined with absolute rest, was the best therapy for TB.

Unfortunately, a bedridden machinist can't earn a living while taking the rest cure and there were no hat-making factories in Saranac Lake. So my mother was compelled to take in laundry and baby-sit to support the family. After one year of bed rest my father decided he couldn't stand the idleness any longer. He borrowed money from his sisters and opened a small grocery store in Saranac Lake. His doctors told him he would be dead in six months.

The store was an immediate success and my father outlived his doctors by many years, although he continued to have relapses of TB until the 1950s when new "miracle drugs" all but wiped out the disease. Dad lived to be 92 years old!

The grocery business provided well for our family until the late '20s when an A&P market was established next to our store. Fortunately my father had an early warning of this and sold before the disaster. Dad then went into the taxi business, usually with just one car. This was the source of the family income until his retirement in the 1970s.

We three Sporck children (I have an older brother and a younger sister) were blessed with parents and one grandmother whose only purpose in life was to provide for us. Providing didn't mean spoiling. It clearly was hard to spoil kids when the provider often came home with $3 a day or less. But we never wanted for essentials and we always felt we were better off than most.

Certain things were of prime importance to our parents. After food came education, education, education. Since my parents had so little schooling, they were committed to their kids getting thorough educations. This commitment resulted in university degrees for all three of us, all from Cornell.

I never was as serious a student as my brother and sister, both of whom did very well in school. They qualified for scholarships that paid for much of their college tuition. My brother did especially well, setting standards of excellence at Saranac Lake High School which are remembered to this day. I, on the other hand, was a mediocre high school student, finding much more satisfaction in sports, school politics and raising hell. I played on the football team, the basketball team, the track team and the ski team, and was elected president of the student council.

All through high school my primary ambition in life was to win an appointment to West Point and become a professional soldier. My goals changed during my senior year when I met Jeanine, the girl who was to become my wife. (As I write this, Jeanine and I have been married fifty years.) The idea of spending four years at West Point without her companionship suddenly seemed less attractive.

I enlisted in the Army in June 1945 and my two years in the service convinced me that engineering was a better direction to take than West Point. My military experience was not distinguished. I entered as a private and exited as a private. Actually I did take a competitive exam and won an alternate appointment to West Point. But my service experience, especially a West Point preparation class at Fort Benning, Georgia, inspired me to withdraw my candidacy for the academy.

My only "interesting" experience in the service occurred after leaving Fort Benning and being assigned to Carlisle Indian barracks at Carlisle, Pennsylvania. In 1946 this was a school for the Government of Occupied Areas. Here, officers were trained for occupying government areas in Germany. I worked as a "gofer" for a colonel teaching civics. The student officers arrived from all over the country in very dirty autos.

Since I had a lot of surplus time, I started an on-base car-cleaning business with a number of part-time G.I. employees. This was a very successful enterprise for about two months. Five dollars got you a clean car. However, trouble arrived when the outfit's executive officer, a major, told me to get his car washed. I told him it would cost him $5 and he disagreed. Thus ended my car wash business and started me in my new occupation: *cutting grass with a bayonet.* This was probably the main reason I was never promoted beyond private.

I finished my Army hitch in 1947 and spent one term as a student at the new Paul Smith's College in Saranac Lake. The classes I attended in

1948 were Paul Smith's very first. It was then, and still is, the only private college in Adirondack Park. The college was founded by the heirs of a local entrepreneur who did well in the resort hotel business. I studied calculus, among other subjects, while waiting for the Fall term to begin at Cornell.

Much later in my life I have participated actively in the growth and development of Paul Smith's College, and as I write this I am a member of the board of trustees of that fine institution. We are all proud of the fact that the college is now accredited to grant four-year bachelor degrees in several disciplines important to the economy of the Mountain Lakes area of the Adirondacks.

I entered Cornell University in September 1948 as a student of mechanical engineering. Two objectives were foremost in my mind:

- Earn enough income to get married.
- Finish school and get started on my long-term financial goal of reaching $10,000 a year.

The first objective was reached quite soon. Between the G.I. Bill, waiting on tables at a fraternity house and other part-time jobs, I was in pretty good shape. At the end of my sophomore year I became a co-op student in the General Electric Company's engineering program. This, plus my future wife Jeanine's income, amounted to enough for a young couple. We got married in October 1949 in Saranac Lake at the Presbyterian Church where my family were long-term members.

One interesting point about the wedding: Right after the ceremony Jeanine's favorite uncle congratulated me and welcomed me to the GE "family." Uncle Frank was a lifelong employee of GE and his welcome was a sincere expression of his strong loyalty to his employer. How the world has changed.

My second objective took a lot longer to achieve. Indeed, I didn't earn $10,000 a year until I joined Fairchild Semiconductor 10 years later in 1959.

I was an average scholar at Cornell except in math and physics, where I did quite well. My interest in co-op assignments was stronger than my interest in school work. The Cornell co-op program at that time involved working three to four months with a participating company, going back to the Cornell campus for a term, then repeating the sequence. This was excellent experience. I had assignments testing gun turrets for B-36 bombers in Burlington, Vermont, quality testing of water coolers in Bloomfield, New York, and, finally, testing jet engines at the Evandale, Ohio plant.

The last assignment was a godsend. The Korean War was on and testing jet engines was critical work. I worked 12 hours per day, 7 days a week. Jeanine got a job with a construction company building a new factory for GE and she worked the same hours. We saved $3,000 in three months, a fortune for us. A godsend, actually, because Jeanine was pregnant and stopped work in our senior year. The $3,000 saw us through the rest of our college experience.

The years went by and I was totally unaware of anything happening in California. I may have read about the invention of the transistor, and I may have seen Shockley's name in print, but I didn't know anything about semiconductors and I wasn't curious about them.

I was in my ninth year as an employee of General Electric, and involved in the manufacturing of power factor correction capacitors. In addition to my nine full-time years, I had been in the GE co-op program for two of my years as a mechanical engineering student at Cornell University.

GE was a good place to work. When I was hired they assigned me to a three year manufacturing management program and made sure I was exposed to many different supervisory situations. Back in those days, GE was primarily a manufacturing company, and effective management was an important component of profitability. When I first went to work for GE, the company had 35,000 workers in Schenectady alone! Now there are only a couple thousand employees left in the Schenectady works, a sign of GE's shift from manufacturing to financial services.

GE's Hudson Falls facility had a compensation system for factory workers that was based on what were called group incentives. In other words, a worker could make a little more money if the group turned out more finished products. I was assigned to develop some manufacturing methods not directly related to the way things were being done. We did the development work at a location away from the assembly line. It seemed to me that we had, indeed, worked out better ways of doing things, and there was a promise of higher productivity.

When we proposed our improvements, the union objected. Unions were very strong at GE and had a lot of influence over work methodology and compensation. There was a big union protest rally staged to keep out the new methods. I was burned in effigy, and GE caved in. They chose not to install the improvements.

I went home that evening and told my wife, Jeanine, that the time had come to look for work elsewhere. I began to read the recruiting ads in *The Wall Street Journal* and *The New York Times*.

I spotted a small ad in August 1959, seeking a production manager for a company in California called Fairchild Semiconductor. I answered the ad and a little while later I was invited to a job interview at a Manhattan hotel.

The two gentlemen who were supposed to interview me must have been at the designated hotel quite a while before I showed up, because they showed obvious signs of a great deal of liquid refreshment. They were laughing at each other's mumbled phrases and only marginally interested in conducting a formal interview. After some conversation they told me I was hired and instructed me to report to Mountain View, California, at my earliest convenience. I was to be paid $13,000 a year, which was $5,000 more than I was earning at GE. I accepted their offer on the spot.

Jeanine was surprised that I would leave Upstate New York and the Adirondacks. We agreed that we would spend two years in California and save the difference between my new salary and the old sum. At the end of two years we would have $10,000 saved up to expand the small motel we owned in Saranac Lake. It was our plan to move back there and live out our lives as innkeepers.

We sold our house, put all our belongings in the car and headed for California. I reported to the new Fairchild facility in Mountain View in the fall of 1959, ready to take up my assignment as production manager. But when I arrived at the reception desk, nobody knew who I was. They didn't recognize my name. They had no idea what to do with me. Apparently, the men who had hired me in New York never bothered to tell anyone at Fairchild. After quite a bit of asking around, I finally found one of the men who had been at the New York hotel, and he dimly remembered our meeting and the job offer.

They showed me to an office where I found another man, also newly arrived, who had been hired for the same job. The two of us were assigned to the same office, with the same job, wondering what to do. Bob Robson, our general foreman, was also assigned to that office and he reported to both of us.

I honestly can't remember what happened to the other guy. But in a matter of days he was gone and I was in charge of making strange devices called semiconductors. As was true for so many of those early-day recruits, I didn't know exactly what they were, or how they worked. Everything I know about semiconductors was learned on the job. Fortunately, many of my new knowledgeable associates were generous and patient with their explanations.

My first impressions of Fairchild: A group of people with enormous technical abilities, enthusiasm and confidence, but little or no structured manufacturing organization. I was accustomed to the well-defined environment of General Electric, with strict standards for everything from cost accounting to ethics. Fairchild had virtually no competence in the handling of labor and labor unions. I brought this competence to my new employer.

Thanks to Ed Baldwin's early leadership, the Mountain View plant was as modern as anyone could make it in 1959. The diffusion areas were like laboratories, with arrays of tube furnaces, exhaust hoods, pipes running everywhere with various gases, small darkrooms for the photolithographic processes, and workers in dust-free smocks.

The assembly area had long rows of benches and chairs. Each station had a binocular microscope and precision manipulating equipment. It was possible to fabricate a great many transistors on a single wafer, and it was possible to process many wafers at a time in batch diffusions, but then every individual transistor had to be assembled by hand in a series of painstaking steps. And each finished device had to be tested in a number of ways, again accounting for a lot of labor.

I was totally occupied with the challenge of manufacturing, and from my point of view, certainly, manufacturing was the keystone of Fairchild's growing business. With hindsight, however, I now know that developments in R&D and marketing were every bit as important.

Charlie Sporck with Sherman Fairchild, probably 1965

CHAPTER FIVE

BOB NOYCE'S SUDDEN FLASH OF INSIGHT:

The Birth of Integrated Circuits

Important as the Planar Process was to the achievement of higher fabrication yields, there was another benefit of Planar geometry that would soon, in my opinion, make it one of the most important technological developments of the 20th century!

It had been obvious from the very beginning of silicon transistor manufacture that there was something illogical taking place at the cus-

**Dr. Robert N. Noyce.
Photo from 1965**

tomer end of the process. The device manufacturers produced wafers containing hundreds—or even thousands—of individual transistors.

Then the transistors were separated, assembled onto individual "headers" and sold to customers as discrete devices. The customers, in turn, inserted the headers into printed circuit boards and interconnected the transistors.

Why not interconnect the transistors at the wafer level? One approach might have been to use very thin gold wires that spanned the etched channels between those original mesas. But you could only overlap so many wires before they threatened to touch each other and produce unwanted connections. And the little wires did not hold up well in the shock and vibration tests that were imposed by military customers. That approach was not promising.

When Bob Noyce looked at Hoerni's Planar Process, he had a moment of illumination. He saw that there were no physical channels to bridge on the wafer and no exposed junctions. If some passive components, such as resistors and/or capacitors, could also be fabricated on the wafer along with transistors, all of the elements needed to achieve true electronic circuits would be present.

Noyce, with the collaboration of Jay Last, envisioned the deposition of a thin layer of aluminum over the passivated surface, making contact through holes etched through the passivation layer to selected portions of each transistor and the related components on the chip. Finally, a mask-and-etch operation could be used to remove the unwanted areas of aluminum. What remained was a pattern of thin aluminum lines that functioned as conductors.

Because everything was done with thin films of directly deposited material, there would be no problems with shock and vibration tolerance. And because there were no exposed junctions, the devices could be expected to exhibit long-term stability.

Noyce envisioned all of that at once. In whatever time it took to have the thought, Bob Noyce invented monolithic integrated circuits.

But there were still some technological problems to be solved. Because the various components were all neighbors on the same small piece of silicon, they experienced undesirable electronic interreactions.

Izzy Haas and Lionel Kattner worked hard in the R&D department to solve the problem. One interim approach that was soon abandoned involved turning the wafer over and etching away the superfluous silicon material almost to the top surface. It was an electrical success but very difficult to produce. The ultimate answer, worked out by Last, Haas and Kattner, was yet another diffusion, one that passivated and isolated the boundaries of the various components.

At one point in the development of integrated circuits, probably in September or October 1960, Tom Bay attended a staff meeting where Last reported on his integrated circuit progress. Last remembers Tom Bay announcing, "Jay Last has pissed away a million dollars on this integrated circuit project. I say we should shut it down." Tom Bay's attitude also reflected business conditions at the time. There was a recession and business was not exactly booming.

Many years after the fact, when I asked him about his original attitude, Tom Bay said that he took an anti-integrated circuit position because Fairchild had a lot of business in transistors and diodes. Sales of discrete components were growing rapidly, and, at the time, the factory was having a tough time meeting the market demand. It was difficult to make and sell those first *Micrologic*/RTL integrated circuits, which were not well received by customers. But they were the first monolithic integrated circuits ever offered for sale, and they heralded the birth of a mass-production technology that would lead, inevitably, to the complete microprocessor chip. Fortunately for Fairchild, Tom Bay's negative attitude did not prevail.

In one of those coincidences of human inventiveness, Fairchild filed a patent disclosure for the "Noyce Process" of device integration just a short time after Jack Kilby of Texas Instruments disclosed the sort of interconnection scheme described on page 66. Kilby's proposal used thin wires interconnecting the individual devices on a wafer. The Kilby disclosure was filed on February of 1959 and the Noyce disclosure, for aluminum conductors deposited on a planar device surface, was filed in July of that same year. Both Fairchild and Texas Instruments claimed to have invented the integrated circuit.

It was soon obvious that the Texas Instruments approach, while inter-esting in the laboratory, could not be practical on a commercial level. Indeed, Fairchild scientists called the Kilby demonstration a special case of a hybrid circuit. But the Fairchild Planar Process was immediately use-ful for the mass production of diodes and transistors as well as for the integrated circuits that soon became commonplace.

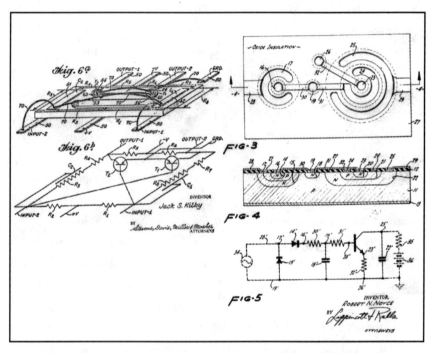

Integrated circuit patent drawings. On the right, the Fairchild submission, filed on July 30, 1959. On the left, the Texas Instruments submission, filed six months earlier, on February 6, 1959. The Kilby (Texas Instruments) concept, although a bit earlier, proved impractical even in 1959, and would have been impossible in today's microprocessor environment.

There was a legal battle between Fairchild and Texas Instruments as each company claimed the invention of integrated circuits. Meanwhile, the entire industry gradually adopted the Planar Process under license from Fairchild. (The TI/Fairchild controversy was eventually settled 10 years later with a cross-licensing agreement.)

Jack Kilby was recognized by the Nobel Committee and named as a co-recipient of the Nobel Prize in Physics in 2000 for his pioneering work on integrated circuits. It seems obvious to me, and to many others, that Bob Noyce would have been afforded at least the same degree of recognition, and that Jean Hoerni also deserved a Nobel prize for his development of the Planar process. Unfortunately, the committee honors only the living, and Noyce and Hoerni did not live long enough to collect the honors they so richly deserved.

As the integrated circuit moved from the good-idea stage to the factory floor, Jay Last and Jean Hoerni were being wooed by Henry Singleton to set up a semiconductor operation for Teledyne Corporation. Jay Last insisted that any new venture be located on the San Francisco Peninsula, and ultimately, he and Jean Hoerni organized Amelco Semiconductor, a wholly owned subsidiary of Teledyne. Gene Kleiner, and Sheldon Roberts, two more original founders of Fairchild Semiconductor, also participated in the Amelco startup. Last remembered Hoerni's comment on the departures as *"There was just too much talent at Fairchild."* Amelco focused on military products and became a very successful company with strong technology. Some years later, Amelco was renamed and became known as Teledyne Semiconductor.

Hoerni, who Last described as *"most productive when he was discontented, and he was usually upset over something,"* eventually "got cranky" at Amelco, went to Union Carbide, and then became one of the organizers of Intersil, another Silicon Valley spinoff semiconductor company.

When he thought back to his departure from Fairchild, Last cited the emerging organization of the company as the trigger that started him thinking about changing jobs. "Bob Noyce was general manager and Gordon Moore was in charge of R&D and I was working on device development under Gordon. It was no longer my company. I was just another employee and it was time for me to move on."

Last also said he was affected by Tom Bay's negative position on integrated circuits, and had some reservations about Fairchild's negotiations with Olivetti and Telettra, which put up the money, to establish SGS in

Italy with Fairchild technology. "We gave up Europe to that consortium," said Last. "It was just another sign that the company was growing in directions that didn't involve me. But my main reason for leaving was that I wanted to work on integrated circuit applications. This wasn't going to happen soon at Fairchild, and Henry Singleton at Teledyne wanted to do it right away."

All of the evidence seems to indicate that the pressure to set up SGS in Italy came from Fairchild's corporate office on Long Island, in Syosset, New York, and that Noyce went along with the directive as a good soldier and not as an advocate. Don Rogers, Fairchild's sales manager, was sent to Italy to manage the sales effort and Harry Sello, who had been manager of sustaining engineering in California, ran the operations side. Ownership of the Italian company was divided equally between Fairchild, Olivetti and Telettra.

36 Years Before TIME MAGAZINE's *Man Of The Year*

Andy Grove, Bob Noyce and Gordon Moore, probably around 1968.

Andy Grove, chairman and CEO (at the time of my interview,) of Intel Corporation, was named 1997 *Man of The Year* by TIME Magazine. Thirty-six years earlier, he was just completing his Ph.D. in fluid dynamics at the University of California, Berkeley, and looking for a job. Andy described his education as very heavily mathematics-driven, and he almost certainly would have been a success in any of the emerging technologies of the day.

The Cold War was at a peak and Grove saw his career possibilities divided into two categories: What he called "The Lockheed Class" of military-oriented companies contrasted sharply with the more commercially oriented outfits. He interviewed with both types of company and kept notes. General Electric turned him down because of his lack of specific technology experience. Hewlett Packard offered him a job and assured him that he would rapidly learn whatever he needed to know. Grove described HP as a company *"with the sense to look for bright guys."*

Andy's Fairchild career almost didn't happen. Never a man to mince words, Grove told me about the strange ordeal of joining Fairchild . . .

"I wrote Fairchild, saying I wanted to come out and interview. They wrote back a condescendingly disgusting letter, along the lines of 'We like our young men to interview with us when they have finished interviewing with everybody else.' You know—go away and come back when you're ready to graduate.

"The first thing that was wrong with it was, it was kind of arrogant. The second was that I was graduating in February or March. I finished (University of California at) Berkeley in two and a half years with a Ph.D. They thought I was going to get out in June, and really I was all done. So I gave up on Fairchild.

"Then in the fall of '62 or very early in 1963, I got a call from somebody at Fairchild. It was somebody I never heard of who was coming out to Berkeley and would love to get acquainted with me. He was John Waring, head of the chemistry department at Fairchild R&D, and he didn't know anything about my earlier application. It was typical of Fairchild, behaving like a big place even then; two pieces of paper would never cross in that place.

"Waring went to Berkeley and asked who the best students were and got my name, so he called me at home to invite me to meet him when he came to Berkeley. Very quickly I realized I didn't want to work in the chemistry department. Then I met Gordon [Moore] and it was love at first sight. I have my notes to this date, by the way. I can dig them out. I kept notes for everything because I was interviewed by so many places, I was so unsure about what was going to happen, so I typed up notes after each interview.

"Here's what I wrote about Gordon: 'Young, very bright, got the essence of my thesis in minutes. Unbelievable that at his age he would be in charge of a big laboratory—fantastic guy—what a wonderful guy to work for.' Something like that. Thirty-three years later, it proved to be pretty correct. So that's how it started. It was March 20-something, 1963.

"Tom Sau was my boss that I'd never met because he wasn't around. Gordon hired me on behalf of Sau, who was off somewhere. He was there in the morning and left in the afternoon to go to some meeting. He sat me down (that first morning) and walked me through how he wanted me to do an analysis of MOS capacitors and taught me what he knew about it and left.

"He was gone for the rest of the week, and by the end of the week I published. We had a data center. Computers were not widely used, particularly not at Fairchild at that time, but I used to write programs in Fortran at Berkeley, so I was an ace. I planned out the report, wrote it up, put a bunch of curves in it and had it ready for Tom for Monday. I published it.

"Bob Noyce got a copy somehow. I don't know the mechanisms of distribution. A few days later I got a note (which I still have) from this guy Bob Noyce, on intercompany yellow stationery: 'I read your report on MOS capacitors. Very nice work.' Signed Bob. Bob who? Then they told me he was the big boss.

"I was 27. So I found it OK. Not bad for the first week or two. In fact, the stuff I did on that report was the beginning of the MOS analysis and all that stuff. MOS had just started. The company hired Bruce Deal to do better oxides. Bruce arrived within weeks of me, and we didn't know about each other.

"Anyway, Bruce was hired in R&D, Exnal was hired in R&D. Exnal did ion migration type work for his Ph.D. at the University of Utah or at Utah State, and then there was me. I don't exactly know who hired who, but the three of us were working on different branches of the same general problem. It took us weeks, a good number of weeks, before we discovered each other—in the cafeteria: 'What are you doing? I'm working on this, I'm working on . . . etc.' Nobody bothered to coordinate us (probably this doesn't come as horrible shock to you) and out of the three of us plus Tom Sau, since he was the boss, published 20 papers, some of which turned out to be costly—but this is how we met. In fact I met one of them (I don't remember which one), and he told me that "There's another guy," and then the two of us went and found the third. We hit it off OK and we were perfectly matched in terms of attitudes."

Andy Grove couldn't have known it at the time, but he and Gordon Moore both got into semiconductors because somebody was searching through resumes in search of exceptional talent. Shockley had found Moore's resume among others at Lawrence Livermore Laboratory, and John Waring found Grove's resume at the Berkeley campus of the University of California.

Grove's comment about the lack of organization at Fairchild ("*two pieces of paper would never cross in that place*") was symptomatic of the raw backgrounds of so many. Very few of the semiconductor pioneers had grown up in a formal company environment. They were forever reinventing (or ignoring) systems and procedures well established in older industries.

Floyd Kvamme

Floyd Kvamme (*Quam'ee*) was
another 1963 addition to the
Fairchild staff with an interesting
story to tell about the Fairchild
"mystique" which was beginning to
manifest itself. Again, in his own
words, here's Floyd's version of the
way he landed in Silicon Valley . . .

Floyd Kvamme

"After getting out of Berkeley, I
went to work for a little company called Electronic Systems
Development Corporation in
Ventura, California, and became a design engineer with this
new stuff called transistors. I had a bachelor's, and when I got
my degree, I didn't know anything about business because at
Berkeley, it was a highly theoretical thing. So, seeing semiconductors—I'd always wanted to go get a master's, but I didn't
know what in—and, seeing semiconductors, I said, 'I've got to
get a master's in semiconductors.'

I wrote to probably 40 schools in America, but only two
offered semiconductor master's programs in 1970: Purdue and
Syracuse. Syracuse was GE-sponsored, with GE Semiconductor
being in town. And Purdue, where—a lot of people don't know
this—N.A.D. Crane found the transistor effect three weeks after
Shockley. And of course, nobody knew that because Crane was
three weeks late!

I know this is a lengthy passage, but I have included it because it illustrates one of the big reasons why established large corporations did not
become leaders in the semiconductor business. Kvamme's story about the

internal complications at General Electric is probably typical of the way things were at ITT, RCA, Raytheon, etc. In addition to the mastery of a new technology, the startup companies, such as Fairchild, were managed informally enough to jump on new ideas and processes as they emerged. Try to imagine a bright young engineer struggling to stay on the cutting edge of an emerging technology in the GE thicket of established procedures . . .

"[My wife] Jean was pregnant and I had to work and so I decided to go to Syracuse because I could get a job at GE Semiconductor. I was taking my master's part-time at nights—every night—finished it in two years—didn't see Jean for two years in the snow. For San Francisco natives, that was exciting.

"Actually, there's a little story that I thought of as I remembered this: I got to know the guy who ran engineering back there very well, Len Meyer, who became the general manager at GE Semiconductor a little after that. About eight weeks into the program they had a little thing for these guys who were going to be their semiconductor gurus (and I was one of them.) Meyer said, 'A very important guy is visiting. This guy is a genius. He started a company out in California. His name is Bob Noyce.'

"It was the first time I had ever heard of Bob Noyce. I mean, you would have thought that God himself was walking through by the description of Len Meyer, and it made an incredible impression on me.

"That was 1960. And it would have been about the fall. Bob visited what was called 'The Electronics something Lab' at Syracuse which was a little thing where they were doing work on epitaxy and some of that stuff, and he gave a little talk to a group of about 20 of us. I guess GE was considering taking a license in the Planar Process. That was the basis, I think. He wanted to meet the semiconductor guys. But I'll never forget the buildup that Bob got at that time.

"I worked as an applications engineer and got my master's at Syracuse in semiconductors in '62 and I wanted to go into marketing and they wouldn't let me. So, I decided 'I'm not going to stay here.'

"Accounting set the prices. You had to go through channels. I was assigned as a sales rep to GE Computer in Phoenix to get them to design-in our germanium mesa transistor because I was doing my Masters in high-speed switching and what caused the transistor to switch. They figured I could sell the product by explaining the technology. I got the computer people excited about it. It was the 2N996—I still remember the part type.

"You had to go to accounting to get the prices you'd quote to customers. In those days, a guy named Berkley Davis ran the electronics components division, and his office was in Owensboro where they ran the tube division, and their accounting team had to approve our semiconductor pricing. They weren't even in Syracuse with us. It was crazy! It took forever to get a quote done, and the notion of forward pricing, or [our forecast] that yield was going to get better, or once you got—I mean, it was totally foreign!

"Everything was run by the tube guys, and it was terrible. I mean, the guys at GE Computer really wanted to buy our transistors, and it was almost impossible to do business with a sister division.

"Once I was invited to a GE general managers' meeting at Skaneateles. They had this big house built in the Depression years, and I was supposed to go up and talk about some of my master's [degree] work. We thought we knew how to predict how fast the transistor would switch and frankly had some pretty good stuff and we were putting in additional parameters as performance got higher. So we talked to these general managers and I gave my little pitch and then I sat down and listened to some of the discussion.

"A guy says, 'We don't give a damn about how fast they switch. We can't figure out how to do business with you guys! You take forever, your prices are noncompetitive. I mean, come on! That's wonderful that the kid knows how fast the transistors switch.'

"And I just sat there, and they were absolutely right because I had experienced that same frustration by being the sales guy at GE Computer. The *coup de grace*—that actually created the Skaneateles meeting—was that we had a transistor called the 2N404 which was competing with RCA's 2N396 which was the big deal in those days, a big volume part. GE Military puts out an ad, center spread, in *Electronic News* saying that the RCA 2N396 was the best germanium alloy transistor in the world, and the guys at GE Semiconductor went crazy and said how much work we had to do. And that's what created that meeting, and in that meeting it was brought out that the problem was you couldn't do business with them.

"Oh, and the other problem in those days was that the other divisions had access to our financials. Things were run so accountingwise that they [buyers from sister divisions] could get in and see what your costs were and you couldn't arbitrarily quote prices to a sister division. It was crazy. It was just really nuts-o. Can you imagine? Accounting set the prices!

"I left GE and looked around and actually talked to Fairchild at that time and I don't remember why they weren't interested, so I decided "Screw it. I will go and get a Ph.D." So I talked with UCLA and, again, couldn't afford to go to school full-time.

"So I went to Space Technology Laboratories in Manhattan Beach, California, and was in charge of a design group for some circuits for one classified satellite program and a thing called OGO, which was the Orbiting Geophysical Observatory satellite.

"I went there because STL would pay for my schooling at UCLA and I started to do the work and in fact completed all the course work and was thinking about starting a thesis again in silicon. But you had to have three expertises at UCLA and computer architecture was one, semiconductor was another, and I forget the third.

"At STL we were called on by a very aggressive Fairchild salesman named Chaz Haba and he came in one day and there's a funny story about it. I had done a lot of work in charge analysis and how fast transistors switch and we needed a very fast diode. I needed a very good forward recovery, and he had a device (can't remember the number of it now) that he thought was going to be fast, and he brought in a guy—he said he had a diode expert coming down that day and so, we talked about the diode. They came into my office and we went over it, and I asked them all these questions because this guy was the diode expert, from the diode factory.

"Every time I asked the guy a question, Chaz interrupted and answered the question. So I said 'Look guys, let's go down and plug it into my circuit and I'll tell you in a minute if it works.' So we waltz down the hall and Chaz was giving me all these excuses, like 'They haven't been tested yet,' and I put the diodes in and they worked fabulously. It was the FD-6 family, one of those fast forward recovery types, which was exactly what I needed. So, all the way back to my office, Chaz was telling me how it was 'absolutely what I told you.' Well, a few weeks went by, and he said 'Hey, you really ought to come to work for Fairchild,' and he introduced me to Mel Phelps who hired me. I decided to truncate my education, so I never finished my Ph.D.

"I went to work for Fairchild April 1, 1963, as a product marketing engineer in the digital IC area. I remember very shortly after that Chaz talked Jerry Sanders, who was running the Los Angeles region then, into having me come down to give a seminar on transistor switching. I did, and there was that guy I met when I was at STL, the 'expert' from the diode factory. I said, 'Gee, what you are you doing here?' It was Marshall Cox! He said, 'That day, I could have shot Haba! Because I was from the legal department at 9:00 a.m. on a Rockwell call; I was from the factory on your call!' He was in training! He didn't know a diode from a rock, it turned out, and he'd just come to work as a salesman. I've never forgotten it. And Marshall and I have laughed about that because Chaz was quite a salesman.

"I remember going in to say hello to Bob Noyce just after joining Fairchild and reminding him of having met him those years before. He recalled the visit, mostly because GE wanted some impossible set of terms (he didn't tell me what they were) to do the Planar patent or whatever, because they had some planar stuff that they were working on—I just don't remember those details at all. However, I did go in to say hello to Bob."

What I like about both Andy Grove's and Floyd Kvamme's stories are the mentions of informal contacts with Bob Noyce. In one instance, Bob took the trouble to send a congratulatory note to Grove for his first paper as a new employee. In the other instance, Kvamme dropped into Bob's office to say hello and to remind him of an earlier meeting in Syracuse. Bob was just that way. Everyone, from assembly workers to R&D scientists felt perfectly at ease speaking with Bob, popping into his office to say hello or stopping him in the corridor to make a comment or ask a question.

GE's Semiconductor Failure: Food for Thought

General Electric was, and still is, a company with a habit of success. When Floyd Kvamme worked for the GE semiconductor division, there was certainly no shortage of resources, and the company had access to all of the technology that was floating around. But it wasn't long before GE abandoned its outside sales effort, even though the company continues to pursue R&D work in semiconductors.

GE fell victim to the same cluster of problems that forced most of the other old-line corporations out of the semiconductor business. The industry simply moved too fast for the corporate structure to accommodate the changes. No sooner had a production line been established to manufacture some device with an apparently high sales potential, and all of the work assignments had been cleared with the union, than a new development would make the device obsolete. Workers had to be reassigned, factory equipment had to be modified or replaced, and entire organizations had to be dissolved and re-formed. By the time all of the requisite approvals moved through the chain of command and all of the conferences had been held, important market opportunities were missed.

Pricing was another important issue. Out in California, where a new generation of management viewed the "learning curve" model of pricing as a normal way of life, radical price erosion was taken as a given. Newly introduced devices, much in demand by leading-edge equipment manufacturers, sold at premium prices. Within a relatively short period of time, as yields increased and manufacturing costs plummeted, and as competitors brought similar products to market, prices moved sharply lower. A "new" semiconductor company incorporated this process into the collective consciousness and lived with it. But old-line corporations could not accommodate that kind of fluidity. They insisted on rigid plans with unrealistic sales predictions. And even when they tried to remain competitive, the many layers of management and the strong influence of their accounting departments slowed down their response to the point of ineffectiveness.

It was a situation that should have taught some valuable lessons about the management of a company engaged in a leading-edge industry, but history repeated itself when personal computers emerged. Once again, the old-line corporations started out with an advantage over the startups, and once again their rigid structures presented insurmountable obstacles.

Almost alone among all the other established corporations, IBM seemed to appreciate this process. IBM always had a strong semiconductor operation, but resisted the temptation to take its products to the open market. And when IBM entered the personal computer business, it set up an autonomous operation many hundreds of miles away from their other facilities. Even so, IBM has had great difficulties keeping up with start-up competitors who were more flexible.

Transitron

According to Bob Swanson, now CEO of Linear Technology, Transitron was the country's second-largest manufacturer of semiconductor devices in 1962. Based in Boston, Transitron was the brainchild of the Bakalar brothers, and rapidly grew large enough to threaten the primacy of Texas Instruments. One of the brothers, David, was a bona-fide technical person and the other one, Leo, had run a company making shoe lasts. Their first factory was in a former bakery, in Melrose, Massachusetts. A feature story in *Fortune* magazine around that time was illustrated with side-by-side photos of the CEOs of TI and Transitron, and had a headline referring to "David and Goliath."

It now appears that Transitron was not a particularly well-run business. There was something about an investigation by the Securities and Exchange Commission after Transitron went public. Stockholders allegedly claimed that the prospectus omitted important information, and things went downhill from there. But Transitron recruited and trained some of the best people in the semiconductor industry, including Bob Swanson, Pierre Lamond, Wilf Corrigan, Jim Diller and others.

When Bob Swanson decided to leave Transitron, he interviewed with Sylvania and Fairchild, among others, and he was invited to visit

Fairchild by Fred Bialek, who was running the San Rafael, California, diode plant.

The morning interview must have gone well, because Bialek had some other employees take Swanson out to lunch. Swanson, naturally, left his briefcase and overcoat in the plant. While the others were away, Bialek looked through Swanson's briefcase and found a letter from Sylvania offering him a job for a stated salary.

When lunch was over and Bob Swanson returned to Fred Bialek's office, Fred offered Bob a job at exactly $25 a month more than Sylvania had offered. Swanson thought about it for a moment, and then said, "The offer is too close to the Sylvania offer to be a coincidence. You must have looked in my papers!"

"*Of course I looked,*" Swanson recalls Bialek as replying. "*Isn't that why you left your briefcase behind?*"

The story tells a lot about Fred Bialek. He was never one to pass up an opportunity to get "one up" in a business deal. And his determination to hire Swanson was just one more example of Fred Bialek's ability to iden-tify good people.

Bob Swanson would go on to become a major factor in the success of National Semiconductor, and after that, the founder of Linear Technol-ogy. Swanson's Silicon Valley company has become one of the world's most successful manufacturers of linear integrated circuits.

CHAPTER SIX

THE SOUTH PENINSULA BECOMES SILICON VALLEY

There was, obviously, a time when Silicon Valley did not have that name. The San Francisco Peninsula extends southward from the city of San Francisco for a distance of about 55 miles, ending at San Jose. The entire area was traditionally known simply as the Peninsula, with the southern part, known as the Santa Clara Valley, mostly agricultural until the rise of the semiconductor industry.

There were some well-established industrial companies in the San Carlos/Redwood City area, and a few technology-oriented companies in the Stanford University Industrial Park, but from Mountain View to San Jose the small towns were separated by broad expanses of fruit orchards, vineyards and commercial flower growers. Just about the only significant nonagricultural activity in Mountain View was Moffett Naval Air Station, with its enormous blimp hangars and long runways. When I arrived in 1959 the Bayshore Freeway had just been completed, making it possible to drive to San Francisco from San Jose without the annoyance of cross traffic and red lights. San Jose Airport, today a bustling commercial terminal, was then just private with two or three rock-bottom commuter operations. During the early '60s, an outfit called California Time Airline flew passengers between San Jose and Burbank for $11 a trip!

Fairchild Semiconductor set up shop on the south side of Palo Alto, and very shortly expanded to new facilities in Mountain View, almost directly across the Bayshore Freeway from Moffett Naval Air Station. As new ventures spun off from Fairchild and put up their own buildings, the movement was gradually southward from Mountain View into the heart of the Santa Clara Valley.

In those days the most influential trade paper was *Electronic News*, a weekly that carried a combination of industrial statistics, genuine news and a lot of new product press releases from equipment and component manufacturers. The local EN office was in San Francisco, but just about all of the area news was generated by companies in the Santa Clara Valley.

A reporter for *Electronic News*, Don C. Hoefler, was one of the first writers to realize that the area was becoming a world center for semiconductor development and production. He was fascinated by the way key people from one semiconductor company would leave to establish another firm, and then suffer their own agonies of attrition as their key people, in turn, spun off to form still more companies. Don wrote periodic stories outlining the "family tree" of the area. And when he made reference to the semiconductor community of the Santa Clara Valley, he called the area *Silicon Valley*.

As far as I know, Don Hoefler invented the name, and if it wasn't totally original with Hoefler, he certainly deserves credit for promoting it. It wasn't long before Silicon Valley was accepted all over the world as a collective term for the cities of Palo Alto, Mountain View, Sunnyvale, Santa Clara, Cupertino, Saratoga, etc. Nowadays the companies that participate in the business of Silicon Valley stretch across the lower end of San Francisco Bay through San Jose to Milpitas, Hayward, Fremont and neighboring towns, but Silicon Valley remains a linguistic icon used and understood all over the world.

Don Hoefler eventually left EN and started a subscription newsletter that dealt very candidly with the internal goings-on at various Silicon Valley companies, and as time went on he became a "wonderful and terrible" institution in his own right. His readers enjoyed the gossip-style information he published about others, but they hated to see him coming their way to ask questions. Much later in this chronology, when Fairchild had a new management team and an extremely complicated business situation, Hoefler was especially tough on Wilf Corrigan, who was struggling to do his best for the Fairchild shareholders. When Hoefler died, it wasn't hard to find at least a few corporate executives who breathed a sigh of relief.

If they ever get around to memorializing Don Hoefler, he deserves credit for naming Silicon Valley.

CHAPTER SEVEN

MANUFACTURING, ECONOMICS AND UNIONS

Fairchild started with sales for military applications, and those components had to satisfy some requirements that vendors had not previously encountered. In addition to exhaustive environmental testing on the finished units, which included shock, vibration, temperature cycling and life tests, all of the raw materials had to be identified by lot numbers that were traceable back to the original supplier. Those requirements called for additional employees to keep records and certify the tests, adding to the manufacturing cost. Representatives of the various military services, and of the prime contractors, were admitted to the semiconductor manufacturing facilities where they added their own oversight to the in-house programs.

It is undeniable that the cumulative effect of all that quality control was the achievement of exceptional device reliability, but the extra steps were costly. Overhead kept rising.

As time went on, improvements in yield kept pace with competitive pressures. Even though the selling prices dropped over time, costs dropped even faster and profitability was maintained. In some cases, the price erosion was very dramatic. The 2N696/2N697 transistor family members sold initially for $150 each. By the time the Planar Process was established and plastic packaging had been developed, equivalent transistors were selling for ten cents each!

If Fairchild was to prosper, the extremely competitive high volume consumer and computer markets would have to be exploited, and throughout the operation, cost control would have to become paramount.

Looking for Cost Reductions

Continued improvements in silicon ingot production resulted in larger-diameter ingots, with correspondingly larger-diameter wafers. Before long, it was possible to produce thousands of transistor dice on a single wafer, and batch diffusion processes could accommodate dozens of wafers at a time. There were great improvements in wafer fabrication yields, but, obviously, the resulting cost improvements on a per-die basis were extremely small. All of the "science" was being focused on wafers and fabrication processes. But even if a way could be found to cut the cost of wafer fabrication in half, when you could get as many as 15,000 dice from a single wafer, the savings for any individual die were not significant.

The most significant cost area was in final assembly. Human workers had to position one header at a time in a special fixture under a microscope, pick up a die, place it within a very small target area on the header and hold it in place while a combination of heat, pressure and ultrasonic vibration produced a good mechanical and electrical bond. Then gold wires thinner than a human hair had to be fastened between contacts on the die and posts on the header. It amounted to a lot of separate manipulations for each transistor. And that wasn't the end of it. A hand-guided resistance welding operation was required to seal the caps to the headers.

Following final assembly, each device had to be tested for electrical performance. Individual transistors were inserted in test fixtures and readings on meters or panel displays had to be noted. Experienced workers could do these tasks rapidly but, even so, the final assembly and test labor component was the biggest challenge in a drive to reduce costs. We kept finding ways to mechanize various operations, but the assembly process persisted in being extremely labor-intensive.

An Anti-Union Attitude

Some of us at Fairchild had worked in establishments with unionized labor and rigid work rules. I had spent years at General Electric and Bob Noyce had been at Philco, where union contracts defined the work rules for employees. But because of the nature of our new industry, where we had to deal with constant change, we were highly dependent on the skills, adaptability and creativity of every employee. When cost factors are seriously addressed, *everyone* has to be involved. We needed input from our employees, and we needed their help in refining and mastering the skills that helped us boost final assembly productivity. We were all very young and none of us was tradition-bound. Compared to the long-established East Coast management structures, we were extremely people-sensitive.

It seems to me to be no contradiction that we were also strongly anti-union. We were more than willing to pay competitive wages and benefits, and we were proud to provide good working conditions, but the last thing in the world we needed was a union contract that specified what each rigidly defined category of worker could and could not do. We were in a state of continuous modification of methods, fixtures, instruments, etc.

There was a time when most of the large, old-line electrical-oriented corporations had semiconductor divisions. Companies such as RCA, GE,

Sperry, and many others tried to get into what was obviously an industry with a bright future. All of them were unionized, and all of them failed to make a commercial success of their semiconductor operations. I'm not laying the blame totally on the unions, because the rigid, hierarchical management style of those long-established companies (as was so vividly described by Floyd Kvamme when I interviewed him,) also played an important role in their inability to capitalize on a new technology. But it is hard for a union leader to sell the rank-and-file on constant changes in procedures and work rules, and back in those days it was unusual for unions to collaborate with management in cost-reduction and productivity-boosting efforts.

We were determined that we would not fall victim to the paralysis that we thought would accompany union organization of our company. And when a union attempted to get a foothold by organizing our diode factory in San Rafael, California, which was being run by Fred Bialek, we fought back with as much vigor as the labor laws allowed.

It may not have been the deciding factor in the election that defeated the union's attempt to organize our diode plant, but we were delighted to learn that the business manager of the union was earning considerably more than our general manager, Bob Noyce. We made sure that our employees knew about it the evening before the election. And in the end, our representations regarding the fairness of our compensation plans, the fairness of our treatment of employees, and our obvious need for ad-hoc modifications and revisions on the factory floor won the day. It was the last time a union organization effort at Fairchild got all the way to an election.

In all of our subsequent expansions, we were careful to confine our searches to locations where unions were not likely to have an unfair advantage in influencing the way we manufactured our products. I know there are arguments on the other side of this issue, but that's how we felt. Even now I feel that the absence of unionized labor was a factor in our ability—and the ability of our entire industry in Silicon Valley—to innovate and retain a technological lead.

Branching Out from Silicon Valley

Automation was the established semiconductor industry's general response to final assembly cost pressures. Texas Instruments, Motorola and Philco had made great progress in factory automation, but at a correspondingly great expense. There was no way that Fairchild could fund that sort of effort; we were a small company still in the start-up phase, and the money wasn't available.

The other approach was to find some place where labor costs were lower than they were on the San Francisco Peninsula.

Fairchild's real market growth potential was in computer and consumer semiconductor applications. Those were high volume, low price markets, and Fairchild was not ready to compete for that sort of business. If the company wanted consumer and computer business, it would have to dramatically reduce the assembly labor costs that were becoming so dominant.

Even before the semiconductor industry came to the San Francisco Peninsula, the area was not a cheap place to live. Houses and apartments in the established residential areas were more expensive than in most other parts of the country, and other costs were correspondingly high. Labor rates were not out of line for the area, but the multiplier effect was significant. As Fairchild sales grew, assembly workers had to be added, and their salaries were a big cost component. I began to look for locations where labor was available at advantageous rates, and where factory facilities would be reasonable.

My administrative assistant, Don Kobrin, drew the assignment of finding another assembly location within the continental United States and he approached the task methodically. This is how Don remembers the project:

> "After some initial research, we narrowed the possibilities to the New England states. We invited the various state industrial development people to meet with us in a Boston hotel. Unfortunately,

there was a huge blizzard on the scheduled meeting day and travel was just about impossible. The Massachusetts representative was based in Boston and had no problem getting to the meeting, and the Vermont contingent drove down through the snow, but none of the others could make it. Vermont lacked the population centers that would support our need for employees and labor rates in Massachusetts were on the high side.

"I went to New Hampshire and interviewed 100 women at the state employment office. When asked why they wanted a factory job, the answers tended to focus on 'extras,' such as adding a room to the house or buying a boat. Elective purchases. Most of them said they expected to be paid regular union wages.

"Maine was a different story. The state employment people placed a radio notice of interviews, and many women showed up. They expressed a desire for work based on the unemployment of their husbands. It was clear that they needed jobs. When they asked us about pay, we said we would pay the prevailing minimum wage, and that seemed to satisfy them. Almost all of them indicated a hatred for the labor unions, which had not provided any protection as the industrial base of Maine gradually slipped away.

"The Portland area had a lot of advantages. There was enough of a population base to provide an initial work force of 500 employees, it was possible to drive down to Boston to attend continuing education classes, the people were anti-union, and we knew of an empty supermarket building where we could get started at a reasonable cost.

"There was another advantage—Raytheon had recently closed a transistor plant in Lewiston, and we knew that it would be easy to find technical and engineering people. The South Portland plant was a great success from the very beginning, and even now, under a different ownership, it continues in operation."

We did, indeed, find many valuable people when we established the South Portland plant, including Jim Smaha, who later became vice president and general manager of the semiconductor division at National. And even though labor costs in Maine were lower than in California, they were still not low enough to satisfy the competitive pressures from other semiconductor companies that were developing automated assembly processes. Clearly, we needed a better answer to the assembly end of our business.

Transistors on the Reservation

Don Kobrin also got involved in a series of negotiations leading up to the establishment of an assembly plant at Shiprock, New Mexico, on the Navajo Indian Reservation. The venture had every promise of mutual benefits to ourselves and to the tribe, because Fairchild needed additional assembly capacity and the Navajo Nation was seeking a combination of economic development and employment opportunities.

The Navajo project involved many considerations. The federal government made available some attractive grants for training workers. The Navajo Tribe offered an initial start-up location and promised land for a permanent building with some early-year tax concessions. And there was a large pool of potential assembly workers, eager for an opportunity to work in a leading-edge industry. Indeed, we found that the women were well adapted to fine work and they had no difficulty developing the necessary skills.

But, in my opinion and in the opinion of some others, we seemed to be making a destructive contribution to Navajo society. There were new social problems created by the fact that money (from wages) was going into the families through the women, weakening the leadership role of the men.

Fairchild later determined that it was more economical to assemble products in Southeast Asia than in satellite plants around the country and the Navajo plant was closed. They told me that some of the women employees were so distressed that they chained themselves to the girders inside the building.

Pioneering in Southeast Asia

Bob Noyce had an investment position in a small radio company in Hong Kong, and he suggested that we look into that part of the world as a possible assembly location. I visited the Hong Kong radio factory with Julie Blank, and Blank's description is worth quoting.

> "The way I remember it now is that Bob had an investment in a radio company over there. As a matter of fact, Baldwin worked there for a short time. Actually, Bob had the investment in that radio outfit before Baldwin."
>
> [The Baldwin reference is to John Baldwin, not related to the Ed Baldwin of Fairchild's first months.]
>
> "Then Jerry Levine went over to Hong Kong for a visit. I think he just happened to be in Hong Kong. The way I remember it is, when Noyce mentioned it to me, he thought it was something we ought to take a look at."

Jerry Levine and Bob Noyce had been roommates at MIT and Jerry was working for Fairchild Semiconductor. He was on a vacation trip, and Noyce asked Levine to look in on the Hong Kong radio plant in which Noyce had an interest. Julie's narrative continues . . .

> "I remember Jerry Levine coming back and talking about the fact that this is an opportunity. I remember being very cynical about it. You know, I wondered how the hell are we going to get these people to assemble semiconductors? Although Bob's experience with the radio operation had been disappointing, he still felt that we should consider Hong Kong as an assembly

location. He sent you and me to go through that radio operation. Do you remember how awful it was? All those people
just sitting there, doing nothing. I think we just sort of stum-
bled into Hong Kong. I think Jerry Levine has to be given the
credit.

"Noyce felt strongly about Hong Kong. He supported it, but
[John] Carter didn't. I remember listening to him saying, 'Those
guys, the Red Chinese, are down your nose. You're going to get
run over and you can't trust that crowd over there.' You know,
he had all the reasons why it was an unstable place, which was
partially correct.

"Gee, I remember your case of the trots. I remember looking
at you at the hotel room—you looked like death warmed over. I
never saw anybody look so green."

Julie got *his* just a few days later! Everyone who went to Hong Kong in
those days came down with some sort of intestinal distress. And John
Carter was right about the Mainland Chinese giving Hong Kong a hard
time. They controlled the fresh water line into Hong Kong and they
sharply limited the amount of water they sent. I remember that Hong
Kong was allowed only one hour of fresh water each day, from 4:00 P.M.
until 5:00 P.M. Everybody ran into the hotels at 4:00 to take a shower,
and at first the water ran brown because it had been standing in the pipes
for 23 hours. But we did put a plant in Hong Kong.

We took an old factory where they had been making rubber shoes, on
the Kowloon side of Hong Kong. Ernie Freiberg, the most can-do plant
engineer I've ever known, turned it into a semiconductor assembly and
test facility. Norm Peterson, who had been the manager of our silicon
crystal growing operation, became Fairchild's first plant manager in
Hong Kong. John Yih was the engineering manager and John Baldwin,
who had managed Bob Noyce's radio plant, became our first manager of
finance and administration. Everyone else was from the local population and everyone we hired was very competent.

That initial offshore plant of ours developed the first plastic transistors made by anyone and, in operation for only one year, Hong Kong shipped 120 million devices!

Fairchild's establishment of a Hong Kong facility in 1963 was the first Southeast Asian manufacturing venture of any American semiconductor company. The plant provided an immediate cost advantage in both direct labor and overhead, and overnight it challenged the wisdom of most investments in assembly automation by TI, Motorola and others. In fact, we started a trend toward assembly plants in Southeast Asia, one that was adopted by many other companies as time went by.

Although we went to Hong Kong for direct labor savings, we found that we could hire engineers and other overhead people at dramatically lower costs as well. In many cases, they had been educated and trained in the United States and they were highly capable technicians and supervisors. Their availability and their overall caliber made the decision to go offshore immediately successful.

When I think of that Hong Kong plant, I remember an amusing incident involving our engineering manager, John Yih, who had been educated in Asia, and his wife, Nancy, a delightful Chinese woman who had gone to school in the United States and was thoroughly Americanized. I was over there on one of my periodic trips when somebody organized a picnic outing. I asked John if Nancy was going to accompany us, and he made some excuse for her, saying that she had another commitment. This was not unusual, as Asian wives did not participate in their husbands' business-sponsored social affairs, as they do in this country.

We all gathered at the designated assembly point, and there was Nancy, all smiles, dressed for a picnic and carrying a basket. Her American ways were at variance with the Asian tradition. At first John was unpleasantly surprised and I remember that his face reddened with distress. But he recovered and the outing was pleasant.

History has a way of repeating itself. Fairchild was the first semiconductor company to establish a facility in Southeast Asia. The second such establishment was a spin-off, led by John Yih!

**A meeting in my office, probably 1960. John Yih,
Chris Coburn, Don Valentine, myself and John Baldwin.**

At that time, when wafer fabrication costs were not as significant as assembly and test labor, U.S. manufacturers, led by Fairchild, dominated the world semiconductor market through their lower labor costs in Southeast Asia. The Japanese companies that were entering the semiconductor industry did not set up offshore plants. They, too, had comparatively high labor costs (relative to the prevailing labor rates in Southeast Asia,) and therefore did not compete seriously with American companies on the world market.

It was only when complex integrated circuits shifted the cost burden to the chip fabrication level, where the Japanese had developed an advantage, that the Japanese semiconductor industry took off outside of Japan.

It is undeniable that we exported a lot of American jobs, and nowadays the job issue is hotly debated. In those days, however, reducing labor costs was a matter of company survival and there was no choice.

Success in Hong Kong led to searches for other assembly and test locations, and Fred Bialek was in charge of foreign expansion. His stories make great reading. Here are just a few samples of Fred's take on the period of Fairchild's international expansion . . .

"I could spend all day telling you Korea stories! But if you're thinking about the real cold thing, one night, it was so god-damned cold—actually the New Korea Hotel is where this happened. Ernie Friburg [a plant engineer who set up several offshore factories], had sort of a semi-suite with a curtain between the bedroom and living room—and that's where we used to stay. It was so friggin' cold in this thing that we would sit there and keep our overcoats on when we were in the room because they literally had no heat!

"We'd go down into the dining room where it was warmer, and then we'd go up the room and sit around in our overcoats and drink bourbon just to keep warm. It was that kind of thing. This would have been the winter of '66 when we were building the building. The windows in this place hadn't been washed in 10 years at least and Ernie's wife was complaining about it, and complaining and complaining, and they never came to clean.

"We were sitting up there trying to keep warm, drinking bourbon and all of a sudden there was a knock on the door, and it's 9:30 at night, and we opened the door and there's these two guys with buckets to wash the windows. At 9:30 at night! And there's a blizzard out! They came walking into the chilly room with their buckets and their sponges and they walked directly over to the window, opened the window, one guy leans out and starts washing the filthy windows and the snow was coming in! I mean, the room just got ice cold in nanoseconds!

"They started washing the windows, and the guy took his sponge, and it just froze right to the window! They couldn't figure that out. Anyway, Ernie grabbed one of them by the seat of his pants, threw him out the door, grabbed the other guy, and we got rid of them. It was very funny. I'll tell you, the Koreans were just—back in those days—they were such innocents, you know? They were absolute innocents. They sure got over it, though. Boy, they sure learned fast!"

The inability of the hotel to provide adequate heat inspired Ernie Friburg to make a close inspection of the boiler. He actually took it apart and reassembled it so that it did a better job of keeping the guests warm.

Fairchild's assembly plant was the first U.S. satellite operation in South Korea. Bialek's offshore adventures included a few episodes that seem funny now, but must have been extremely uncomfortable at the time.

"The airport incident was kind of funny. Actually, more than that happened that day, because this is back when the Han River was just a culvert—a big, wide dirt culvert. There were only two bridges over it then. Now there are something like 39 bridges over it. They had this huge storm.

"Bob Napoli was in Korea with me at the time, and he has his own story. I had sent him out to Chosun University, I think, to talk about recruiting engineering guys. He was in a Jeep and on his way back, the storm had gotten so bad that the road literally had flooded up probably three feet high, and the Jeep got stuck. He jumps out of the Jeep, the driver jumps out of the Jeep with him. They were in water up their waists, and the driver pulls out an umbrella to keep Bob dry!

"He and I were going to meet in Tokyo that night, and we were on two different planes. He caught his plane finally, and I was on my way out to the airport, and it was late. It was pouring, pouring rain, and I got in this little taxi—in fact in those days all they had was these little Bluebirds, little small cars that were only three feet wide. We were heading out to the airport in this driving rain, and all of a sudden this baldheaded old man on a bike pulls directly in front of us. The cab driver swerves to try to avoid him, hits the guy, and the guy goes flying 20-30 feet in the road. The cab goes flying off the end of the road, drops about 10 feet onto a little dirt road below that, hits again, and drops another 10 feet into a rice paddy.

"In the meantime my head is bouncing up and down inside the car, my bags are bouncing around, and we finally get down to the rice paddy. We hit and all the doors of the car fly open—the bags fly out, and I fly out, face down in shit—dressed in a suit. And I had to get my plane, and of course the car was stuck. So, I grabbed my bags and I start climbing back up the hill, and I couldn't climb up because it was all muddy.

"Then a bunch of Koreans who had gathered there sort of made like a human rope and I climbed up on them with my bags in my hand. I got to the airport with dung all over me, smelling like a son-of-a-bitch, and it was cold. It wasn't in the middle of winter, but it was cold.

"The airport there also had no heat. This was back in the old days when it was like a big, empty hangar. And it turns out the plane was late, so we had to wait around for an hour, and this stuff just dried on me—because my bag had been checked, so I couldn't change, thinking I was in a hurry. So this stuff all dried on me and I really stunk! You can imagine. When I got on the plane, luckily it was mostly empty because they moved everybody else to the other end of the plane and stuck me away so people wouldn't have to smell me!

"I got to Tokyo, and I got in one cab, and actually, the driver refused to take me! So I finally got into my hotel in Tokyo and took a shower and although I preferred to throw the clothes out, I had them cleaned instead.

"When I first went to Korea, we went over there, if you recall, to do a joint venture with Gold Star. After I sat around and talked with the Gold Star guys and sort of not really negotiated, but discussed, the general parameters, we finally decided we wanted to do our own deal. As part of that, of course, I was looking for pioneer benefits for going in there.

"We took a look at their 'pioneer tax law,' which was really only in its beginning stages of being drafted—it wasn't even written yet. I looked it over and basically said to the government guys, 'This is a piece of shit. It doesn't cover the bases, it doesn't really give us what we need. It won't attract people into the country, etc., etc.' I volunteered to help them to write the pioneer tax law, but we were on a deadline to get going.

"So I said to them, 'I'll tell you what I'll do . . . I'll make you a deal. I will take this law and I will work on it and revise it to what I think needs to be in this law for you to attract foreign investors, but I want a better deal than I'm putting in here. If I put in eight years of pioneer, we want 10. If you like what I've done, you give me my deal. Is it a deal? Deal.

"This was like the beginning of the week, and they asked how long it would take, two months? I said, 'No. I'll be done with it by Friday.' So, Friday I went in and gave them this law, which they adopted practically unchanged. We got our deal. Korea turned out to be an interesting experience—

"I think Korea, in hindsight, was probably not the right place to go because we should have recognized some of the Korean temperaments and some of the things that were going to happen there. At the time, however, it was very successful.

"Here's a story for you (I think I told you this) on the bribery stuff: One of the deals I made when we first went in there is that we would not put up with any bribery. Period. We had major discussions with the Korean government guys, who said this was the only way they made their money.

"I said 'Look, that's your goddamned problem. If you don't get paid enough, we're not going to augment the salary. Period. We will not deal with bribery,' and they agreed. And, you know, there were a couple of little incidents that happened that weren't very important and we resolved.

"Napoli was down at the airport trying to clear some equipment, and he called me and said 'We got a problem down here.' I said, 'What's the problem?' He said, 'This guy's got his hand out. He won't release the goddamned equipment without a bribe.' I said, 'Give me your phone number. We'll call you back.' I took our lawyer and we walked down the street back to the government building to the guy who made the deal with me. I walked in there and said to him 'Hey, we got a problem.' What's the problem? I explained it to him.

"OK. He picks up the phone, dials the number—the call was done all in Korean, and of course I couldn't understand a word—so this guy asked a couple of questions and basically gave some instructions. I looked over at my lawyer, and the lawyer turned white—just absolutely went white. Then the guy hangs up and said 'It won't happen again, Fred.' Good, so we left. We got down the street and I asked the lawyer, 'What the hell happened in there—what'd he say?' He said 'He just took care of it, Fred. It's OK.' I said 'What do you mean?' He said 'Don't worry about it. He took care of it.' And absolutely nothing ever happened again as long as I was involved.

"I do think that to run a successful plant in Korea, you have to be a certain kind of manager. You have to manage it like Koreans manage it, really, and even they have their problems. That was quite an experience.

"The couple of years I spent over there were probably one of the more enjoyable overseas experiences, just because the Koreans are such a kick. I mean, talk about some of the parties we had over there! They were wild. Those guys are wild men! Absolute wild men!"

Some years later, after I left Fairchild to run National Semiconductor, the manager of the Korean plant, Dave Heck, fired the accounting manager and brought in a new supervisor from the United States. This action was not received favorably by the Korean staff. Their reaction was to lock Dave Heck inside the plant for a number of days until the issue was resolved.

Bang-Bang the Kamikaze Driver

I'm getting ahead of myself, but while Fred Bialek has me thinking about
Asian adventures, I recall a later adventure in Indonesia when National
Semiconductor put a plant in Bandung, Indonesia. Bandung is primarily
a university town, located a considerable distance from Jakarta. It was
possible to fly to Bandung from Jakarta, but the airline just didn't have
the appearance of reliability that we were accustomed to, and it seemed a
lot safer to drive between the two places.

The roads, however, were terrible. They were narrow and clogged with
traffic. We employed a driver, who called himself Bang-Bang, to handle the
frequent trips. Bang-Bang must have been inspired by tales of Kamikaze
pilots from World War II. He could drive from Jakarta to Bandung in two
hours, but by the time he got you there you would have lost ten or fifteen
pounds from sheer fright. Conversations with Bang-Bang revealed the
interesting fact that he had one wife in Jakarta and a second wife in Bandung. We used to joke among ourselves that we couldn't decide whether
Bang-Bang was escaping from one of his wives or speeding to the other.

My wife accompanied me on one of my trips to Bandung, and at the
conclusion of the wild over-the-road adventure she swore she'd never
again risk her life that way.

The Best of Two Worlds

Both Fairchild Semiconductor and National Semiconductor placed a
heavy reliance on manufacturing facilities in Southeast Asia. But the
management and coordination issues were not insignificant. Communications were not as easy as they are these days, we had less of an understanding of the cultures where we located our facilities, and we had to
invent new approaches to scheduling, transportation, etc.

At both companies, Ed Pausa was the key individual in managing
those difficult interfaces. He had managed factories in Southeast Asia,

including Fairchild's Hong Kong plant, and at National Semiconductor he was vice president in charge of all Southeast Asian operations. He was a major factor in the high efficiency of those facilities and he exhibited a highly effective management style.

Like so many other top management people who spent years working for Silicon Valley semiconductor companies, Ed Pausa became a successful consultant. He is still recognized as an expert in the management of Southeast Asian manufacturing facilities.

CHAPTER EIGHT

FAIRCHILD MARKETING:

"Take No Prisoners"

Fairchild had tremendous technical talent from the very beginning, but what is often overlooked is the marketing strength of the company. Fairchild's marketing department played as important a part in the company's success as the superiority of the products. And just as certainly, the Fairchild marketing team and the way the members behaved was a direct reflection of Tom Bay.

As I write this book and send it to press, Tom Bay is very much alive, a frequent tennis opponent and guest in our house. In a way, it seems a little strange to talk about Tom as he was 40 years ago, but that's when he had the most influence on the development of Fairchild Semiconductor.

Bay came to Fairchild Semiconductor with an excellent background. He had taught physics at the university level, he had held responsible marketing positions with other component manufacturers, and his reputation was strong enough to put him in the running to be general manager of Fairchild Semiconductor. But he refused to consider the job, convinced that he could do more for the company in a marketing capacity.

Everyone remembers Tom Bay as the absolute image of a successful salesman. Long before the idea of "dress for success" gained so many adherents, Tom's wardrobe was impeccable, he stood straight and tall with a commanding presence, and he appeared to be unflappable. His voice was well modulated and his gestures were spare and effec-

Tom Bay

tive. Customers were sure that Tom considered them to be the most important people in the world, and he seemed capable of bending Fairchild in whatever direction it took to meet a customer requirement. It seemed to customers that Bay had the authority to make any decision on the spot, without contacting the home office.

Given all of that, it is interesting to revisit Bay and Noyce's first meeting with IBM, when Fairchild was only a few weeks old. Fairchild had no factory, no product, and no track record. IBM was accustomed to doing business with reliable vendors who published detailed specifications. Somehow, Bay and Noyce convinced IBM to order a small quantity of transistors at a high price, manufactured to specifications that the two men invented in the course of that first meeting. It was a triumph for Noyce's technical competence and Bay's overwhelming presence as a salesman.

As the weeks went by and it became obvious that Fairchild would, indeed, be able to deliver those first transistors, Bay found himself shuttling back and forth between California and New York. He found other groups within IBM that needed silicon transistors, and sales volume built rapidly. As Tom tells it,

"The first guy I hired was Howard Bobb, who was a Hughes type. I felt, since our first customers were on the East Coast, we had to have someone back there and not have me flying back and forth. At that point I was the only sales employee in the whole company and we needed somebody to baby-sit faraway customers when there were problems, which we knew there were going to be. So Howard came on. One of the reasons the Hughes people were heavy at that point in our biz was, they were the biggest in silicon diodes.

"Howard was a peddler and I guess he did a reasonable job for Hughes. As I said, we had to have someone back East to take care of IBM as the two IBM plants were our only customers in early 1958. As far as IBM was concerned, they talked to me and talked to Noyce, but Howard was there if they needed something or someone to come by and hold their hand. He was there to do it. He was there helping other customers, too, but we needed someone to work on the IBM account at the same time. Anyway, Howard certainly did an acceptable job there and through Howard, we hired Don Rogers who was the second guy we hired. Also from Hughes.

"When we hired Howard, we had no sales volume at all. We had the orders from IBM. Maybe we'd gotten a second order for a thousand pieces at $35 each. We obviously needed someone to call on the other accounts on the East Coast. And Howard was the guy to do that."

(Howard Bobb would soon become a key founder of two other semiconductor companies in Silicon Valley, thus becoming one of the pioneers in the "spinoff" movement.)

At Howard Bobb's suggestion, Tom recruited Don Rogers, who had been selling Hughes semiconductors to Hughes Aircraft. Bobb continued to represent Fairchild on the East Coast, and Don Rogers began to call on prospects in Southern California. Bay gives Rogers a lot of credit for moving Fairchild from a start-up operation to an established company.

"Howard is the guy who said you ought to talk to Don Rogers because all he's been doing is selling to Hughes Aircraft for Hughes Semiconductor. And of course, again, that was military business. Military was the only reason for a need for Fairchild at that time and we wouldn't have been able to build a company at that time without the military business.

"Don Rogers was one of the most influential guys in making Fairchild happen because he went into [North American Aviation's] Autonetics at the time that they were making headlines about how important reliability was on the Minuteman program. The vendors chosen for that program were going to be made. The guy who was in charge of components said it [the Fairchild transistor] looks like a nice product but you're too late because we've already chosen what we're going to use.

"And Rogers, being the kind he is, said we're going to get our product in there. And he went and talked to engineering and had about 20 guys telling the boss: 'We have to get that Fairchild 2N697 in this program or it will never make it.'

"Our competition was the Texas Instruments 2N3367. It was similar to the old MADT at Philco's. Inside, it had a bar mounted up in the air and it survived the early stages of the Minuteman program and after that it was never used anywhere else except in the Minuteman program and once it was in that program it was used forever.

"Don Rogers got both the NPN and the PNP transistors, as well as some diodes, into the Minuteman program. That was, without any doubt, our biggest coup, because the program had gotten such publicity nationwide about how important reliability was and how the products that were going into the Minuteman missiles were going to be the absolute best. It put Fairchild on the map because it was during 1959, early '60, that we were actually chosen to be one of the suppliers to the Minuteman missile. That involved an expense on our side, but prices of the devices were more than able to sustain our costs."

Fred Bialek remembered that some of the Minuteman program diodes sold for as much as $45 each!

Don Valentine and Bob Graham

Don Valentine

Fairchild Semiconductor was barely a year old, but the quality of Fairchild transistors and the ability of the small startup outfit to penetrate at least two large accounts was noticed by a couple of component salesmen at Raytheon Semiconductor, one of the pioneers in germanium devices.

Don Valentine was a graduate chemist who had served a hitch in the Army Signal Corps, and then spent some time as a component salesman for Sylvania in New York. When he concluded that Sylvania's commit-

Bob Graham

ment to the semiconductor business did not match his personal forecast for the future, he went to work for Raytheon, largely because he wanted to move to California and Raytheon promised him the move.

Valentine struck up a friendship with another Raytheon salesman named Bob Graham. And the two of them discussed their dissatisfaction with the Raytheon product line.

Then, as now, Don Valentine had a systematic approach to their situation. As he tells it,

"We were unhappy about the quality and nature of the product line and the Raytheon commitment and all the rest of it. We jointly interviewed other semiconductor companies and we largely divided the universe alphabetically. He [Bob Graham] took something like A through L, and I took M through Z, and we began trying to find out about the other companies that we were competing against.

"Graham was much more of a Los Angeles-based, West Coast person than I was. We both wanted to live on the West Coast, and we both wanted to be in the semiconductor business. We went methodically through the damned alphabet, and Fairchild became our target company. This is now late in 1959. I ended up joining in about December.

"Just about then, anecdotally, I remember Bob and I then dividing up and doing a more systematic search of the companies, based on the quality of their product line. Clearly TI was a very dominant and attractive company. Motorola was launching the germanium product line. But there were very few start-ups compared to what happened a short time later.

"There were two guys you would know, one guy you wouldn't know. Don Rogers and Bill Conrad. To me, Conrad was considerably more impressive than Don Rogers in his analytical understanding of the business we were in. He knew which customer was the target based on information from the factory about the product line and things, where the factory wanted to go in terms of product line, and he had a phenomenally analytical approach to attacking markets and customers. Don normally did it with charm and entertainment; Bill did it with incredible tactical tenacity."

It is ironic that Don Valentine and Bob Graham began their Fairchild careers at almost the same time, and as colleagues from Raytheon. Graham remembers that he joined Fairchild first and recruited Valentine, but the time interval could not have been significant. As later events proved, both were men of extremely high intelligence, both of them were successful in obtaining new accounts and large orders, and both of them had distinguished careers at Fairchild. As the company grew, Valentine became a top executive in the field sales operation and Graham had a corresponding position in product marketing.

Bob Graham remembered a much different Don Valentine than was apparent some years later. Valentine was described as an outgoing man with a great sense of humor and as much appetite for fun as the rest of the sales force. As time went by and Valentine was promoted within Fairchild, he became far more serious and methodical in his approach to his work. Some would say, introverted. It was an evolution that would serve him well in a later career as a venture capitalist and adviser (and board member) to many other companies, but Valentine's gradual shift toward a much more serious approach to his work puzzled some of his former colleagues. Bob Graham remembers that Valentine's shift toward seriousness coincided with Valentine's reading of the novel *Atlas Shrugged*.

Don Valentine did, indeed, become a far more serious person, but he still had his moments. There was a time, some years later, when Don and I were in Italy on a visit to SGS just outside of Milan. We ran into some people we had known from past dealings, and somehow wound up in an establishment where we got into a contest to see who could drink the most grappa. Grappa is a raw, high-proof, brandy.

Valentine was an aggressive competitor, and took on a heavy dose of the stuff. At the end of the party we hailed a couple of taxis to take us back to our hotel, and Don and I were in the lead car, with others following us. As we approached the vicinity of La Scala, Don said he wanted to speak with someone in the other car, and with that he opened the door and stepped out. Our taxi was moving and Valentine went rolling over and over on the pavement. He didn't appear to be injured, and we were able to get him to his hotel room and safely into bed.

The next morning, Don didn't show up as expected and there was no answer when we telephoned his room. We got a hotel employee to let us in, and there was Valentine, still marinated from the previous night's grappa.

Ultimately, years later, Valentine and Graham collided at the vice president level, and only one of them could remain with the company. Valentine stayed, and Graham, without any dishonor on his part, left to hold a series of executive positions with other companies.

Bob Graham was vice president of marketing and then general manager of ITT Semiconductor in West Palm Beach, Florida, he was the first marketing manager at Intel Corporation and he was instrumental in starting a very successful semiconductor manufacturing equipment company.

CHAPTER NINE

FLASH AND FIRE:

Jerry Sanders

Jerry Sanders

Jerry Sanders had his first contact with Joe Van Poppelen, the man who would end Jerry's Fairchild career many years later, in 1959, but it wasn't at Fairchild. Sanders was a design engineer at Douglas Aircraft, dealing with Motorola sales reps. His story makes for a series of amusing mental pictures.

"I designed this thing working with the Motorola guys, and the first thing I observed was that the Motorola sales people who were calling on me were better dressed, drove better cars and clearly made more money than I did. And they knew very little.

"I saw an opportunity to make some more money, and while I was dealing with the Motorola people, I saw an ad. Motorola was advertising for sales engineers. I thought this was an absolute win-win deal. They *needed* somebody like me, so I applied for the job. I got an interview with a guy who at the time was the national sales manager (maybe the worldwide sales manager) for Motorola. His name was Joe Van Poppelen.

"Joe Van Poppelen met me at the Hollywood office of Motorola, and I only owned one suit, and it was one that I had worn through my last year of college, and it was a navy blue suit. I remember it very well, because as I was going in for the interview, I stopped off in the men's room to make sure I was looking presentable, and I noticed that my collar had frayed through and the white lining was showing.

"So I quickly went down to an office supply store, bought a bottle of Scripto ink, which was a particular blue you may recall from those days, put some on my finger, and inked the white spot on my suit so I wouldn't look quite so ragged. Unfortunately, I got ink on my finger, which made me look a little bad, but as engineers go, I wasn't so bad.

"I went in, had the interview with Joe Van Poppelen, and I think we had a good conversation. Joe suggested that while I really wasn't experienced enough to be a sales engineer and call on customers, they had a headquarters sales applications engineering slot in Phoenix, Arizona. They would train me to be a sales engineer if that was to be my career. So, I accepted that job and packed up and moved, and that was in 1959."

Jerry Sanders soon moved from Motorola to Fairchild. The story as he tells it is too detailed for this report, but here are his words, edited for brevity . . .

"I was not in the field. That came later. I was at Motorola from July of '59 to April of '61. My first year was in Phoenix, Arizona working at headquarters, answering technical questions; in fact I wasn't even there one year, probably three to six months in Phoenix, basically a training program. Then I was assigned to the Chicago office.

"Chicago was my home town; I worked for an area sales director named John Gray. My job there was basically to back up the sales force. There was a guy there named Ray Kimball. There was another guy there named Bob Thomas, who was one of those razor-haircut, polished fingernails, shiny shoes, professional sales guy, who in my view, was unqualified for the job. From my brash point of view, he didn't know a P-N junction from pinochle. So, it was an interesting experience to watch this—these guys were relying heavily on me for technical support, far beyond the compensation I was receiving, compared to what they were earning.

"But, at the time, it all seemed like one team, and I was really quite content there. I mean, I was well regarded by the people at Motorola, I liked the people, Les Hogan was a good guy, John Welty was a good guy, Leo Dwork was a good guy. There are other guys whose names escape me for the moment, but it was a good bunch of people, I was given a sales territory. I had all the ragtag accounts.

"The ragtag accounts means I was given mostly the accounts in Southern Michigan, Southern Wisconsin, Northern Indiana, but all the choice accounts had been removed. The other guys had them. But I also had Magnavox and Bendix, and I did quite a distinguished job there. My Magnavox contacts, later on, resulted in my having some successes at Fairchild, but it was while I was calling on those accounts that I came to the attention of the Fairchild area director, a guy named Bob Majors. Bob was looking to expand Fairchild's sales force in the Midwest, so he set up an interview.

"This was the spring of '61. Motorola was a household name, especially because of the TV business, Motorola TV. I was a

Chicago boy, although I did have aspirations to get back to California. I'd had some conversations about that with the Motorola people. By the way, a lot of people who were far senior to me in the organization, in experience in some cases, and in age in every case, many of those guys wound up working for me in subsequent years as AMD [Advanced Micro Devices] has grown, or even at Fairchild, for that matter.

"But at that time, Ed Farrell was in charge of the West Coast, and the thought of working for him was not particularly appealing. Again, he had been a GE guy. There was a big GE influence because of Rudolph, who had gone from GE to Motorola as their marketing manager. The good news about the GE influence was that these guys were experienced managers and there was good feedback. The bad side was that there was a regularity and a uniformity of expectation. You know, they weren't looking for any stars. At least that was the impression I had.

"I remember meeting with Bob and it being suggested that I go out to Mountain View and meet the people. Bob Majors was a wild, aggressive guy, but not a guy who persuaded me that there was any vision of where this company was going to go. But, being a California-influenced guy as I was, the chance to go out to California for an interview on a Friday gave me the chance to spend the weekend there, or as my plan was, to spend the weekend in Las Vegas! So, I booked my flight out there, and Fairchild gave me the tickets, and I promptly changed them for tickets which allowed me to come back through Las Vegas. I went out to California and I met the people and it changed my life!

"I met Tom Bay, I met Don Rogers, and I met Bob Noyce. Those are the ones that stick out in my mind. I don't think I met you [Charlie Sporck] until later. On that particular trip, first of all, Don Rogers was such a wonderful, persuasive guy, and so full of enthusiasm. He had a background from Hughes and he

was a real salesman's salesman, but he did have some understanding of the product, and that was a real noticeable difference, that there was some knowledge of the product.

"Then when I got to meet Tom Bay, this was a major event in
my life. Here was a guy with the wingtip shoes, the button-
down—you know, he looked like an executive, he carried himself well, he had an understanding of where the market was
going, and this guy was clearly a cut above. He also was wear-
ing a cast on his wrist, and I learned he had broken his hand
pounding on the table."

(It was during an argument with me.)

"Yeah, I heard this story about you, and I thought, well, these
guys must be pieces of work! But anyway, the energy, the enthusiasm was there. Bob Noyce blew me away! I mean, the man
was a flat-out genius. You know, he's every guy's image of the
kind of guy you'd like to have as the chief of the group. He was
a good-looking guy, he was articulate, he was bright, he was
sports-minded—the guy was great!

"So, meeting these guys, it was pretty clear to me [where I
was headed]. Then of course, I heard about the technology
and I must say the guy who really sold the technology—who
was just crazy over the technology—was John Ready. John
Ready just talked about everything, you know, unstoppable—
Irish demeanor. 'You have no idea, Jerry, of everything we're
telling you; we're just scratching the surface. What we're
showing you is so little compared to what we really have, you
know, we've got this Micrologic . . . ' Well, I didn't know
Micrologic from a hand grenade, but that was the first of the
integrated circuits.

"There was not a lot of revenue being generated by Micrologic in March-April '61, but the concept was pretty clear to me.

So the combination of batch processing, silicon-Planar, Micrologic, the quality of the people, I said, this is the company I want to work for.

"Then I told Don Rogers who wanted to hire me and was supposed to close me, that I had one problem, and the problem was that I wanted to work in Los Angeles. Don Rogers was the sales manager in Mountain View. He's the guy who recruited me, he's the guy I spent the weekend with. I wanted the job, I wanted Los Angeles, California.

"Rogers was an action guy and he said, 'That's done, but we gotta take care of this guy Bailey who's the area sales director, because you're going to go work for him!' So, basically, Don made it pretty clear, which he probably shouldn't have done (and that was the difference between the GE management and the Don Rogers management), that Bailey would have to give me his blessing, but that was a lead-pipe cinch. That was gonna happen, so I was in!

"That was Don Rogers. So we had a good rapport immediately, and I joined Fairchild. That's where I got the 900 bucks a month! I thought I'd died and gone to heaven."

Dating the Boss's Girl

At risk of turning this into a biography of Jerry Sanders, one more priceless story came out during our conversation. Try to imagine the picture: While he was working for Fairchild in sales, Jerry Sanders was hosting a dinner for two engineers from IBM, and, as an unrelated coincidence, Noyce, Hodgson and Sherman Fairchild were having dinner at the same restaurant.

At the time, Sherman Fairchild, in addition to being the chairman of Fairchild Camera and Instrument Corporation, was also the chairman of the executive committee of IBM. The IBM engineers would normally never come into contact with Mr. Fairchild, but they certainly knew who he was.

Here it is, exactly as it is on tape. The indented text are Jerry's words and the questions are mine:

Sherman Farchild

"There's a story that Hodgson tells about a time when Sherman Fairchild had just dedicated a building at Stanford. He and Hodgson and Noyce were at the L'Auberge Restaurant in Menlo Park having dinner, and—this is Hodgson talking—he invited you over to join the table. He introduced you and the two IBM guys, who were very impressed, to Sherman Fairchild, and after the introductions, you turned to Sherman and said 'Sherman, I understand we're going around with the same girl.' And Sherman said, 'Yeah, who's that?' You said, 'That's the receptionist out at . . . '"

    "It was probably Sperry."

"And Sherman says, 'Is that right?' And he pulls out his little black book and goes through it—"

    "He recalled her name."

"He said, 'Oh yes, you're right.' What's your recollection about that?"

    "Almost nothing except what you just said."

"That's a hell of a funny story."

    "I cannot believe—"

"I can imagine these two IBM engineers shrinking out of sight. Because this guy is in his 70s at this stage!"

"Was he that old?"

"Absolutely!"

"I'm really embarrassed because I don't remember the girl; I remember the event. I remember the girl telling me she had dated him. I don't know how it happened, so I'm really in the dark here."

"You want me to depend on Hodgson?"

"It's absolutely true! I have this vague recollection of dating girls in Long Island in this time frame, because as I said, I had this national responsibility and—this is going way back! This has to be before I was married. This means it was in the '61 to '65 time frame, because I got married in November '65. That's when I was doing that entertainment job and I was involved, going out to—and in those days I also had—I remember the conversation. Sherman, by the way, was not offended. We had a good relationship."

The story is a good one on its own, but even better when you know a little bit more about Sherman Mills Fairchild. His father had been one of the founders and the first chairman of IBM, and Sherman himself had inherited a lot of IBM stock. He invented a particularly good aerial camera, started a company in 1924 to build and sell the cameras, and then he started an aircraft company in 1927 to make airplanes to fly his cameras around. Thousands of Fairchild airplanes were built and eventually were used around the world by feeder airlines that served smaller communities.

Fairchild had 30 patents to his credit, including a carrier for fruit picking, which he invented at age 73. He invented a flash camera in 1915 to help take pictures for *The Harvard Illustrated*.

Sherman, who was born in 1896 and died in 1971, lived in the same era as Howard Hughes. It is interesting that both of them loved aviation, both of them were very wealthy and the two men had similar interests in women. Young women. And it makes me smile to think about the two

IBM engineers who were, in those days, constrained by a strict company code of behavior. Jerry Sanders, a salesman from Fairchild in his 20s and Sherman Fairchild himself, in his late 60s or early 70s, both dating the same girl!

CHAPTER TEN

SCHOOL DAYS

Much of the strength of the Fairchild marketing organization was related to the way the Southern California group trained and monitored each other. Led by personalities such as Graham, Valentine and Jerry Sanders, the Southern California approach spread to other offices throughout the country and was responsible for Fairchild's development of the premier marketing organization in the industry.

It was obvious to everyone that semiconductor components were the key to enormous progress in electronic devices of all sorts. Because of their small size, high reliability and greatly reduced power requirements, they made it possible to develop unprecedented improvements in computers, consumer products, weapons, space exploration systems, etc. And as the semiconductor manufacturers accelerated their device development programs, new devices became available before the circuit design engineers knew how to apply them.

On the customer side, as circuit designers caught on to the capabilities of transistors, they began to come up with requirements for which there were no suitable devices. Fairchild's small sales staff in Southern California began to operate an after-hours "school" to share information as it became available.

The catalog of transistors, identified by a combination of letters and numbers, as in 2N696 and 2N697, expanded to dozens, and then hundreds of individual types. Even so, there were not nearly as many manufacturing processes. Many of the designations reflected a distribution of performance characteristics as determined in the final testing stage. A good salesman had to know more than the electrical performance of each device; he had to have a grasp of the factory production yields in order to bargain effectively with a buyer. It was also important to know as much as possible about customer applications, so that a good device recommendation could be made to some other customer. It was a definite plus to have had experience as a working circuit design engineer.

At least one evening a week, instead of going home after the conventional work day, everyone assembled in a makeshift classroom. The job of making a formal presentation rotated according to the experiences of the week just finished. At times, an engineer from a customer company would be invited to address the group.

It was the beginning of a very exciting time for the men (and in those days all of the sales representatives were male,) involved in the new industry. Information came along rapidly and had to be shared on a timely basis. Fairchild's salesmen spent more time with each other than they did with their families.

Some sense of the spirit that ran through Fairchild's field sales engineers is obvious in Jack Gifford's story of the events leading to his presence in the group. I hope Jack will forgive me for paring away some of his commentary, which was extremely detailed . . .

"I went to UCLA and graduated as a electrical engineer in 1962.

"One of my job offers came from a company in Pasadena with nine guys, every one of them out of CalTech. They were masters and Ph.D.'s and I was basically a gopher. For some reason, one of them liked me and offered me a job. They did studies. Basically their field was EM theory and microwave and communications and in those days you could make a lot of money selling proposals. The government would buy anything, like hanging antennas out on stars and the Star Wars kind of thing. They did very well and after I was with them about four months they got bought by a company called Electronic Specialties, and this is where Fairchild comes into the picture.

"Electronic Specialties was about a $30 million company growing very fast toward $100 million and they were into military electronics. They had built power supply systems and front-end communication systems, antenna systems, and receivers for ECM equipment and they had a good expertise in rugged small power supplies. They bought this systems company, consisting of these nine guys plus me, about at the same time they landed a $400 million order from the government.

"All of a sudden this $40 million company has got this $400 million contract to build 200 pieces of hardware that's got phased array, planar antennas, all kinds of signal processing, and little boxes. One went in every F4 fanjet.

"So the company gets this contract and all hell breaks loose. There's about 40 employees in this $40 million dollar company, and all 10 of us became overnight, well, anything you could do, you had to do. I ended up, the year I got out of school, running this department to design a major piece of electronics and here I am 23 years old. I learned a tremendous amount of things as a circuit designer and in high frequency. And we were designing and building as fast as we could and of course the systems had to be solid state and you couldn't do the designs that we had to do without the products Fairchild had.

"We had money to burn. These little green and white Fairchild boxes were all over the place. Fairchild just gave us the samples. It was the classic Fairchild sales approach. Every day one of those guys, Chaz Haba or Tom Williams or Jerry Sanders would be in there saying try this one, try that one. Then we all converted to Fairchild and there wasn't a part in this thing that wasn't Fairchild.

"And then I got to meet these Fairchild guys, but never did it occur to me to become a salesman. It was fun to look at them but I never thought about being one of them. I was making $650 a month and it's funny, I had an opportunity to play professional baseball and if I did that I could get $450 a month. I got to meet, well, these guys, Tom Williams, Chaz Haba, I was so impressed by these guys, I liked them. They were just my kind of guys.

"One day Jerry Sanders and Chaz Haba came over. That was unusual. They took me to lunch and they looked at each other. I first told them I was flattered but I really wanted to design circuits. I really didn't want to be a salesman. One of them said, 'Why don't you sell for a year? Then you can come into the factory and design circuits.' Then they came back and said 'We've talked to our management and we're going to give you the best account in the world, our best account.'

"I didn't know what that meant but I could see that it meant a lot to them. They did say something that *did* mean something to me: 'On top of that if you come to work for us today we're going to go to [a sales meeting in] Hawaii next week for a week and *you* get to come.'

"That was it. I swear to God that did it. I had no idea I would ever go to Hawaii in my life and that was it. I can remember thinking, if I could ever make $20,000 a year that's all I ever needed. And these guys were going to take me to Hawaii. So I joined."

Jack's salary jumped from the $650 a month he had been making to a princely $750 a month! Plus a bonus plan based on his sales results. Gifford's sudden immersion into the Fairchild field sales 'culture,' if I can use the word, made a deep impression. Remember, he was just starting his Fairchild career . . .

"For one thing, I had never seen such a bunch of wild guys in my life, I mean, Jesus Christ, we got onto the airplane and there wasn't a woman that was safe. Not only on the airplane but that whole week in Hawaii. They made the Navy look like . . . it was unbelievable, I'll never forget it when that week was over, Hank O'Hara, I mean, we were waiting in the airport to go home, and Hank was leaning up against the post at the airport sound asleep. These guys were so trained, they could sleep standing up, I mean, they didn't sleep at night. It was amazing.

"I was impressed by, and in awe of, that sales system. I mean, the product training and the sales training. I'm sure I owe almost all of my success to three things in my life; one being my competitiveness and my desire to win in sports, the second being my engineering education at UCLA and third, the lessons I learned about business and selling skills from Fairchild Semiconductor. I mean, the quality of people was unbelievable.

"I've told many people this: If I had to pick one year out of my life where I learned the most, it was that one year selling in L.A. I learned skills that caused me to succeed in life.

"The company could count on the sales guys. They were committed and so I came back after that week in Hawaii realizing that these people were unbelievably good. They were dedicated.

"When I first got there, I would hear stories about Jerry Sanders. I hadn't been around Jerry too much, other than we would go in the office one night a week and we would do practice selling. Did anyone ever tell you how those went? You sat there on a chair and they would put you through this. It was like school. You think sales were out there drinking and screwing around? We were in there from 6:00 until 11:00 at night.

"There was no bullshit, boy, it was serious. I remember Don Valentine, at one of these school sessions, firing a guy for being five minutes late. I mean, he would sit there like a drill sergeant. I remember two guys that got fired because of that. That was the discipline in the sales office that was run by Jerry and Chaz.

"Jerry was flamboyant. Don Valentine, to his credit, had absolute control of Jerry Sanders, not that it was even necessary but there was nobody bigger than the company. Nobody was bigger than that chain of command and that's the thing you saw, it was like the Marines.

"Then we would go down to Hamburger Hamlet and have a few beers or whatever the hell we did and get home and some of us never getting home, and getting up in the morning. I remember sometimes I'd go to bed and spend all night thinking about what I had to do in the morning and then I'd get up and do it. Maybe today they'd say that was a nervous breakdown but it didn't occur to me that that was it. That was the intensity level that we were operating at.

"And here's this guy running this very disciplined sales office and I would hear these stories about Jerry. I remember one story where he had come in with a purple suit and a yellow shirt. He got up on a desk in the lobby and danced around and 1,500 people from all the buildings came in to see Jerry Sanders talk about Fairchild. He was like a barker, and that's a true story.

"There were two sides to Jerry. He wanted to be a show, he had a great love of Hollywood, of stars. The office was located there because of that and he would hang out wherever he could be around them.

"One of the buyers told me that Valentine was a son of a bitch. They didn't like him. He was the toughest. I had a

$100,000 order once and I wanted to give it to Don Valentine personally, and I called him up to say I had this order for him, and he says something unprintable which meant, 'I don't have the time to come to you.'

"We were not the most sensitive of people either and when we lost a order, it was a personal affront. We were trained to take it to the limit. In the end, the customer would rather give the order to you than go through the ordeal. And if you lost the order, management knew all of the orders, pending and coming, and so when you lost one you went through a kangaroo court and it wasn't just to harass you, they were going to go back with you and get the damn order.

"We had the Brooks Brother suits, the wing-tip shoes, we looked alike, we all looked like Tom Bay. We all copied Tom Bay. We all had this killer instinct. They looked for that trait."

Jack Gifford turned out to be much more than an excellent salesman. He had an outstanding career at Fairchild, and then, later, went on to form Maxim Integrated Products, a company that specializes in analog integrated circuits. Gifford's leadership qualities contributed to his extraordinary success in the industry.

CHAPTER ELEVEN

RUNNING THE FACTORY

By the end of 1959, Fairchild Semiconductor was causing a stir in the industry. Barely two years old, Fairchild had the beginnings of a take-no-prisoners sales force and a product line that included the only Planar transistors and diodes on the market.

There was always a mismatch between the production capability of the factory and the needs of the sales staff. When new devices were announced and significant sales were booked, it wasn't always possible to deliver as many units as the purchase orders specified. The Fairchild organization evolved into four major departments:

Sales, obviously, handled the classical task of calling on customers and writing the orders. Manufacturing was responsible for building the devices. Product Marketing was responsible for interpreting the needs of the customers, coming up with new applications, and accurately assessing the production capability of the factory. And over in another facility, away from the day-to-day confusion of the marketplace, research and development was coming up with new devices and new manufacturing processes.

With success and growth came predictable tensions. Floyd Kvamme reminded me of the time when he and Cloyd Marvin were having coffee in the cafeteria and I spotted Jack Magarian sitting at the same table. I guess I was a little too emphatic when I banged my hand on the table in front of Magarian and said, "When you tell me something has been shipped, that doesn't mean to our own dock!"

Rationalizing Technology Transfer

As envisioned in theory, the R&D department would come up with a new product, prove out a process, develop specific manufacturing guidelines, and then send the specifications to manufacturing. Manufacturing would then follow the "recipe" and begin delivering new products. In practice, manufacturing often found that R&D guidelines didn't work in the factory.

The system looked sensible on paper. Fairchild's R&D facility was located in Palo Alto, in the Stanford Industrial Park, some distance away from the factory and administrative complex in Mountain View. The setting was campus-like and the atmosphere was academic. Excellent product development results flowed out of R&D in an impressive stream.

Sometimes everything worked perfectly. We'd get product samples and written process specifications, and we could follow the "recipes" and turn out thousands of acceptable devices. But there were instances when we ran into manufacturing difficulties that had not been anticipated by R&D. That led to interface problems for which there were no easy solutions.

If R&D sent somebody to the factory to help straighten things out, there was a question of who was in charge. There were occasional frictions between the manufacturing managers, who tended to categorize

R&D personnel as impractical eggheads, and R&D technicians, who viewed the factory managers as unimaginative in some instances, or too literal in other situations. What might have been treated as an entirely predictable consequence of moving a complex process from a research setting to a mass-production environment sometimes turned into a clash of personalities.

There were many meetings devoted to straightening out problems of technology transfer. All sorts of ad-hoc solutions were proposed and tried. Phil Ferguson, in particular, grappled with the challenge of identifying the moment when a product was really ready to move out of R&D and into full-scale manufacturing. But we never came up with a satisfactory way of smoothing out this aggravating state of affairs. In retrospect, I feel that one of the major contributors to our difficulties in this area was inadequate technical capability within the factory staff.

From Czochralski to Epitaxy

Phil Ferguson was a central figure in another one of those passionate debates that came up every so often regarding emerging technologies. As I mentioned in an earlier chapter (pp. 24–26), the production of suitable silicon ingots was no trivial thing. And as we learned how to make ingots with larger diameters, the difficulties of holding the right crystal orientation grew. It also became harder to achieve a uniform distribution of "doping" atoms within the crystal lattice. The answer seemed to be a new process called epitaxial deposition, or as it was usually shortened, *epitaxy*.

Epitaxial deposition was a fancy term for the formation of a thin layer of "perfect" silicon directly on top of a wafer sliced from a silicon ingot. Why the layering? Because the precise distribution of doping atoms within the underlying wafer became much less important. The deposited surface layer could be controlled more easily. With the epitaxial process under control, very-large-diameter silicon ingots could be produced and sliced into wafers. The wafers were polished and cleaned and sent through the epitaxial process. But the process had a lot of variables, required expensive special equipment, involved the use of potentially hazardous gases and called for highly skilled technicians to keep things under control.

Ferguson participated in a side-by-side yield test of integrated circuits fabricated on "standard" wafers against the same devices produced on epitaxial wafers. Ferguson remembered that the epitaxial yields were much higher, settling the issue and establishing epitaxial wafers as the new norm.

The End of Development Isolation

It seemed to me that it was a mistake to have R&D work conducted at a distance from manufacturing. When I became CEO of National Semiconductor I had device development work done in close proximity to manufacturing, and instead of some variation on "delivering" new process specifications, the people who did the development work cooperated with the factory managers in easing new products into the mainstream of production.

Today, as far as I know, the early Fairchild model of a remotely located device development facility is not used by any major semiconductor company. There still may be some basic research programs conducted in quiet laboratories that are away from the factory floor, but device development, and especially manufacturing process development, is done right in the factory environment.

There was another, more serious flaw in the way Fairchild handled device development. Fairchild was an engineering-driven company, and all of the important new products were really the brain-children of the R&D staff. R&D would develop something, turn it over to the factory and, in effect, say, "Make these things and sell them."

That's not how decisions should have been made. Marketing should have been charged with the responsibility of deciding the device development priorities. Fairchild's marketing people were design engineers fully capable of understanding the needs of the customer and the competitive situation from month to month.

None of us ever found a satisfactory solution to our technology transfer headaches while we were at Fairchild. Indeed, the frustrations and aggravations played a significant role in the decision of Gordon Moore to join Bob Noyce in leaving Fairchild to organize Intel. I could see the flaws in our system before I became general manager, and I should have straightened things out when they put me in charge. We made some attempts to change things, such as bringing Pierre Lamond into the factory from R&D, but there was still a considerable gap between development and full-scale manufacturing. The difficulties were evenly divided between manufacturing and R&D. Lessons we learned while at Fairchild were later applied to the organization of all succeeding spinoffs, which located development work within the factory itself.

Regardless of conflicts, real or perceived, I must say that Fairchild's greatest strength was in research and development. The success of Fairchild was fundamentally the result of a superb R&D effort.

What to Make?

Sometimes there were bad decisions, bad luck or a simple misreading of the market.

As soon as Fairchild had the Planar process, it was possible to make devices that combined several transistors with the requisite passive components, resulting in integrated circuits that provided the modular functions of logic diagrams. One of the first product families used a combination of transistors and resistors on a chip and was given the generic name of RTL, which stood for resistor-transistor-logic.

RTL turned out to be more difficult to manufacture than had been originally anticipated, and customers were less enthusiastic than

Fairchild expected them to be. But RTL was the company's first major push in integrated circuits and was aggressively marketed under the trade name of *Micrologic*. The Apollo missile program used Micrologic components.

RTL was a product that came out of R&D under the sponsorship of Bob Norman. There hadn't been any requests for the product from the marketing department, but Norman, along with a few others, thought that it would sell.

Meanwhile, customers were building logic circuits with discrete components, designed along the lines of DTL, or diode-transistor-logic. The DTL idea became so well established that Orville Baker, Dave Allison and a few others left Fairchild for Signetics, where they started a successful DTL integrated circuit capability.

Fairchild's field engineers kept pleading with the factory to make DTL integrated circuits, but R&D stubbornly backed RTL. When the disagreement became passionate, Bob Norman left Fairchild for General Microelectronics (GMe), where he was instrumental in GMe's launch of an RTL product line that was no more successful than Fairchild's had been. Not only was RTL hard to manufacture, but it was difficult to use in circuit applications.

Fairchild was still struggling to get DTL into mass production, but Signetics was growing like crazy with their DTL line and by the time we finally had a product, the market for DTL was fully developed.

Tom Bay, director of marketing, and I met to discuss DTL manufacturing costs and selling prices, and we decided to price our gates much lower than Signetics was asking. At the time, Signetics was getting around $5 a gate. We pegged ours at about 99 cents a gate. (Gates refer to the complexity of a given integrated circuit, and was borrowed from the very first descriptions of digital logic circuits.)

Obviously, we couldn't stay in business if we sold products for less than they cost to manufacture, but we had faith in the "learning curve." As our volume grew, we were confident that we could find the production economies to justify our premature price drop.

Fortunately, our suppositions were correct. Almost overnight we killed the Signetics market for DTL and from a factory perspective, it was a pleasure to see our RTL volume decline as DTL sales skyrocketed.

In another one of those recurring interrelationships between companies in Silicon Valley, Joe Van Poppelen was then the general manager at Signetics, and much later, in an offhand comment, he said that Fairchild's "price bomb" cost him his job at Signetics.

Speaking of costing a person his job, Floyd Kvamme had a story about one of Fairchild's application engineers, a fellow named Maurice O'Shea, who was sent to a General Electric plant to explain how a Fairchild component functioned in an important GE circuit. According to those who were there, O'Shea went over and over the circuit with the customer representative, who couldn't quite follow the explanation. Finally, after about an hour, O'Shea supposedly straightened up in his chair and said, *"I know why you don't get this. You're too damned stupid to get it!"* At which point he stood up and walked out. The salesman had to tell the customer that O'Shea had been fired for his intemperate comment, and from then on Fairchild had to isolate O'Shea from all GE contacts.

CHAPTER TWELVE

WORK HARD, PLAY HARD

Late Afternoons at "The Wheel"

The idea of regular tutorial sessions, started by the Southern California sales group, spread throughout the company. As other sales offices were established in major customer locations, representatives from Fairchild's home office made frequent appearances to update the sales people on new devices and suggested applications.

It was a time of lavish hosting for customers, and after-hours socializing became part of the Fairchild marketing and manufacturing way of life. Instead of heading straight home after the regular work day, management people would remain at the office for a while to discuss whatever needed resolution, and would then adjourn to a nearby lounge for enough drinks to take the edge off the day. In a way, the drinking served a purpose, further cementing interpersonal relations and easing communications between departments.

Some families, unfortunately, suffered. The world of Fairchild was simply more exciting than anything else going on in the lives of many staff people. Sales were growing. Facilities were being added. Salaries were rising. Promotions were being awarded. Wives and children were getting less attention at home. Inevitably, more than a few marriages were shattered.

The combination of gung-ho company spirit and a limitless future was definitely a part of the mystique. Fairchild began to hold annual sales meetings that were a combination of a reward for a job well done, an assembly for the dissemination of new product information, an opportunity to plan strategies for future sales penetrations and an arena for individual displays of courage, cleverness and alcohol capacity. The schedule included formal classroom sessions along with plenty of recreational opportunities.

The "proceedings" of the technical sessions were documented in handouts that could be studied afterwards. The stories about adventures and misadventures experienced in the course of those sales meetings provided conversational fodder for months afterwards.

I mention the drinking aspect of the semiconductor industry because it came up in many of the interviews I conducted decades later when I was preparing this history. People had some difficulty recalling exact events or dates, but clearly remembered some of the more dramatic anecdotes related to too much alcohol. It is tempting to include a few of the detailed accounts here, but there is just enough potential for exaggeration to make me cautious.

The drinking was tolerated because it took place outside of regular hours, or, if it happened at lunch, it was connected with customer hospitality. Clearly, the ability to hold one's liquor was a definite plus within Fairchild, and almost certainly, everywhere else within the semiconductor industry. It seems to me that most of the really heavy drinkers are now dead, and those who survived are now either nondrinkers or significantly more moderate in their choice of refreshment.

The favorite oasis for after-hours refreshment was a place called Walker's Wagon Wheel, which I recall was at the corner of Whisman and Middlefield in Mountain View. It wasn't a fancy place but it was large enough to hold a crowd and it was the site of many business discussions, liberally lubricated with alcoholic beverages. Marketing people would tell manufacturing people about their customer calls and their difficulties with sales and deliveries. Employees of other companies would also show up, leading to a certain degree of cross-communication and eavesdropping. The notorious reporter for *Electronic News*, Don Hoefler, did a significant amount of his "research" at the Wagon Wheel.

One late afternoon, Jack Magarian, who held a manufacturing management position at Fairchild, was refreshing himself at the Wagon Wheel and impressing some girl with his sparkling conversation. Suddenly Magarian's wife, Shirley, came into the establishment with all five of their children, and marched over to his bar stool. Magarian turned and saw his wife and kids and summed up the situation by saying, "Oh shit. Shirley!"

I'm getting ahead of my story, but while I have the Wagon Wheel on my mind, here's a final story about "The Wheel." Years later, after Fairchild had gone through some changes in ownership and I was CEO of National Semiconductor, we bought Fairchild, now much reduced from its heyday as a technological leader.

Tom Bay and I took a stroll through the old Fairchild main factory building in Mountain View and relived some memories. And then, just on a whim, we drove up to The Wagon Wheel. Instead of the crowded, noisy place that it had been 25 years previously, it was now all but deserted. There was one person tending bar and only one customer, a quiet woman, enjoying a quiet drink.

Sure enough, she was one of the employees from Fairchild of long ago.

CHAPTER THIRTEEN

THE LURE OF
MONEY AND POWER

Fairchild Semiconductor's first full year of operation was 1958, and for the first four or five years every day was crammed with exciting developments. New devices were developed, integrated circuits kept getting more complex, applications grew exponentially, and the investment community started to notice the potential of the semiconductor industry. Within just a few years, other companies were interested in starting new semiconductor operations or expanding existing organizations.

This brings up the whole issue of retaining key employees. There are practical limits to the salary increases a company can use as rewards for work well done, or as incentives to keep employees from leaving. The opportunity for promotions is similarly limited. When a competitor comes around with "an offer you can't refuse," it is sometimes impossible for the first employer to prevail.

Stock options are an obvious answer. By giving key employees a large enough stake in the success of the company, they remain motivated and they have a realistic expectation of significant gains in the future. But the top management at Fairchild Camera and Instrument Corporation was reluctant to approve the kind of options that would have been effective. They did not understand that you had to go lower in the organization with stock options, and Fairchild became vulnerable to a siphoning off of high-performing, middle-management people, engineers and scientists.

By the mid-1960s, another aggravation began to eat away at the Fairchild Semiconductor morale. Whatever the actual numbers, it was felt in Mountain View that the Syosset folks were using large profits generated by semiconductor operations to fund acquisitions that didn't make a lot of sense. There was a growing friction between the semiconductor division's management and the Fairchild corporate management, particularly in regard to the duMont acquisition.

What had been a kind of all-for-one-and-one-for-all spirit gradually eroded into what's-in-it-for-me. Some of the results were great successes and some were dismal failures. Consider the case of GMe.

CHAPTER FOURTEEN

GENERAL MICROELECTRONICS

Phil Ferguson and GMe

Phil Ferguson who had come to Fairchild from Texas Instruments, was in charge of device development at the R&D facility. He was one of the first men to grapple with the important issue of technology transfer, and was deeply involved in addressing the question of what constitutes a finished product, ready to move from R&D to the factory.

When I asked Phil Ferguson about the history of GMe, he provided a lively narrative of the company's history. What follows, edited only for continuity, is Ferguson's story.

> "I think it was in 1963. It may have been the summer. We sold it to Ford in 1966. The official name was General Micro Electronics. It was a strange name, but it was picked by the first president, a retired Marine colonel named Mark Lowell. He had been the head of the microelectronics division of the Bureau of

Weapons, and in that office had many large defense companies courting him, including General Motors. Gme was picked so it would look like it could have been a subsidiary of GM, which GM vigorously denied. It was a strange name.

"The way it got started was that there was a company in Chicago called Pyle National, an old-line manufacturer of electronic products, that got started in the 1870s making headlights for locomotives. They gradually built into a not very large company making electrical connectors and various things. The president was a guy named Bill Croft, and he kept reading about ICs in the very early days of ICs, and he was making umbilical cables for the first MinuteMan missiles and making a lot of money. So, they took some of that money and hired a consulting firm to go and see if ICs—because they kept talking about reducing the electrical connections—if ICs would affect their business.

"The consultants, in their wanderings, in talking to people about ICs, came across this Colonel Lowell at the Bureau of Weapons. He was a pretty impressive guy. They came back and told Pyle, well, no, it's not going to affect your kind of business, but it looks like a good business, and we ran into this guy who seemed very dynamic and seemed to be the king of it all.

"So Bill Croft spoke with Lowell, and asked him if he knew anyone who would be a good recruit for a new company. Lowell brought up the name of Howard Bobb, a salesman who had a good relationship with NSA. Croft agreed that there was a good opportunity, and Pyle National had enough cash to fund the new company with $5 million. I was the last straggler. I came in at the very end of the discussions, when it was essentially a done deal. That's how GMe got started.

"The group included Dean Dish, Howard Bobb and Bob Norman, Art Lowell, Don Farina, myself and a fellow named McMillan. (I can't remember his first name right now.) It was unfortunate that our staffing happened that way. We did not realize they were hiring a great number of Fairchild people, not maliciously or what have you, it's just that people contacted others they knew, and it turned out they were all from Fairchild. We should not have done that. It was a mistake because it looked like we were trying to destroy them. But there weren't many places to go for [knowledgeable] people at that time.

"Fairchild sued us. We kept pulling out so many people over four or five months that finally [Fairchild's corporate people in] Long Island said, "You have to do something." Although I wasn't there, I had the impression that the semiconductor division in California was ordered to go after us by Fairchild's corporate office in Syosset, Long Island.

"Unfortunately, Lowell was moving through a reality check. When he was in the military in that particular job, which was when I was in the line in the Air Force, electronics was a big problem. We used to call ourselves the Air Defense Command One, Two Punch because we'd fire missiles and then miss and have to ram them. And probably half the time our radar didn't work, and the fire control systems didn't work, so doing something about the reliability of airborne electronic systems was a big, big problem, and this microelectronics unit was charged with doing something about it. And of course, the first pressure for hybrid components and modules, and all that stuff came out of that group.

"Lowell was, as a full colonel, in a very influential position. He seemed to get mixed up between the time when he was a customer of all these big companies and when he became a vendor. In places like GM and Northrup, after he started GMe, he tried to contact the same people he worked with when he was their customer. He thought a lot of his relationships could be maintained because of his personality, and I think it was a tough time for him.

"Howard Bobb was the marketing guy and Bob Norman was circuit design and Howard Bogart is probably my only good friend because he was the guy who placed the design for that first calculator we built. We set up to do epitaxial ICs which we'd just transitioned to the factory before I left Fairchild. Our goal was to make it on bipolar ICs and I think for a year or maybe two years, we had the best capability of being able to set up a brand-new plant and get it up and running in a couple of weeks. That may be one thing that triggered the lawsuit; that we came on stream so fast. Fairchild had become concerned about the speed.

"And, of course, we were making RTL, which was fatal because all the RTL was used in the SAFE program so you couldn't get visibility because of the security classification, so it was always one of these things that might be around the corner. I think, within a couple of years, we had 98% of the RTL IC market. But of course we should have been dealing with DTL and what have you. But Lowell didn't really know enough about the business or the market to take an active part [in that type of decision-making]. And as I was young and naive, I think I accepted, well, maybe Howard knows something I don't know. I certainly never questioned the RTL commitment like I should have.

"Frank Wanlass had been playing around with MOS. When I first looked at MOS, my first reference to MOS was that a guy named Webster wrote an article in an electronics magazine talking about the MOS structure, and I remember thinking, 'That sucker's three-dimensional, and that could be of great importance.' So even though our whole commitment was to bipolar, on the side we had MOS projects.

"The problem we got into was that we ground up more and more of our money, and Pyle is not a large company, so we didn't have an influx of a lot of cash. As more of these RTL programs got delayed and we were eating money like there was no tomorrow, we started looking for some emergency thing to do to bail ourselves out. We built this calculator out of RTL and then made a couple of MOS circuits and then dramatically we could pull one board out with a ton of RTL on and stick this other board in with one device on it [and get the same functionality].

"Based on that we were able to go back and get a fair amount of funding, $1.2 million, I think, from Victor Comptometer, a company looking to electronic calculators as replacements for their electromechanical products.

"I'll never forget taking a tour of their plant with the president, Benny Bakewell. And I remember saying, 'If this stuff's any good at all, this semiconductor stuff, it's going to wipe all this out.' He said, 'It'll never happen. You could never make that kind of stuff for the kind of money we can make these for. Look at all these automatic presses.' So their concept was that this would be a high-end, prestige 'Cadillac' item on top of their electromechanical items. So, we got that [contract], and we started scratching around and got a couple of contracts from NSA, more from them than from anyone else. As a matter of fact, our first MOS device went up into a satellite [to measure the] radiation belt.

"But to finish it off, it turned out that Bill Croft, the president of Pyle National, had been on the Elgin Watch Company board with a guy who at the time was the president of Philco. I guess the Philco semiconductor people were impressed with what we'd done with MOS and were thinking maybe Philco should buy us and put us in under them. It turned out that Philco was not very happy with their semiconductor group, so they bought us and put their existing operation under us. This created a big problem.

"Yes, I was the general manager. I stuck around; Howard and Bob Norman left. Actually Lowell left after about a year. I was the CEO for the last year. Lowell and Bill Croft had a falling-out over performance. It was always 'next month, next month.' So at some point Croft just had enough and fired him and put me in as the president, and I ran it for a year. We had no way out. We couldn't make reliable MOS devices without burning the hell out of them or what have you.

"Lowell really didn't know what he was doing. He had never run anything in his life; he'd just been in the Marines. I tried, but it was kind of like, well, Lowell had this concept which was very strange, that every division should have its own building.

"So, from the very start we had physical isolation. All this security, and equipment disappearing, and so forth, it was just not—I'm surprised that Croft didn't think about it, that this guy was in the military his whole life and then is expected to run a fast-moving company.

"But there was a lot of partying. There was a party one time we had with people who shall remain nameless. A bunch of them flew out for a meeting, and we started about 9:00 and Art Lowell had spent a bundle of money fixing up his office. He insisted he didn't need a desk, he just needed a table to stand at, with a full bar, sink, refrigerator, what have you. It was very nice and looked kind of like a cathouse. But anyway we started with Lowell breaking out the champagne about 9:15, and by 11:30 we were supposed to go to lunch, but everybody was just blind drunk. Before noon, this one guy from Northrup fell down and beat himself up, and we had all these station wagons arriving at El Camino [Hospital] to escort this guy to the emergency room for 10 or 20 stitches. This is a very famous story. It became a standard.

"I remember one time Norman had a meeting somewhere at a restaurant, and he had all kinds of folks there. This was after we sold the company to Philco and we had a few bucks. So, Norman had all these people at this meeting at lunch, and they were drinking like crazy, and at about 3:30, I couldn't find anybody. I tracked them down and got Norman on the phone and said, 'What the hell are you doing? Those people need to get back here.' And Norman was drunk as a skunk, and he said, 'Well I'll tell you what. We got arguing about whether a Mai Tai in the U.S. tastes as good as a Mai Tai in Hawaii, and I've got seats for 25 people, for all of us . . . '

"Now this is men, women, married, single. 'I've got seats for all of us on the 5:40 to Honolulu and I'm taking them all to prove that the Hawaiian Mai Tais are better than the Californians.' I said, 'You're out of your friggin' mind!' And I fired him right there on the phone and sent down a bunch of station wagons. I really don't know what we would have done without station wagons! They loaded up all the drunks and brought them back. You know, when you have a company with Colonel Lowell and the three of us, there's going to be some liquor change location."

Charlie Sporck interjects:

"Right about that time we were interviewing a salesman from GMe down in L.A. around where Northrup is, and he was telling us that the next day he went in to see this one guy who had a big bandage on his head. The salesman asked how he got hurt, and the guy said, 'We started drinking champagne and the next thing you know, I'm back here, and I'm all bandaged up.' I think he was probably back down in L.A. by 3:00 P.M. Still drunk."

"Howard left first, and Howard always maintained, and I always believed, that Howard's first loyalty was to NSA [National Security Agency] and just government contracts. We had been working with [Howard] Bobb, and to his credit he had gotten some pretty sizable contracts to develop for NSA. He looked at the long shift registers and what have you and decided that this was what we needed for secure encryption. That was very interesting. We started developing circuits for them, but of course, Howard was the one who had them; they weren't really GMe's. They were Howard's contracts. So he went and used those contracts and as I understand it, got a letter from NSA saying we will support this company, to go get venture capital to start AMI. So Howard left and Bob [Norman] did not go. Howard left by himself.

"That was in the fall of 1966, in fact immediately, as soon as we sold it. Bob Norman stayed around a little longer, maybe three or four months. Howard starting working to try to get AMI funded, and then I canned Bob Norman, and Bob went and found somebody with money and started NorTek.

"When Philco bought GMe, Ford was actually the purchaser. And another thing: I'm surprised we didn't all end up in prison or something, because we had this calculator which was based on MOS, and when the Philco president and Croft thought they had a deal, then Ford got involved in it. We actually sold the company to Ford.

"I went back there for a Ford board meeting, and the first time we had the calculator working, I slipped into Pyle for their board meeting so they could see it, and like an idiot, I just got on the redeye with it and bought a seat for it. So I sat on the redeye in one seat, and sat next to it, all strapped in. I took it back off the airplane at 6:00 in the morning in a big, heavy wood box. This cabbie carried it out and put it in his cab and I said to him, 'I'll be back in a second; I'm getting my bag.' The guy was sleeping but said OK. So, I went and got my bag and the cab was gone! Jesus Christ! So, I got in the next cab and got him to radio and ask, 'Who just left the airport and was asleep and has a big box in the front seat?' So, we got together a few miles down the road, which was enough to make me a little twitchy for the day!

"So, I got to the board meeting and put it in there, and of course, did not have time [to check it out] because I was late because I was behind from my adventure with the taxi cabs. I turned the thing on, and the display showed all 8's. I said, 'OK, ring me tomorrow.' So I called up Howard Bogart and said, 'Get another one on an airplane back here.' So they did, and the next one worked and Pyle was very happy.

"Then later, when we were about to sell the company to Ford, I took a calculator back to Dearborn for the board meeting. Of course, I was not invited in, but I took the calculator out and made sure it was turned on in time. I was certain we were going to have a repeat of what happened at the Pyle board meeting.

"I was sitting out there while the board meeting was going on, and I got a phone call from Howard Bogart, saying, 'You know, we think there's 400 volts on that case. We found a problem in the transformer, and we think there may be 400 volts on that case.' And, my God! I'm about to electrocute Henry Ford! But as it turned out, it all went well; they were very impressed. Funny, funny, funny.

"So, anyway Philco bought GMe, and I went back there and talked to Philco; I said, 'Hey guys, these folks were all on stock, and if you pay them off, they're all going to go.' And their answer was 'One time we bought less than all of a rubber company's things and it didn't work out well.'

"When Philco contacted Pyle, Croft, the CEO, said 'This thing is a gold mine.' And I said, 'Bill, don't do anything; I'll be on an airplane.' So I went to Chicago, and in the middle of the night out at Howard Johnson's by O'Hare, I told Croft, 'The markets aren't there, and we can't tell you when they're going to be there, because it's all classified. And this MOS, we don't know why they're failing!' Croft then said, 'They offered us $10 million for it,' and I said, 'I think you should take it.' He said, 'If you think so—.' He was a player; he was ready to go right to the wall, and that's where he would have gone!

"Of the $10 million, $5 million went back to repay what they put in and then we split it some ways, so we got $1.5 million each. It was like in the Army, we put this check in the bank account and then drew checks against it and that was it. But the company really should have done very well.

"So, they [Philco] took over and we had our payday and everybody left. Howard Bobb was recruiting [all our people] for his new company, AMI. We had the contract with NSA. It was pretty important to us. We lost six project managers in one month, and whenever we would appoint somebody, Howard would hire him. Then, after a couple of months, NSA pulled the contract from us and gave it to Howard, and of course, people took off. Electronic Arrays spun off, NorTek spun off, so since they just got gutted, there was no reason for people to stay at GMe. I stayed for 14 months to try to do something and then I left, too."

CHAPTER FIFTEEN

THE LOGICAL CHOICE, UNCHOSEN

(Would there have been an Intel?)

After I left Fairchild in 1967, Bob Noyce brought Tom Bay back from the instrumentation division to run the semiconductor division. And in a short period of time, there were major changes at the Fairchild corporate level in Syosset. John Carter was discharged as CEO and the corporation was looking for a new leader. Clearly, there was only one person in the entire organization with the credentials for that job. Bob Noyce had proven his ability to deal with rapidly changing technology and he had delivered a solid performance as a business manager of a major division for almost a decade. He was frequently quoted in technical and trade publications, he was in demand as a speaker and just about everyone liked him. More important, perhaps, than any of those considerations, Noyce had the loyalty of Fairchild's entire population. He was the only person who could have held Fairchild together.

To Noyce's astonishment, probably, and certainly to the astonishment of the people at Fairchild Semiconductor, Noyce was not given the top job. Gordon Moore gave a concise summary of what happened . . .

"That's when Noyce asked me if I wanted to do something. I was trying to sell Fairchild on making memory products. I told Noyce that it was the first idea I've seen in a long time that could be the basis of a new company. We were just looking at the idea that there was something in memory and that you could do something with it.

"And then, six months later, they fired Hodgson! [Richard Hodgson was executive vice president of Fairchild Camera and Instrument Corp.] And they set up this three-man committee to run the company while they were looking for somebody from the outside to come in and run it. So, Bob was going to be passed over. Did Bob want the presidency of the company? He sure as hell wanted to be asked.

"That was in early '68. Anyhow, Bob had made that one shot earlier in that year, asking me if I didn't want to do something. I said, no, then. In about May he came back and said he'd decided to leave and did I still feel that way. I went home and thought about it, and I was getting frustrated with the [technology] transfer thing. I figured if somebody comes in from the outside, he's going to stir all this stuff up and I probably won't like it; I'd rather leave before he comes than afterwards. So, I said, 'OK, let's do it.'

"We didn't have any real definition of what we were going to do, but memory was the thing I told Bob that you could set up a new company on. We then set about extracting ourselves from Fairchild. I remember I resigned on the 3rd of July and they didn't even pay me for the Fourth.

Fairchild's Search for New Leadership

According to Tom Bay, Gordon Moore and others, Bob Noyce advised the directors of Fairchild to consider C. Lester Hogan as the corporation's new president. There is even some speculation that Noyce approached Hogan on behalf of the Fairchild board of directors and helped convince Hogan to resign from his position at Motorola and accept the Fairchild offer.

It was reasonably expected that Les Hogan would rapidly overcome the difficult transition period and replicate his presumed success at Motorola Semiconductor. Everyone in the industry respected Hogan's achievements, he, too, was much in demand as a speaker, and the company he led was *one of the*, if not *the*, largest semiconductor manufacturers in the world.

When I left Fairchild to become CEO at National Semiconductor, I was pleased to receive applications from a number of highly qualified Fairchild people who had faith in my ability to turn National around and make something out of the potential that had not been tapped. When Noyce and Moore left Fairchild to organize Intel Corporation, another cluster of valuable, experienced employees also left Fairchild. Now there were many important positions to fill at Fairchild.

I was following developments at Fairchild with a selfish motive. I needed a director of marketing at National and I knew that Tom Bay would have to make a choice between Don Valentine and Jerry Sanders to lead the Fairchild marketing team. I had interviewed both Valentine and Sanders and I liked both of them. I knew that whichever one was picked by Bay, the other one would resign and come to National. It was only a case of watching and waiting.

As it happened, the blockbuster news—that Les Hogan had left Motorola to become president of Fairchild Camera and Instrument Corporation—was revealed while the Fairchild Semiconductor marketing department was holding an annual sales meeting in Hawaii. Tom Bay had picked Jerry Sanders to be Fairchild's director of marketing and Don Valentine went off to join me at National. Bob Graham, who had left Fairchild earlier to take over the marketing department of ITT Semiconductor in West Palm Beach, Florida, joined Noyce and Moore at the newly formed Intel Corporation in Santa Clara as director of marketing.

For a moment in time, Graham, Sanders and Valentine were all directors of marketing at Silicon Valley semiconductor companies.

Lester Hogan's move from Motorola to Fairchild was much more of an "event" than a mere change in top management. Fairchild and Motorola had been arch enemies for years, and as the CEO at Motorola Semiconductor, Hogan was the focus of a lot of negative feelings held by Fairchild personnel.

Jerry Sanders had a sense of inherent disaster in the wind. He was very candid in his discussion of the situation . . .

"What is important is that we had a sales conference in August '68, and we were in Hawaii, and the word had come that a whole new team of people from Motorola had arrived. It become pretty clear that Tom [Bay] was going to be out. He volunteered nothing about what any of our futures were, other than to say, you know, things are pretty bad. I believe it was in that first conversation that I first learned from him that Dick Hodgson had told him that Joe Van Poppelen had been hired to be the vice president of marketing.

"That was the job I had. So here I am in Hawaii, married with several children, in my usual state of having no cash, and I was learning that my career, which I had made this commitment to Fairchild as my future just a year before, was shaky. Hodgson was out, Bay was out, and Hogan and his team were coming in. So I called Les Hogan to congratulate him on his new job and to ask if I could have a meeting with him; I wanted to talk to him. He said 'No, enjoy your vacation. Have a good time.' I told him there was no way I could enjoy my vacation, that I really needed to talk to him, and that I thought I could be useful in what was going to be, obviously, a disruptive time.

"So he agreed to meet me for breakfast in a few days to give me a chance to get on a plane and get home from Hawaii. We met at Ricky's Cabana. So I show up at Ricky's Cabana at let's

say, 8:00, expecting to have breakfast with Les Hogan. Wrong.
Les Hogan is there, and he's got his whole team, Wilf Corrigan,
Gene Blanchette, Andy Procassini. Not Joe Van Poppelen! Of
course, in the back of my mind I knew it was Joe Van Poppelen
who'd been hired [to take over Sanders' position.]

"What I said at that breakfast was that I was there to apply for
the job as director of marketing worldwide. And he said, 'Well,
you've already got that job, Jerry.' And I said, Well, yeah, I have
but you don't know me, and when you knew me a few years
ago I was much younger, and so forth. Anyway, we had a great
conversation. These guys fired questions at me. I mean, Dwork
was there! Blanchette, Corrigan, Procassini, as well as Les, firing
questions at me.

"The truth was, I was really good at my job. I really knew
what was going on. I answered the questions, and so Les came
in and said he wanted to have dinner with me at my home, so
within a week, he was at my house, putting his arm around my
shoulder and telling Linda, my wife, 'Jerry's my guy. He's group
director of marketing worldwide, and we're raising his salary
from $30,000 to $45,000 a year.' I thought I'd died and gone to
heaven. I thought this was great."

The euphoria that Sanders experienced was short-lived. Even though
several of the new Motorola-turned-Fairchild executives were enthusiastic about Jerry and his abilities, Jerry was convinced that Les Hogan
really wanted Joe Van Poppelen to have the top marketing job. Hogan
gave Van Poppelen a higher-level corporate position, and Sanders interpreted it as way for Van Poppelen to bide his time until Jerry could be
squeezed out. I wasn't there and there's no way for me to sort out the
complexities of all those different personalities and egos, but the Sanders
version has a certain ring of truth.

It is interesting to contemplate the dramatic potential of a meeting
between Jerry Sanders, Les Hogan and Ken Olsen, CEO of Digital

Equipment Corporation early in Hogan's presence at Fairchild. (Sanders doesn't mention the presence of Wilf Corrigan at this meeting, but Corrigan says he was there, too, and his version is almost exactly the same as Jerry's.) Sanders gave this report . . .

"The issue was, Les [Hogan] had a certain management style; Les had a way of running the business. We called on Digital Equipment together. We called on the founder up there, Ken Olsen, and we had worked our butts off at Fairchild to design in Fairchild's 9300 family of MSI. We were competing against TI's 5474 complex functions.

"We had been really successful. Engineering was on our side, but Digital had no legitimate second source. Meanwhile, TI and Signetics and others and National were going to be in the 7400 business.

"So, we're having this meeting with Ken Olsen, and Ken Olsen and Les are discussing this, and Ken said, 'You're presenting me with a problem. Engineering wants to use the 9300, but I'd rather see us have multiple sources, you know, the 7400 is the industry standard.' So Les asks, 'What would you like us to do, Ken?' And Ken said to him, 'You'd make my life simpler if you'd second-source the 7400s.' And Hogan said 'You got it.' And I was blown away. I could not believe it. It was one of the biggest bonehead moves I'd ever seen.

"We left the meeting. He asked me what I thought, and of course, in my naiveté, I said, 'That was one of the biggest—you just burned up years of work—we *had* this!' He was not happy with me. It was very clear that people did not—I mean, I wasn't the most diplomatic, but I wasn't blunt—well, maybe I was blunt. But with the kind of conversations Les was used to having, I was blunt.

"So, I think that was really an issue. That sort of began my unraveling. Then, we had one other issue, and that was when customers would call up because we were late with delivery. It was a problem, and I was the marketing guy, so Les would send me a note. So, Wilf told me, the way you handle Les is, whatever he says, just say 'Yessir,' and then just do whatever you think is right. He won't remember anyway, he won't follow up, that's just the way he is. And I said, Gee, I can't operate like that. I don't want to make out that I have this sterling character, but I can't operate like that! But Wilf said that was just the way it is. So that was a real problem for me.

"Then, I made my fatal blunder. I walked in and said to Les that I would like to—(this all happened pretty quick. They came in August and I was out by November, so it didn't take very long from 'Jerry's my guy for the rest of his life' to stabbing me in the back)—throw my hat in the ring to be general manager of Fairchild Semiconductor.

"At that time, Les himself was acting general manager. As I think back, that was a big reach for me. I was a marketing guy. So, he gave me the good words and assured me, 'You'll be a candidate' and duh-dah-duh-dah, and 'You were the de facto general manager when Tom was here' (which wasn't true; maybe I was strategic in deciding what to do with customers, but that's a very small part. Being the marketing guy is still a very small part of being the general manager, no question.)

"Then he asked me a question, and in my youth and foolishness, I gave the wrong answer. He asked me, 'What if I choose someone else?' And I know the right answer now. The right answer is 'Les, whatever you decide I will support 100% because I know you're going to make the right decision for the company.' Blow so much smoke I could float him out of the building. But did I say that? No. At 31 years old, I said, 'I can't guarantee my behavior.'

"I can't believe I said anything that stupid! 'I can't guarantee my behavior.' So, it was only a matter of time before he called me in and said he was replacing me. Joe had found a guy at TI whose name I can't remember—Doug somebody—who never really accomplished much. But he brought him in, and Les said it was because I'd threatened him.

"As I look back now, as CEO of a Fortune 500 company, if a 31-year-old guy said to me, 'I can't guarantee my behavior,' well, I certainly would not have counted on him. I don't know that I would have proactively replaced him, but I certainly . . .

"So, that's the way it went. Since that time, Les and I have certainly become—you know . . . I bear him no ill will. I don't run into him very often. I have to say that Les has always been kind to me. He did give me a year's severance pay, which made it a little easier."

Fairchild Semiconductor had always been more than just a company. At first, there was a spirit of *life, fortune and sacred honor* shared by the eight men who left Shockley Semiconductor, full of confidence in their ability to overcome all technical obstacles on their way to success in the silicon transistor business. Then, only a short while later, there was a general feeling of euphoria as the company scored many early successes. The third wave was one of industry-leading inventions as the Planar Process paved the way for integrated circuits.

By 1966 the prevailing atmosphere was one of unlimited growth, steady technological progress, a marketing department that was unstoppable, and overall, everywhere within the company, a co-mingling of personal egos with the general organization. *"Fairchild is good because I am good; I am good because Fairchild is good."*

Jerry Sanders understood that complex spiritual driving force. He had seen Tom Bay's ability to inspire the marketing troops, and without in any way imitating Tom, he had turned on his own brand of charm and showed great early promise.

But now the guts had been torn out of Fairchild Semiconductor. Noyce, Moore and Andy Grove, generally regarded within the company as the inventors of integrated circuits, transistors, semiconductors and, quite possibly, sand itself, were gone. I was gone, and with me, some of the most brilliant manufacturing managers in the industry. Jerry Sanders, with his outrageous, flamboyant, in-your-face demeanor, and his obvious intelligence, was gone. And all through the organization, at the middle and upper management level, people were jumping ship.

It was the loyalties that were disappearing. Les Hogan and his followers from Motorola had a great past, with, probably, even better business success than the Fairchild veterans. But Hogan's Heroes did not have the loyalty of the remnants they found when they took up housekeeping in Mountain View. An explosion of semiconductor talent and capability had erupted from Fairchild and into Silicon Valley:

Tom Bay	Jack Gifford	Don Farina
Fred Bialek	Bob Swanson	Jack Magarian
Bob Graham	Bob Widlar	Howard Bobb
Andy Grove	Roger Smullen	John Carey
Gordon Moore	Mel Phelps	Julie Blank
Bob Noyce	Jim Diller	Vic Grinich
Jerry Sanders	Jim Smaha	Don Kobrin
Don Valentine	Bernie Marren	Ed Turney
Pierre Lamond	Dave Talbert	Ed Pausa
Floyd Kvamme	Frank Wanlass	Max Stanton
Phil Ferguson	Don Yost	Greg Harrison
Ernie Friburg	John Ready	Bob Allen
Nelson Walker	Don Rogers	And myself,
Marshall Cox	Chaz Haba	Charles Sporck

I apologize to the many others who should be on this list. Omissions are unintentional and simply a consequence of the difficulty of remembering names after the passage of so many years.

CHAPTER SIXTEEN

FAIRCHILD II:
HOGAN'S HEROES

Most of the key players in the original Fairchild Semiconductor organization were gone, or if they were still on the scene they were floating their resumes around Silicon Valley. But there was every reason to forecast continued growth and success for the company. Les Hogan, after all, had captained the Motorola semiconductor organization to a solid position of industrial leadership. His academic background was every bit as good as any of the Fairchild organizers and he was a much-sought-after interview subject on all aspects of this dynamic industry. When he left Motorola to take over the leadership of Fairchild Camera and Instrument Corporation, many key Motorola people followed him, and others who had known him in the past began to flow into his new venue.

There are many ways to characterize the differences between Motorola and Fairchild, but perhaps the easiest comment would be that Motorola was a well-organized example of an "Eastern industrial corporation," and

Hoping for the best. Fairchild's marketing department was holding
a sales meeting in Hawaii when Les Hogan was brought in from Motorola
to run the company. Here, smiling bravely and trying to make the best of it,
are Ben Anixter, Chaz Haba, Jerry Sanders, Bernie Marren and Marshall Cox.
They had just gotten the news.

Fairchild was a company typical of the "California high tech" paradigm. It is probably safe to guess that the Motorola troops assumed they could apply their well-disciplined corporate approach to Fairchild and turn it into another Motorola.

Of all the Motorola transplants, Wilf Corrigan provided the most complete perspective. Corrigan had been raised and educated in England, then recruited by Transitron when he graduated. He eventually migrated to Motorola, and came along with Hogan to Fairchild. Corrigan had such a strong reputation in the industry that I had tried to hire him while I was running Fairchild Semiconductor.

What follows is Corrigan's story as he told it to me, edited only enough to remove my occasional questions and comments, and to give some continuity to his narrative.

"Our first thought was, 'Hold on a minute. Let's just figure out
how to get the products out; there's great technology here.' But

it became obvious to us that over the past several years New York [where the FC&I corporate headquarters was located] had been starving the company. We sat down with Tom Bay. We said 'Tom, tell us about the company,' and he said 'We've returned positive cash flow to the corporation for the last two years.' This was the rapidly growing high technology sector, but obviously the corporation was starving Fairchild Semiconductor and supporting all their other strange things.

"So, as we looked at the operation, we thought, 'Hey, the products are fine. The marketing thrust is fine.' The manufacturing in the U.S. was archaic, but by then, I'd been to Hong Kong, and compared Fairchild to Motorola because in the plastic transistor business, you know, since '66, we [Motorola] had just been rolling over Fairchild in plastic transistors.

"When you leave one company and go to another company there's a moment in time when you know all the numbers. So I kind of knew what prices we had, I knew what our costs were, and now suddenly, I could look at the other guy's hand of cards. I was kind of stunned, because I looked at the costs, and the costs out of Hong Kong were actually lower for the same products than my costs out of Phoenix with the automated assembly line. It was a real revelation to me. I'm talking about the packaging costs. The die costs were much, much higher out of California but I figured that was easy to fix. The actual manufacturing cost out of the Far East was lower.

"Motorola hadn't really used the Far East strategy too thoroughly by that time. I suddenly realized that Fairchild was way ahead with its manufacturing infrastructure in the Far East. That was a real powerful weapon.

"The new management hired as their VP of finance [a man who had been involved in] quite a little scandal at his previous job. The 'salad oil scandal' was where Billy Sol Estes had dozens of storage tanks, and they had only one tank full of salad oil. When somebody would come and audit, they'd pump the oil from tank to tank. They would take the auditor out to lunch and pump the oil into the next tank, and then take him out for an afternoon break and pump the oil into yet another tank.

"Well, anyway, the finance guy we had was the same person who had actually had been responsible in the Billy Sol Estes thing and he didn't last very long. So, we didn't have a semiconductor-oriented finance guy for probably a year. Then we got Hazel in from Honeywell and things got all squared away.

"We went through this period of massive adjustment where a lot of our premises weren't correct. Then I figured out that it didn't make sense. If we have low manufacturing costs, yeah, we can cut the chip costs quickly. But our prices were a lot less than what Motorola was charging for the same parts. So I said 'Why are you pricing this stuff so low when you're supply-limited?' Remember, they hadn't been putting capital in, so there wasn't a lot of manufacturing capacity.

"They said 'Well, our delivery times are so bad, that all we can do is cut prices to get the business.' So, they were in this spiral—they were paring the price down but they weren't putting in the capital to increase the capacity. It was clear that marketing was not an entirely separate entity because manufacturing was running the show. The sales guys would go sell whatever they could, and nobody was saying, 'Well, we need to get more sales, and price has something to do with it, and so on.' It was a real education for me.

"Hogan was determined to bring Joe Van Poppelen into the picture. I remember going out on a sales trip with Jerry Sanders and Les Hogan to see Ken Olsen at DEC [Digital Equipment Corporation]. This was in the period before Joe Van Poppelen appeared, and Jerry was coaching Hogan going in to see DEC. So, he's coaching him, saying 'Les, when we get in there, at some point, probably very early, all he's going to say is 'Will you second-source the TI 7400?' and the answer to that is, absolutely not! You know, it's a bunch of shit, and the Fairchild product is far superior and so on. But you must not—whatever you do—agree to second-source that TI product. Because if he's got one product which is second-sourced, no matter what it is, and the other product is sole-source . . . '

"Hogan's got it. And I'm the transistor guy. I'm just going along for the ride or to carry the bags or whatever. So, we get in to see Ken Olsen and you know, I'm kind of an observer. Olsen says, 'I want you to do something for me. Would you second-source the 7400 family from TI?' We tell him we have a better product, and so on. Ken says, 'Yeah, I'm going to look at that as well, but tell me, would you second-source the 7400?' And Jerry is—you know—almost going into orbit at this point. Hogan says, 'OK, Ken. For you, that's what we'll do. You're the customer. If you want us to do that, we'll do that.'

"And I suspect that's what almost created the 7400 business at that point in time, and it really meant that the Fairchild alternative was severely handicapped. It wasn't exactly dead. It was a nice product line, and so on, but it wasn't what it could have been. That's what I saw was missing in Motorola because Motorola was very customer-oriented: The customer's always right—you give him what he wants. So, Jerry asks, 'What can we optimize?' He was a very good strategist.

"Well, we went along for a while, and then Joe Van Poppelen came in to be the marketing guy, and Joe's a very gregarious guy. Joe and Jerry had a long-ago relationship at Motorola, and there was some bad blood from the past that lingered on. Anyway, Jerry left.

"We changed the epitaxial process very fast and started to pump a lot of capital money in. We had an attitude: 'Spend the money if you're going to spend the money.' So we put a lot of money in that. I think we opened an additional facility at the time.

"Even though there was a recession going on, a lot of us were spending a lot of capital. At Motorola Semiconductor, Chicago took care of all the financial worries. I don't think Les Hogan really knew too much about it. I don't think Les was alone in that period at Fairchild, not knowing quite what to do. It was tough to get a decision out of him.

"Les had been a decisive kind of person at Motorola in the '60s. But the industry didn't just enjoy a steady climb. I think what happened with Les was that it really did not go as he expected it was going to go. Things changed on him. I think dealing with a board of directors was a big change for him.

"One thing about Hogan was, if you were around him a lot, he'd tell you anything. He'd just talk to you. As a matter of fact when I first started there, he quoted one of the vice presidents— I wasn't sure what a vice president was. But then I said something like, 'Well, shit. What are these other guys—vice presidents?' He said, 'Oh, OK. Do you want to be a vice president, too?' So there was this proximity advantage. If you put in the time with Les, you got much higher visibility.

"I seemed to get promoted when there were recessions. I got the semiconductor division in '70, a time when we had to cut a lot of people out.

"I was made CEO [of Fairchild Camera and Instrument Corporation] in '79. There was a very aggressive guy named William Ylvisaker who was chairman of Gould. They were then an electrical component manufacturer aggressively trying to convert to an electronics company. I had a sense that he was looking at us as an acquisition candidate. He was positioning Gould to become like a predator sort of company.

"I had to do a good amount of smooth talking to keep him off the board because several board members were totally charmed by this guy. I knew I'd have to handle him carefully. I'd done pretty well with the board, but they were very much an East Coast board, and they were quite a bit older. The West Coast ways of doing things were foreign to them.

"For about a year and a half before '79 there was this kind of pressure, 'Why don't you talk to Ylvisaker about coming on the board?' And I actually talked to him. I met him a couple of times, and it was obvious to me what he had on his mind.

"So I found lots of reasons why we had to delay. If you remember, in the late '70s there were a lot of hostile takeovers; it was kind of a trend. I think it was PaineWebber at the time that had this package where they were kind of the defender of choice if you had a hostile takeover. There was a guy named Marty Siegel who later became a little famous who headed this up. So, we said, 'Well, some of the board were concerned about hostile takeovers, and what are we doing about it?'

"So we paid PaineWebber, I think it was $50,000, to come and kind of prepare a contingency plan for defense should we ever get a hostile takeover situation. Marty Siegel comes out. Another charming guy, and he's done due diligence—they got all data and stuff. This is about a year before the Gould thing. This is in '79. Our stock started to move in a strange pattern. This doesn't look right. So, we had a number of people—Nelson Stone got people—to go start watching what's happening. And it was clear our stock was starting to move in the hands of some of the arbitrageurs. So, we were really getting geared up at this point. Then it was really starting to move.

"I finally called Marty Siegel and said, 'Marty, you'd better get your ass out here. It looks like we really do have a hostile takeover, and we need to start preparing our defenses.' So he says, 'Oh, maybe I have a conflict.' I said, 'What do you mean, you have a conflict?'

"Maybe I've got a conflict."

"I said, 'Look. We paid you to come do this; we gave you unlimited due diligence for the whole company. You've got all the data on the company. You can't tell me that 12 months later—'

"He said, 'But that agreement's expired.' I said, 'When did it expire?' He said, 'Oh, about a month ago.' And I said, 'Are you telling me that you might come in on the other side on this deal.' He said, 'Well, I couldn't say that.'

"So, I said, 'Look, Marty, you're going to get the biggest lawsuit you ever saw if there's any—. You go back, talk to your boss before I do, and you come back and tell me what your position is.' So after about an hour, he called back and said, 'Hey, we talked about it. We guarantee you we will not be on the other side.'

"But by now I know there's another side, so then I got Salomon out. We had a relationship with Salomon, so I got them out and said, 'OK. You've got to start defending me.' The stock kept moving, and sure enough, after a couple of weeks there was an offer from Ylvisaker. He called me up and said, 'Hey, you know, we'd sure like to have a friendly merger of the companies, and so on and so forth.' We'd already prepared what we were going to say, and the whole bit. But clearly, you know, around about that time, it was in play.

"We hired Wachtell Lipton to represent us. We came up with a defense strategy and how we were going to attack. There was a lot to attack with Gould. Fundamentally, when you're doing that sort of acquisition, takeover or merger, you're basically suggesting a partnership. So, I was ready to place two-page ads in *The Wall Street Journal* and the *Chicago Times* which were going to say, 'Let me tell you about this. This the number of SEC citations that they have had. This is how they got polo grounds down in Florida that Mr. Ylvisaker's polo team plays on. By the way, they bought this acreage, and the swamp land was sold to the company, and the flat part of it which was drained was sold to the management and the price differences were this and that, and so on.'

"So, I go to the board and I show them the whole plan, and the board says, 'Mmmm. Impugning their integrity.' I said, 'That's right. I'm impugning their integrity.' They said, 'But a lot of our friends are on the board of that company.'

"That's when I realized that yeah, I guess we really are in play. At that point, I said to myself, 'OK. I guess we just gotta go and see what we can do for the company.' I mean, that's a fairly step-function decision, that you go from saying 'OK. I guess my job now is to get the maximum price for shareholders,' and you kinda gotta go through a door when you do that. So that's when we really got into talking to Shlumberger and General Electric in England and a few other companies, and finally, we got $66 a share for the stock, so all the shareholders came out fine."

Corrigan's experience in dealing with several boards of directors, investment bankers, law firms and other business specialists stood him in good stead after he left Fairchild. Following a brief period in the venture-capital business, Wilf Corrigan organized LSI Logic corporation, a still-successful manufacturer of integrated circuits.

R.I.P Fairchild

When the dust settled, Fairchild Camera and Instrument Corporation was acquired by Schlumberger Corporation for about $500 million. The new board of directors brought in Tom Rogers, a man with no semiconductor industry experience, to replace Wilf Corrigan, who resigned concurrent with the Schlumberger sale. When I first met Rogers, he told me he would "straighten out the semiconductor industry in Silicon Valley."

Rogers probably suffered from culture shock as he tried to settle into Silicon Valley. AMD was coming off a good year, and tossed a Christmas party for its employees at a location in San Francisco. It was widely understood (and reported in the press,) that AMD spent $250,000 on the party, which prompted Rogers to telephone Tom Hinkelman, CEO of the Semiconductor Industry Association, and ask, in an outraged manner, *"What kind of an industry IS this? And this crazy Sanders, spending so much money on a Christmas party?"* Rogers may also have been agitated about Fairchild's construction project in South San Jose, where they were putting up a very large plant. As far as I know, the plant was never used as a production facility by Fairchild.

Rogers never quite straightened out the semiconductor industry. Under his leadership, Fairchild broke up the sales organization into separate product lines. Instead of one rep covering his assigned customer, or a group of customers, multiple sales reps from Fairchild were calling on prospects. The problems persisted and grew worse.

By 1985–1986, Fairchild was a total disaster. We (National Semiconductor) bought the whole company for $122 million. With all of its troubles, Fairchild had a very good transistor business, a very good logic business, was well respected in the custom analog business and had an excellent high-speed RAM product. The company was still doing about $500 million a year in sales and there were many highly qualified people working for the company.

We sold the Fairchild Korea property for $15 million, we sold the R&D facility for $15 million. We got $10 million for Fairchild's operations in Brazil and we sold the rights to Fairchild's microprocessor for another $10 million. Then we sold the memory plant in the state of Washington to a Japanese company for $100 million. By my calculations, that works out to $150 million in outright cash for an investment of $122 million, $500 million in new business, some impressive new products and many very fine new employees. We shut down the Danbury [Connecticut] plant but continued to operate the wafer fab plant in Portland, Maine, and the assembly and test facility in Singapore.

A decade later we sold the transistor and logic business for $500 million, making what had been a good deal a far, far better deal.

Today a reborn Fairchild Semiconductor, under totally new ownership, is still operating from the South Portland, Maine, location, and showing increasing strength in the industry.

(I've described the terminal agonies of Fairchild in a separate chapter a little later on in this narrative.)

CHAPTER SEVENTEEN

JERRY SANDERS AND ADVANCED MICRO DEVICES

Jerry Sanders was, and still is, a fascinating combination of two personalities. During his long and successful career as a salesman and later, as a top marketing executive, he exhibited a unique, flamboyant manner in the way he lived, dressed and expressed himself. Underneath the public Jerry, however, there was and is a very keen, analytical intellect and the same human emotions that drive all of us.

Jerry also happens to be a very articulate person, much more expressive than most of us who worked in the Silicon Valley environment of the past few decades. When I asked him about his experiences following his abrupt departure from Fairchild, he shared some details I hadn't known. Our session was question-and-answer, and I have edited Jerry's comments only insofar as they make the narrative clear. We began with my question about Jerry's feelings immediately after he was forced out of Fairchild . . .

"I was devastated. I was in shock. Deep doo-doo.

"This all happened in November 1968, just before my anniversary, and as usual I had no money. I'm sure I didn't have $1,000 in the bank. I didn't know what to do. I was really down. I did get a meeting with Les [Hogan] within a week of the fateful day when he told me I was being replaced. Actually, he really wasn't firing me, he was giving me another job, but it was pretty clear I should go somewhere else. That's when I met with him, and we agreed on a one-year severance pay.

"Now, November 13th was my anniversary, and in this time frame, I'm out of a job. I'm at L'Auberge, having dinner with Linda, out of a job, no prospects, had no clue what to do, and now I'm getting feedback that Joe Van Poppelen has had a meeting with all of my [former] sales organization worldwide. [He said something like] 'No more of this Jerry Sanders stuff; we're going to run this like a business.'

"And I'm thinking, 'God! Not only am I out of a job, but now I'm being vilified, and no headhunters are calling me up. I'm not getting any phone calls. I'm scared!'

"I had to figure out something to do, so I rented a beach house in Malibu for a month, and it was $600 a month, and it just about cleaned us out, and I rented it for the month of December. It was in December because December's not a very desirable month in Malibu and rents are cheaper. And we stayed down there while I figured out what I was going to do.

"I looked into the possibilities of being in personal management in the entertainment industry. I thought about getting into a car dealership because my father-in-law was in the car business, and he thought I had a great sales personality. During that same time I even talked to you [Charlie Sporck]. We had dinner at the Velvet Turtle, and you suggested I get into something where sales is really important, like having a travel agency!

"But you did come through later, Charlie. We had another conversation. That first conversation might have been on the phone, but there was one conversation with you, at the Velvet Turtle, which I'll never forget because you were really, really great. When I had this conversation with you, and you played a key role, I said I was going to try to become the assistant to a president somewhere. You said, 'Why do you want to do that?' and I said, 'Because I want to have my own company some day. I don't want to be subject to the vagaries and the whims of a person of power. I don't ever want to give anybody that kind of power over me again. This feels too bad. This is awful. I want to be in charge.' And I thought in those days that being in charge meant being president or CEO. I didn't know you had share-holders and all that because I was naive. What I really wanted to be was king, but they don't have many jobs like that!

"But anyway, you said, 'Why do you want to go do that? Half the presidents don't know as much as you know now,' (which was not true, but you were very kind) and you said 'Basically, you know how to sell stuff. Get somebody to make stuff and you got a business.' So, gee, here's Sporck, a man I admire, a guy who's run an operation—he's not a marketing or sales guy, so he's got a much different perspective—and he says, 'You can be the president of something. Just get somebody who will make something.'

"Well, I was starting to get phone calls, and the most impor-tant one (there were two of them) was from John Carey who had basically been in charge of digital ICs at Fairchild before the Motorola guys came in and Gene Blanchette walked him out. And Jack Gifford, who had been involved in linear ICs, and both of these guys suggested forming companies. Well, John Carey had the idea that we could form this company to make CTL, because CTL was a real opportunity, and only Fairchild made it, and I said, 'That's not of any interest to me.'

But I liked the concept of John being a process guy and being able to make stuff. John was a very smart guy.

"I started talking to Jack Gifford, and he had a group of guys that wanted to make linear circuits. I knew there was a real opportunity because of the success National had had with the 101A and later the 108A, and these were high-margin deals, and you didn't need huge capacity. So I liked the linear deal. Jack also had some hybrid guys, you know, a couple of guys from India. I remember that because hybrid always seemed to have a lot of Indian guys, so there's a lot of engineering mumbo-jumbo. This is not batch processing. This doesn't take advantage of the technology. I didn't want that.

"So basically, I had a tough task: 1) I had to persuade Jack to dismember his team and jettison the hybrid guys and 2) I had to persuade Jack and John that we should get the two groups together because while the linear business might be a good place to start, the world was going digital. We needed to be in digital. The analog world was just going to be the interface. We needed to be in the digital business.

"Fortunately for me, the greed of Jack Gifford's partners to have someone who could raise the money and get a company started overcame their allegiance to the hybrid guys. They jettisoned them like a hot rock. Then I found out that Jack had been trying to raise money for over a year and couldn't get arrested! Never got any deals.

"They wanted me to raise the money. Somehow they thought I could raise the money. John Carey seemed to me much more knowledgeable on how the operations side might go. To me, he was the other half you talked about that I didn't have. Then somehow I had to juggle and get these guys together. I brought in Sven Stevenson who was a design guy. Somebody has to make them, but somebody has to design them. That was Sven.

"And then I added Ed Turney to the mix. Ed was my best man at my first wedding. He was my best friend, and I wanted him to run sales, and he also ran administration, which was a surprise to Gifford and his crew, because they thought I was going to be the sales guy. I told them I couldn't be president, raise the money and be the sales guy. I'll set the vision, which I always have, but there's got to be somebody in the trenches, day in and day out. Of course, what I didn't realize at the time was that I was just setting up for Jack Gifford and Ed to be at loggerheads in the future.

"It's interesting that there's not a single one of the founding team still here [at AMD] except me. All of them left at the $1 million level, or the $5 million level; it's kind of interesting. So, AMD was born by me getting together with John Carey, telling him I wanted to be in the 9300 MSI business because Les Hogan had blown it, and it was a superior solution and there was no alternate source. National was making hay on 101A's and linear and 7400, but I couldn't make gates!

"I knew I couldn't compete on cost, so I wanted to be in the value-added business. I wanted the niche business of linear to get me going and then I wanted to migrate into building blocks with ever-increasing complexity, which is what we're still doing today. So we've gone from simple transistor functions to 20 million transistor functions.

"Without our initial linear business we wouldn't have survived. It turns out the 101A and the 108S were our largest revenue producers in the first year. (Both of these are National numbers.) We also made the 741 and the 747 and those were big, big deals for us. But the really brilliant thing I did in those days—the one that gave AMD its impetus—was first and foremost, everybody else was using their own numbering system and they used cross-reference charts. I just said, 'No, we'll make an AM-741.' Fairchild had a UA-741, National had an

LM-101; I just said, 'We'll have an AM-101 and an AM-741,' and I got letters from every lawyer in town. But you couldn't copyright the numbering system.

"So suddenly the distributors didn't have to explain a cross-reference to anybody. My deal was, 'Plug it in. If it doesn't work, send it back.' I mean, so that really made us. So then I knew distribution was the key—I'd learned that in commodities and from Don Valentine. I went to the distributors.

"Then I offered the distributors better margins. I didn't change our list price, I just gave these guys a big margin and a rebate program if they met certain goals. So, in effect, they made more money selling an AM-101A than they did selling an LM-101A. A lot of customers didn't want to buy from a nonrecognized guy, but we got our start.

"Then the third piece of my puzzle was military standard for free. It turns out that wasn't really that big a give-up, since I was making only hermetic packages, everything I made met that spec anyway unless I had a manufacturing problem. So, again, I overcame all the resistance. I think that AMD's success is entirely attributable to being market-driven before that was fashionable. Up until that time, Silicon Valley had always been technology-driven, engineering-driven. Whether it's silicon gate or C-MOS or whatever it was, it was always engineering-driven.

"My deal was, again, getting back to my fundamental principles, 'How do we take care of customers? What will satisfy the need?' The customers we were looking for needed a second source at lower cost. I knew long-term you couldn't survive without adding value because, otherwise, you couldn't afford the R&D to keep up. Of course, I'm still fighting against Intel and TI and Motorola. How do you stay current on the technology when you're a $2.5 billion company and they're both $10 billion companies?"

When I asked Sanders about his long-running legal battle with Intel, he was just as forthcoming . . .

"Fundamentally, what happened is this: The Japanese were taking over the semiconductor industry. That was the fear. Everybody was scared. When we started the SIA in '77, we had HP saying that the Japanese quality was superior. Things were tough.

"Andy Grove believed, in the '81-'82 time frame, that there was no way the U.S. semiconductor industry, and that included Intel, was going to be able to survive the onslaught of this enormous Japanese juggernaut. They had to find ways to make alliances to leverage resources, and so, what he wanted to do was have AMD as an alternate source.

"[Intel] was heavily influenced by IBM. But that could have been a very straightforward deal. Grove could have just made us their second source. We could have paid a royalty. But he wanted someone to augment Intel's design capability, and he thought we could be that company. It turns out we didn't do a very good job there, and there's a lot of reasons for that. Partly, the reluctance of companies to really work with competitors, and you know, always trying to have the upper hand, and so forth.

"Today, it's different. No, today I think you could make win-win deals. In any event, we made this deal in '82, and Intel didn't fully appreciate that the microprocessor thing was going to be as big a deal as it became and that the licensing rights they were giving us would enable us to participate in a huge market. Moreover, they really didn't think that AMD was going to be able to produce 8086's and 8088's and 80286's as quickly as we did.

"They were stunned by our ability to use their database tapes. We converted our processes to—well, we called it NS8-I. It stood for an N-channel semiconductor process; the "I" stood for Intel because we modified their process. We had to change their mask set. So, suddenly we were a competitor in the marketplace; we were cutting their price as far as they were concerned. That's what second sources do. That's how you get business as a second source.

"Moreover, we were starting to annoy them in the e-prom market, which had nothing to do with the deal, and since AMD was a kind of 'in your face' kind of competitor in e-proms, eroding their margins. There was some bad blood.

"I think Andy came under some criticism [at Intel], because he cut too good a deal with us, and he couldn't keep us under control. That was all well and good; it was just an annoyance as long as business was good. In fact, I remember getting a letter from Gordon (Moore) at the end of fiscal '84 (which would have been March '84), where we had our second 60% growth year back to back. 60% growth! He wrote me a letter saying, roughly, "This was a hell of an accomplishment for a company our size, and 60% is a big number . . . blah, blah, blah.

"Everything was good. Bob Noyce and I were friends. Andy Grove and I, as far as I was concerned, were friends. We skied together. There were no issues. Suddenly, business turned bad. The PC market collapsed in the summer of '84. Intel sales plummeted in the summer quarter; our sales held up, partly because we'd booked a lot of business. Gordon had said to me, 'If it's not real, I hope you'll give us back some of the business you bought.' I said, 'That'll never happen!' It was still all pretty much camaraderie, jocularity, because the market was big enough for both of us.

"Then, business really got tough. And Intel didn't want a second source. So they weren't going to give us the 386. They weren't giving us updates of the 286. In that time frame, in the '86 time frame, when things were really grim in the industry, Intel lost a hundred million dollars in e-proms. That's when the dumping thing was going on; that's when we had the U.S.-Japan trade agreement. And Andy [Grove] and I engaged in a number of conversations with the idea of combining our two companies.

"We had secret meetings, including one over at Ricky's Hyatt House, and basically we were trying to figure out how we could put these two companies together and what role I would play. There were very substantive agreements, and then, all of a sudden, Andy said that there was no reason for having further conversations because my valuation of what AMD was worth and what they thought it was worth were so disparate.

"Well, my view of what AMD was worth—frankly Charlie— was whatever the stock market said it was worth. The [sudden shift in attitude] was very strange. I've never had a chance to get resolution on what happened there. But Andy told me, 'You should be happy with what you got.' They weren't going to give us the 386.

"That's when I said, 'You give me no recourse.' By the way, this is all documented in the courts. 'You give me no recourse. I have to file for arbitration.' And we did. We filed for arbitration. They then filed to cancel the agreement. They like to give the impression that they canceled the agreement and then we filed for arbitration. That all came out. That's bull! That's bogus!

"The bottom line, as I see it, why it went wrong? Andy felt, rightly so, we had gotten a much bigger benefit out of the agreement than they had. I think that's true, (measured in dollars and cents.) But I won't make that case. We won the lawsuit. We do have the rights to Intel microcode. We did honor the agreement. They did breach it. We were awarded damages. Those damages were confirmed in the California Supreme Court. We won. They lost. They breached, because he didn't want a second source, and the bad blood has always been at the Andy level.

"Today, if he came in here, I'd say, 'Andy, I don't know what happened. You're on every cover! You're a multimillionaire! You built a fantastic business! You write books! You're the guru of advanced technology. What's your problem here?' I still don't know. My view is, Andy feels he was bested in the deal, and his only way to deal with it is that the deal was misinterpreted. When they put on their defense of why we didn't have the rights to the microcode, it was an entirely made-for-trial argument.

"Charlie, I could never be behind such an argument if this happened the other way around. I couldn't tolerate it. Don't get me wrong. I'm not saying anything is wrong with having your lawyers give you the best defense, but I could no more justify the Intel defense than I could the exoneration of O.J. I mean this is crap! And they won the first time, mostly because they doctored dates on documents and hid documents. We found that out; we got a new trial, and in the second trial, both Andy and I testified. Neither one of us testified at the first trial.

"We kicked their butt because truth was on our side. The lawyers tell me, 'That's interesting, but not depositive.' That's true, but at the end of the day the agreement went bad because we were benefiting too much, and we were prepared to make a unilateral adjustment in the deal. What we weren't prepared to do was walk away from it.

"Today, we have a new patent cross-license. We now have successfully concluded an agreement wherein we will have all the intellectual property necessary to provide software-compatible Microsoft Windows processors to Intel's instruction set, including incremental instructions, which they'll be coming out with. No one else had that.

"Even today, Intel doesn't want us to promote that. They agreed to let us make the statement that we have all the Intel intellectual property necessary to make software-compatible processors to Intel's instruction set, but they don't want us to elaborate. They don't want us to promote it, because they want to maintain, to the extent possible, their dominant position. I don't understand that.

"I don't really understand why they play such hardball. I'll use a football game analogy: The winning team generally wins because they outplayed the other team that day. There's nothing wrong with the losing team, and they usually say, 'Hey, they outplayed us today.' You don't usually hear the losing coach saying, 'We got screwed. We got robbed. It wasn't fair.' What you hear is, 'Hey there are some good days and some bad.' Intel, in my view, has in some of its management a character flaw that any loss can't be attributed to them. It must therefore be the result of some extraneous circumstances. To me, that's a character flaw. That's not intellectually honest.

"There is a feeling of arrogance to some extent at Intel. It was manifest in that minor Pentium bug. The simple response would have been to say, 'Hey there's 4 million transistors here, and there's exponential variations on the way those signals can go through. This particular bug has very limited impact on anyone, but if you feel like this is a bad product, we'll replace it!' And that's what it eventually came to, right?

CHAPTER EIGHTEEN

INTEL: THE TOP
OF THE PYRAMID

Bob Noyce, Gordon Moore and Andy Grove were all employees of Fairchild Semiconductor when they made the decision to try their hand at the business on their own. This makes Intel the most successful spinoff in Silicon Valley, and possibly the most successful spinoff of all time.

The history of Intel has been told many times, in many publications. Both Gordon Moore and Andy Grove have been the subjects of in-depth articles, and when TIME Magazine designated Andy Grove as *Man Of The Year* for 1997, a lengthy essay provided quite a bit of insight into the great entrepreneurial adventure that led to Intel's domination of the semiconductor industry. But Noyce, Moore and I were all close working associates when we were at Fairchild and our friendship continued after we had gone on divergent paths. Some fascinating details of Intel's history still remain to be told.

As I said in my introduction to this book, I wish I had started this project while Bob Noyce was still alive, because his first-hand insights would have been invaluable. Fortunately for all of us, Gordon Moore was more than patient with me when I asked him about the founding and first years of Intel. Here is how our discussion went, edited only for continuity and the occasional informalities of a face-to-face conversation.

"When you started Intel, how was the financing done?"

> "We hit it just right. First of all, 1968 was one of these heyday years of venture capital; there was a lot of money around, and people were interested. Bob and I had enough money out of Fairchild, about a quarter of a million dollars each. Art [Rock] got good numbers for the money, and we put in $245,000 each. Art put in $10,000 to round out the first half million bucks, and then the second two and a half million, we marked up five times and sold through Art's friends."

"So it was $3 million that started Intel."

> "The good old days."

"And then you set off to make a memory device?"

> "We started out with memory as the objective . . . To look at it more broadly, what we wanted to do was make a complex device. At that time, you guys in the TTL business, your chips were costing you less than the packaging, by a bundle, and it was hard to define anything that was of real complexity that you could make in volume. We thought semiconductor memory was a chance to make something complex, in volume. So, the processing of the silicon would be an important part of the business again. That was kind of the way I viewed it: Semiconductor memory was the place to do that."

"So you specifically wanted to build something where the chip was the dominant cost factor?"

> "We could take advantage of our ability to build something complex. Yes. We set off to develop three new technologies. In retrospect I call this our 'Goldilocks strategy.' We wanted to do

Shottkey clamp bipolar, which we did. MOS, which at that time, individual transistors were the only devices anybody had seen. Bell Labs was doing a paper on them. We had duplicated them in the laboratory, so yeah, you could make a silicon gate transistor, but not in production quantities. And we were going to do multi-chip memory logic. A whole bunch of things together.

"The Shottkey bipolar turned out to work so easily that it wasn't much of an advantage for several years. We sold bipolar for several years, but right away, anybody who had a bipolar processor got into it. Our first product was a 64-bit bipolar memory. MOS turned out to be just perfect. Very lucky choice. We figured we had about five years to get established before the Dallas companies came around after us.

"When we were all focused on silicon gate, we got by a couple of pretty hairy problems reasonably well. But the companies that were not devoting all of their talents to solving those problems really got hung up on them. So we kept silicon gate to ourselves for about seven years. If the technology had been more difficult, we wouldn't have made it; if it had been easier, we wouldn't have had the advantage, which turned out to be just perfect."

"During that period there were ups and downs, with recessions."

"Yes, there was the '71 recession; '69 was a soft year, too, but that was a development year for us, so it didn't make any difference. The next one came along, I guess it was '71, and we'd just got our DRAM out, the 1103. We had to set up a second source, and we started dealing with this company, M.I.L. in Canada. Bell Canada supported the separate operation we'd set up to do semiconductors, so we did a technology sale to them, which carried us through that period. Now, I remember that as not being much of a problem.

"My view of the Intel startup was that it was fantastic! Things went on schedule, we got them done on budget, and everything went fine. Andy [Grove] views this as the toughest part of his life because he was afraid things were going to fall apart at any moment—Art [Rock] more nearly sides with Andy than with me. He thought we were on the verge of running out of money or something like that. Andy worries much more than I do. That didn't surprise me so much, but Art having a view like that . . ."

"How were you organized after you got started? What was your structure?"

"Bob [Noyce] and I were kind of an office of the chief executive from the beginning. You know Bob. Bob was not a manager. He was a leader, and he didn't like to manage anything. I'm not much of a manager, but I'm oriented a little more in that direction than he was. We had a separate group that was doing the product design. Eventually Andy did something like run R&D. We set up in the beginning with the idea we wouldn't have a separate development facility. We wanted to avoid the transfer. We took just about a year to develop our first product, the technology and the product.

"Those were useful products, but they didn't serve huge markets. During this time we were looking for another application where we could build a complex device. We started looking for a calculator company so we could make a complex device we could sell in volume. The established calculator company had already signed up with others, so we ended up with a Japanese company that was laying out a 13-chip calculator system. There was no way in heck we could make 13 chips. We hired somebody out of Stanford with more systems experience than any of us had. He started looking at this, and said, 'Gee, you can make all of these calculators with a general-purpose computer architecture and the whole thing, I think, will be about the complexity of the memory chip we're making.'

"We polled the Japanese on the idea of abandoning their 13 circuits that had been laid out, and going with a standard architecture that we could do. We only had to do one CPU chip and then a RAM and a ROM. And of course, we were doing the memories already. He [the systems person] saw that this would be useful for a lot of other things too. I remember elevator controls and traffic lights being two things he suggested. I got very enthused about this."

"This was when?"

"That would have been back in '69, I guess. We shipped our first one in February '71. So having this idea, we not only expanded our engineering, but hired Federico Faggin to run the group and actually implement the microprocessor."

"How did you guys get into the wristwatch business, which resulted in so much dilution of the semiconductor effort."

"The reason we did it was that Bob Robson had set up this little company and it was intriguing as heck. And we thought we saw the beginning of a personal electronic system, adding a lot of functionality to the watch."

"I'd like to have you comment on that, because we at National did the same thing. I believe that the reason I did it is because it was probably during one of these recessions in which you're not growing like you want to grow. We were searching for other ways to grow faster than the marketplace was allowing us to grow. I view it as a terrible mistake. You lost $15 million. It caused us to do a number of things that represented a hell of a lot more dilution. Was it a search for complexity or a product to make or was it . . . ?"

"We went looking. If Robson hadn't come around with something like the watch [it would have been something else]. We isolated it sufficiently so that the dilution of the semiconductor effort was minimized."

"It also demonstrated a level of arrogance that we had."

"Hubris!"

"We thought that we could go into a completely foreign area."

> "We probably underestimated a lot of the difficulty in that.
> Probably my engineer's view is that a watch is a thing I wear to tell
> time, to wake me up in the morning. Maybe we were naive."

"I think we all were very terribly naive. At least you guys got out of it
a lot earlier than we did. We at National Semiconductor continued
to fight the stupid thing and were sitting around picking out watch
faces."

> "When we got out of it, the pushbuttons on the side of the watch
> cost more than the chips. It didn't go the way I expected it to go at
> all. You know, the best thing TI ever did for me was to drive us out
> of the watch business. You know, we were going along, selling
> $150 watches. Then $19.95, suddenly, and $9.95 the next year.
> We finally said hell with it."

This fleeting mention of the wristwatch business deserves another
word or two. I tried to remember the exact chronology of Silicon Valley's
ill-fated venture into timepieces and compared my impressions with
those of Bob Robson, the founder of Microma. According to Bob,
Microma came out with the first "complete" digital watch in 1972. It had
an LCD display. Several semiconductor companies had been selling the
actual chips, time-keeping modules and/or the display units to well-
established manufacturers, and at National we actually built the complete internal works on a ceramic substrate. But Robson's Microma
company was the first in Silicon Valley to go all the way with a case and
packaging, etc. Shortly thereafter, a few of us tried to do the same, and
none of us managed a business success. There are bits and pieces of commentary from others about the watch business. It is not remembered
fondly as our best enterprise.

"OK. What were the other major milestones? I think probably the
IBM choice to use an Intel CPU in their PCs?"

"Yes, that was a really big deal. And that was one of those things where we were really pushing for a design win. We had a goal of 2,000 design wins that year. One of those design wins was for the IBM PC. We knew it was a good design, but we had no idea how much better it was than the others. It was another big turning point.

"IBM's product was introduced in '81. I guess the choice was probably made in '80. Do you remember '83 and '84? You didn't think you could build factories enough for all of the stuff. Everybody told us how much they wanted, and we looked at those damned things and built factories as fast as we could. We couldn't imagine making enough 286's and 186's for the universe. So we put second sources in places all over hell to protect our customers, and then the demand didn't . . . Prices . . . our EPROM price fell over 90% in nine months because our most profitable product was a bust.

"We looked at the 386, which was just coming out and except for the AMD deal—that they hadn't delivered on—devices were not coming to anybody. So, I remember having a meeting and saying, 'Look, the software is going to make the 386 successful. Everyone will have to buy it. If our customers are short on processors, the hell with them.' We decided not to second source the 386. We virtually stopped. That was the first time we really regained control of pricing. But always before that you had to give away your process."

"I asked you about the consumer products, the watches. How about add-on memory?"

"We only had add-on memories for a couple of reasons. We had to do memory systems just to understand what was going on, but the biggest potential for memory was on IBM machines and the only way to get at it was to buy it.

"So we caught up with a group out of Honeywell that had the capability. I engineered a memory for the 1103 system that nobody else in engineering wanted to build. The system business for memories was bigger than the microprocessor business for nearly all of the 70's but we were so busy we didn't have the time.

"You got involved in a lawsuit with Cyrix; what is your feeling about a license agreement with a third party that gave Cyrix access to Intel patents?"

> "Catastrophic. It was the dumbest damned ruling I could ever have imagined coming out of the court system. Surrounds the whole idea of the patent cross-license! Geez! I can't believe that that's the law of the land now! All of the decisions have gone against us. That one bothers me the most."

A bit of explanation may help the reader to understand this short conversational exchange. I may be oversimplifying the issue, but here's what we were talking about:

Intel had entered into cross-licensing agreements with SCM Microelectronics in Europe, and IBM, a company with a lot more going on than just computers and software. And one of IBM's operations was—and probably still is—the fabrication of wafers for other semiconductor companies. In other words, a company could bring a set of masks to IBM and ask that IBM produce finished wafers ready to be cut apart into individual chips. In the industry, this is called the foundry business.

Cyrix had produced masks capable of reproducing some Intel products, and asked IBM to do the foundry work, which IBM accomplished capably. Then, when Cyrix marketed products that were, in effect, copies of Intel products, Intel sued Cyrix for patent infringement.

The judge hearing the case found that IBM's cross-license with Intel entitled IBM to make and sell products patented by Intel. As the reader might imagine, this was not well received by Intel.

"I feel the same way about that as I remember looking at the original intent. What does it mean they can do? What, for example,

can some startup outfit get away with and what can't they get away
with in terms of copying ..."

"If they use a fully licensed foundry, they can use all of our circuits
and our architecture . . ."

"But is that really true?"

"Yes! That's what Cyrix is doing!"

"I know what they're doing, but I thought you still had some ways
of restricting the design in some fashion, or the software."

"The only thing we had was microcode. The microcode is not a
patent, and we haven't licensed microcode, so that's a copyright.
Where we could find them, something like that, we could still get
them on copyright. But, in fact, the patents were the original things
we cross-licensed. We renegotiated many of the cross-licenses
now that specifically preclude the foundry . . ."

"So, is there a way to stop this? Or is this just going to fade away,
because there hasn't been a proliferation of this going on since
these rulings."

"I think if you anticipate it, you can write your legal agreements so
you're OK on it. You know, this one just caught me right in the
throat."

"It strikes me as being a way to take the profit out of the guy who
did the original work. I'm dismayed."

"You know, we had two cases, and we won one and lost one."

"What happened with AMD?"

"All the darn things. Our agreement was for the first couple of
things before AMD had anything to trade. They were promising all
the future stuff—on the come. And we never got anything back.
So, after not getting anything back, we finally decided to look at
what we wanted to do. And the thing that really made it a mess
was that by the time we got to arbitrate it, it just laid the

groundwork for everything else. So while we were fighting on that damned arbitration . . ."

"Did you try to get together?"

"I got together with Jerry. . . . "

"One last question. About other companies that make the peripherals. Long term, what's going to happen?"

"We started out doing all the peripheral functions. Then we just blew it. We blew a generation. Actually, on the Pentium-based systems, we're supplying most of the chips. We're going to lose market share this year, because the other guys are finally coming in. We're going as fast as we can. So, we're having to do more of the peripherals. I suspect what we're going to see is a deal where Intel tends to supply a fairly large percentage of the new ones for a while and then loses the dominant position in peripherals."
[NOTE: These comments were made during a discussion in 1996—CES]

"Do you see the CPU absorbing products of peripheral companies?"

"Some of them, but not all of them. For example, right now we're touting something we call native signal processing. You know, the thing with the sound thing and it has a whole separate sound system. If we can pull that kind of function onto the CPU I think it'll happen, and it'll make the whole system simpler and a lot easier to maintain."

"There are many small companies that build peripherals."

"From the days we first started selling integrated circuits, we didn't count on peripherals. The people that recognize that and take advantage of the fact that their proprietary advantage this year is next year's commodity can do pretty well. But ones that try to retain their proprietary advantage where it was, are going to get steamrollered. That's the trouble they're having at Compaq right now. You know, Compaq's our biggest customer, and we're doing a horrible thing—we're enabling their competitors. What was their proprietary advantage a year or two ago, we now sell to everybody, and they don't like that. But the technology drives us that way. We're not going to make them happy."

Gordon Moore has a way of looking, sounding and behaving as the quintessential gentleman scientist/entrepreneur. As I listened to the tapes of my interview with Gordon, and as I reread the transcript, I wondered whether he would come across to readers of this book as the complete human being I've known for so many years. Perhaps this little anecdote from my own experience with Gordon will fill out the picture a little . . .

The Fairchild marketing department was conducting one of their annual sales meetings at The Hawaiian Village Hotel in Hawaii. Gordon and I, as members of company management, were expected to attend and make some inspirational remarks. We arrived from California quite a bit later than the main body of attendees, perhaps as much as a day later. It was a gorgeous evening, and we found ourselves some distance away from the Hawaiian Village. We decided to walk along the beach toward the designated hotel.

There was a lineup of intervening hotels between our starting place and the Hawaiian Village, each with a waterfront cocktail lounge. We stopped at the first hotel and each of us ordered a Mai Tai. Then we tried to walk on to the next hotel, but a fence along the property line went right down to the edge of the ocean. So we waded into the water, around the fence, and made our way to the second cocktail lounge. We each had a second Mai Tai.

And so it went, through a series of Mai Tais, wading around property fences and more drinks. By the time we finished working our way through the lineup of hotels we were well under the influence of strong spirits. We finished our journey by walking up the center of the main street, or perhaps *weaving* is a better word than walking, in an advanced state of inebriation, in our soaking-wet business suits and our squishing shoes and stockings.

CHAPTER NINETEEN

ANDY GROVE ON INTEL

Looking over the transcript of my long conversation with Andy Grove, I found many incomplete sentences and seemingly disconnected phrases. Not because Andy has any difficulties expressing himself, but because his mind is so quick that he grasped the point of my questions before I finished asking them. Andy had an intuitive sense of where I was going and guided the conversation by hand gestures, facial expressions and body language.

It is not, in any way, a reflection on others I interviewed to say that Andy Grove has a unique brilliance that transcends a question-and-answer format. For that reason alone, I have elected to supplement Andy's remarks with as much of my own narrative interpretation as is needed to understand what he communicated in a clear, but sometimes nonverbal, manner.

Grove was not a party to the initial discussions between Noyce and Moore that led to their decision to leave Fairchild and establish a company of their own. His first inkling of the incipient spinoff was a chance conversation with Gordon Moore at a professional conference . . .

> "I was at the International Device Conference in Colorado, and Gordon flew in. He came from a planning meeting, so we went for a walk when he arrived. I was interested in what happened and what came out. He was kind of perfunctorily reporting it.
>
> "We were up in the mountains in Boulder, walking in our shirtsleeves, and he says, 'I've decided to leave Fairchild.' And I said, 'I want to go with you.' So the irony of all of this—I was never asked to join Intel."

"You volunteered."

> "I volunteered, and as sort of an analogy, I never asked my wife to marry me, either. I just started to talk about 'when we get married.' Just from one moment to the next, I sort of took it for granted, and she went along with it and we got married 40 years ago! Then, later on in that walk, he [Moore] told me, 'By the way, Bob Noyce is involved with this.' I said, 'Oh.' I was not happy about that."

"Why not?"

> "I found Bob aloof, indecisive—watching staff meetings where people were devouring each other—and Bob would look detached."

"Bob never really liked to say no."

> "No. And he never could handle controversies. Neither of them can."

"Gordon's a little better than Bob at that; that's my opinion."

> "Actually, in the early stages of Intel, some people needed to be booted out and Bob did all the dirty work. He waited until Gordon was on vacation, and he did it. Anyway, so I thought he was very superficial and all of that stuff. In time I got to love Bob, but my first reaction to hearing that was, 'Oh, shit!' But that's how I got there.

"Then I quit to Tom Bay, [at the time, CEO of Fairchild Semiconductor] and Tom Bay went through the routine very lackadaisically. I mean, I don't think he cared about anything at that point. Everybody he cared for had left, but there were still a lot of people that were good. It was a miserable thing to leave—probably for you, too."

"It was very tough. It was heart-rending."

"There was something about that place. And people nowadays say the same kind of stuff about Intel."

"It becomes almost a family."

"Yeah."

"Who else was involved? Bob Graham was involved, too."

"I never met Bob Graham before Intel. He was ex-Fairchild, but I never met him at Fairchild."

"He had been at ITT Semiconductor in West Palm Beach, Florida. First as director of marketing, and then, for a short time, as general manager. Did you guys have a specific target? I assume it was memory, but did you start knowing exactly what it was you wanted to do?"

"We weren't sure about bipolar vs. MOS, so we were going to do both. We did both technologies. And we were going to do a module, we were going to do it with MOS memory arrays and bipolar decoders with flip chip assembly."

"Pretty damned ambitious—flip chip."

"I hated it. All kinds of funny bonding. You know, 30 years later it's still tough. Fortunately, we were pretty successful with our bipolar effort.

"Your first memory product—was that 1101 or 1102 or something like that?"

"1101, yes."

"I seem to remember that when you guys first started working on that, you had a lot of trouble getting yield. Is that right?"

> "At that time, it was very true! And then later on—the biggest thing was—you, National—had a shift register that we competed with."

"Ken Moyle; right."

> And when we first passed National in shift registers—[pounds table] [laughs] it was a great triumph."

My conversation with Andy Grove then shifted to the way old animosities gradually faded away with the passage of years. We agreed that people who, 30 years ago, for one reason or another, disliked each other, eventually came to grips with everything that happened. Don Valentine and Jerry Sanders for example. Don Valentine and Bob Graham. They all started out as close friends, then were at odds with each other. When you talk to them now, they say, 'Well, the reason was we were in two different responsibilities, and those responsibilities tended to clash.' It's interesting. The other point that's interesting is that history gets rewritten to conform to what people want to see in it.

My conversation with Grove reminded me that Bob Noyce once had the idea of combining Intel and National Semiconductor. It must have been around 1972, and I asked Andy if he knew about it.

> "It's one of those things that I can't swear I remember, but there is a familiarity—"

"I think the deal was, according to Gordon, Bob felt that we had some manufacturing strength to bring, and Intel had the product— the technology strength, and it would be a good combination. Then he got Gordon and me to meet to talk about this, and then I just don't remember—"

> "So it went that far—the two of you talking?"

"I don't remember the details."

"I have to tell you one story that has become germane to this. Bob [Noyce] had enormous respect for you. I'm not surprised. Bob Graham was using you to beat me up."

"That's probably where Bob got the idea."

"Bob Noyce?"

"Yes."

"He certainly supported it to the extent that you became this larger-than-life manufacturing genius . . . "

"Solver of all manufacturing problems, right."

"Which is not an unreasonable evaluation [of your abilities]. But we were just starting. We were a little R&D outfit starting to turn out products. You know? They put me in the job there, and it's kind of like, 'Well, listen, Andy—you are no Charlie Sporck!' So, I lived with that for quite some time—a very sensitive time.

"So, fast-forward. We were hanging around at some cocktail party. This is much later. You don't know this. You were there; I was there; some people were surrounding you. I wanted to tell you how you were used as a standard of comparison as my coworkers criticized my performance—by that time this was humorous. This is about 10 years later. I never could get your attention. People were buzzing around, and it's a story I really wanted to tell you. So, this is part of what I mean. Who knows how many people hogged the shadow of somebody and competed with somebody else?"

"OK. So, you guys were pursuing these three avenues, I gather. You had the MOS memory devices and the bipolar devices and the modules. At some stage you dropped the bipolar—"

In '73–'74—five years later. Our first fab was in a Mountain View building. We built our first building on the Central Expressway. It was a bipolar fab area. In '71, bipolar was definitely going to be a factor but we never expanded it out of that one fab area, which was at one point the bigger half of our operations. We shut that down maybe in the late '70s"

"Was there a time when you said that's not going to be for us? Even before you shut it down? That we're going to concentrate over here in MOS memory products?"

"There may have been but it was no big drama. The 1103 was very successful and we had one key bipolar product in development. We had two-layer metal. We had a very hard time with that. We actually introduced it, but never sold more than 2,000 pieces. On the other hand there was a reason for bipolar to exist because all the decoder circuits that went along with it were bipolar.

"So, pretty gradually the charter for the bipolar stuff became the kit part. Then the static RAM business started up, and the static RAM business went faster and faster, so we pulled the plug on this one bipolar development.

"We had done all right up to that point. The first bipolar device was 64-bit. Very successful and paid the bills for a while. Then we had a 256-bit, which was also pretty successful. It was the 1K level where we were having trouble. That's when we had to go to two-layer metal. So there was a charter for bipolar for a long time beyond memories.

"So the answer is: Nature took its course with respect to memory, and it would have been a big drama if we had to shut down. But since we had another reason for it, there was no big drama. The big drama for us was in '85 when we got out of memories.

"Before you get there, how about your modules?"

"They were dead in six to nine months. You know, actually what killed that business was more than factory technologies, per se. The yield was awful. I mean, we are talking two-die-per-wafer-stuff.

"And to build that bonding system up, you lose half of your good dice—you know, the stuff that you pull before you put all that crap on—half of it is dead. I mean, it was kind of a sin to take a wafer with four good dice and put bumps on them—and we would come out with one!"

"Tell me about the microprocessor. Or I guess it was first a micro-controller—that right? 4004?"

"I don't think those distinctions existed at the time. There is a much-told story: Somebody—a big calculator company—came in with a request for 13 custom circuits for a calculator. Bob loved all that—Bob loved everything. Gordon figured out we could never design 13 circuits, given that our total history consisted of two or three original designs. So, somebody, either Bob or Gordon, asked Ted Hoff (I was not involved) to work on it and it became a totally programmable microprocessor. We knew its potential so well, we gave away full rights to the whole !&@! thing to Busicom!"

"It always pays to plan ahead."

"You're right! We sold $1 million worth of that first design. We were very happy with it. It turned out to be a good development. Then we went to Japan and bought back our rights."

"When did all that happen?"

The business was done in 1970. In '71 I was working on the big ramp-up of the 1103 so I was not very happy about producing two big chips that were quite different. They were screwing up my very fragile production line.

"When did you guys realize what you had?"

"Later. I thought it was something really useful. But [in terms of sales], I had no idea where it was going."

"How about when IBM made the decision to use your CPU?"

"Well, it was a big deal. But memories were a bigger deal then."

"When did IBM make their decision?"

"Late 1980, early '81."

"Memory started being a problem for you when the Japanese started coming in. They started coming in the late '70s, didn't they?"

"Well, we were pretty big in static RAMs, 2147's and 4K statics. We had a pretty big business. We had three strong businesses around that time. E-proms, static RAMs and D-RAMs. This is late '70's.

"Microprocessors were not a big deal up to that point. Around the late '70's—around the 80/86 times—Davidow [vice president of marketing at Intel] was going around writing memos: 'DEC only sold 30,000.' Davidow was here then. I hate to admit to it, but that was one of my recollections—how DEC altogether sold 30,000 PDP-11's or whatever, and we had to be careful not to have too high expectations.

"And then Gelbach came, and Markkula was—"

"Markkula was already here. Graham hired Markkula as product marketing manager. I didn't know marketing people from sales people. I mean, sales people I could understand because I would go on customer calls and see what they did."

"The guys in between—"

"I thought they were turkeys! Markkula was always very nice to me, but I didn't have much use for him. The reason it's important is that five years later—1978—I pick up one of those pink message slips from my secretary. My secretary gives it to me with a big grin. It says 'Mike Markkula, Apple Computer, please call him back.' I said, 'Apple Computer??'

"I called Mike, 'What is this Apple Computer?' I mean, it was funny! I thought it was a joke! Anyway, he wanted me to come over, and so, in '78, he shows me around Apple. I'm still trying to answer your question about when we realized what we had with microprocessors. I met the two Steves. At the end of the day, Mike wanted me to join their board and offered me a chance to invest.

"What's Apple got to do with my answer to your question about when I knew we really had something? The two Steves were very interesting because they were kids, you know, and they had this device, and there was Mike at Apple Computer! So, I put a little bit of money in it, I mean a few thousand dollars, against my best judgment, and I said no to the board offer. That's how much I knew in '78.

"But I guess the incident left an impression because I started paying more attention to those little computers. I went up to Moscone Hall in San Francisco to the early personal computer shows. I started going—they were playing 'Pong' on personal computers and various other jazzy things. So, it had a little impact.

"But then comes 1980-81, and we have two big wins at IBM—the Displaywriter and the PC. There was no question in my mind which one I celebrated. The Displaywriter could type! We had five of them in the company, and there was that Tinkertoy PC! And I was just wrong about that!

"So, further, about marketing people. Our product marketing manager was in charge of all that. In an internal presentation two or three weeks before we heard about the IBM design win, he declared the 8088 was the Edsel of microprocessors. I gave him a plaque sometime later with that phrase.

"So, you know, things happen. But the random motion is not broadly recognized. I mean, there's some kind of magnetic field that drives us in a particular direction, but in between, when you look at us microscopically, the industry visions were not all that clear. Bob [Noyce] was much more of a visionary than the rest of us, to his credit. He was mesmerized by all this stuff. "

"Noyce had a very inquisitive mind. He was always interested."

"At one point, he said at a staff meeting, 'Now that we are in the computer business—- dah, dah, dah.' Gordon went berserk! 'What do you mean we're in the computer business!? We are not in the computer business! We will *never* be in the computer business!' I don't know when that was, but it was around the time when Ted Hoff put together the first development system—a very early version of it—and Bob was, in a way, right. He was just 15 years ahead of his time!"

"A couple other questions: You guys went into the watch business. Why did you do that?"

"That you have to ask Gordon."

"I asked Gordon, and got his answer, and it doesn't conform to the reason I think most of the semiconductor companies did these things. We all did it. I think they were mistakes, but . . ."

"Well, I think we did it because Bob Robson came and charmed Gordon into putting C-MOS into a watch module—which of course we didn't have. This is operations manager Andy saying, 'What kind of bullshit? We don't have C-MOS! Of course, we can develop it.' But I mean, we developed C-MOS technology because of the watch business, and that C-MOS technology did us no good 10 years later."

"I happen to think that the dilution of effort that semiconductor companies went through, diddling with a lot of consumer and system products—National did it—was a mistake. TI stayed in it for a long time, but they never made any money from it. But, even if they were successful to some degree, the dilution was a mistake.

"The reason, I think—the reason why National went in—is that we got conned. Part of it was arrogance. This business that we've got these chips that you can make a calculator with or a watch with, and obviously these people who build and sell watches are stupid idiots and we're the smart guys. We can really dominate that market. I mean, the chip is meaningless in a watch.

A watch is jewelry. What the hell do we know about jewelry? The same with calculators. The other thing was that there were periods, cycles in our business, ups and downs, in which things were damned slow. And we were looking around, saying, 'Well, the semiconductor business isn't growing very rapidly. We need another opportunity, an opportunity to dissipate energy."

"Two years later, approximately, I got promoted and I inherited Microma. This time it was mine, and for a while I was trying to make something of it. It wasn't working. Of course, it's easy to understand in retrospect. Imagine what a moment of truth to me that was when I found out that Timex had 250,000 points of sale for their watches. Our biggest annual record run rate was about 250,000 pieces. So we had to work a year—and all that labor was supposed to equal one lousy watch per point of sale for Timex. One. I mean, we didn't belong in that business."

"None of us did. It was stupid."

"The successful companies turned it into a commodity business. Casio, specifically. It's not even jewelry; it's very functional. It lasts forever. It'll last longer than a PC!"

"And when it doesn't—I mean, I lose them—"

"And you go to the nearest store and buy one for $15."

"Please tell me about the AMD issue—it's probably a sensitive subject. Tell me what, in your opinion, caused it, and why did it drag on so long?"

"AMD? It's not a sensitive subject. It's been litigated for so many years it's tiresome.

"This is my personal perspective. Sanders followed us around in the latter part of the '70's, early '80's, and copied us as best he could—I mean in the minutest details. So, we had kind of friendly competition. I would tease him about this. I would compare the early annual reports from both of us. He copied the fonts, the style.

"I mean, his whole strategy was kind of making himself look like a second Intel. I don't want to go through all the details, but at various times we started working together and there was this final deal that we litigated over. And the first key product in the deal was the 80286. We were short of those 286's, so we made AMD a special deal to get the customers off our back.

"AMD never delivered what they were supposed to in exchange. So, comes the 80386, and we were saying that we were not going to do that same stupid deal that we did with the 286; we want real performance from AMD. We made various suggestions—we had discussions over royalties.

"Then they backed off. They said 'No, no, no—we'll wait. Let Intel come to us. You'll want us to take the 386 to the world market. You won't be able to produce it. It has a big die—dah, dah, dah.' I said, 'No.' They didn't honor the original deal. I said we're going to raid our e-prom factories and generate a capacity for making microprocessors. The rest is history, as they say. Those guys miscalculated. They bet on history repeating itself. History didn't repeat itself. So, they came after us with the arbitration. From there on, after that . . ."

"AMD started the suit?"

"Oh, yeah. They made a demand for what they weren't getting. The arbitration went on for four or five years, actually longer than World War II. They were stretching it out. I don't know why they were hoping to stretch it out because naturally, even if they won in the end, they would have gotten a product that was long obsolete.

"So they evidently concluded somewhere along the line, halfway in the arbitration, that they were not going to get the 386 out of this trial. They started to develop their own product using our microcode. Then we sued them for copyright infringement.

"From my standpoint, I resent being hounded for a decade by a company trying to right a bad miscalculation. So, that's much of my bitterness."

"I haven't talked to Jerry yet. (*I did, eventually, speak with Jerry Sanders, and his side of the story is presented in Chapter 9 of this book, beginning on page 112.*) One last issue: The memory decision—dropping that. Tell me about that."

"What happened there is—the gist of the whole scheme is—we got beaten out of it. We had several plants at the time. Only one of them was good. We were in deep denial of that situation. Then the IBM PC business dried up, you know, the crash of '84 came on, and all the stuff that permitted us to indulge in burying our heads changed.

"This was—"

"1985. And I remember it very well. We went out the revolving door, came back and we did it to ourselves.

"That's a very appropriate way to look at that. I guess you were honoring your emotional attachment to the business—"

"It took a year to face up to the situation."

"You were losing money on memory then."

"O, God, yes."

"Everybody was, including the Japanese."

"I just couldn't see a clear path for us to get well. The problem with all of this was—I've told this any number of times, and it's true—let's suppose we worked it all out. Let's say we put the product development work and dumping stuff and everything, into the equation. We still needed to become a 10% factor to make it work. It would have required $600 million of capital! This was in 1985. And we were only a 2%—3% player. We had no success strategy. We just fell back on slogans—you know, 'technology driven.'"

"Technology driven is a big temptation."

"So I grew up as a manager over that issue."

You know, in many respects, Andy, the Japanese did us a big favor because they took most of the U.S. companies out of commodity products and forced us to focus on design-rich products, which most are in now and are doing very well. Although, I must admit, the people who stayed in memory because that's all they had are doing well."

"That's right."

"I think that's only because there's a shortage of memory right now."

"Well, actually, that's interesting because it's only based on two major things: First of all the Japanese capital—"

"They stopped investing in domination of the market."

"And the PC happened. If the PC hadn't happened, things would have been different. And the PC happened because all these American companies developed microprocessors and Internet chips and—"

"Design-rich products."

"Right! So, Adam Smith had it right. And there was a major transformation in the industry, sort of 'creative destruction'—but in '85, I only recall the 'destruction' part!"

"I must admit in '85, I really was depressed about where the Japanese were going—I really was depressed."

"I remember that."

CHAPTER TWENTY

THE NATIONAL SEMICONDUCTOR ADVENTURE

I finally get to run my own show.

The history of National Semiconductor began in 1959, when some employees of Sperry Semiconductor spun off to form National. Sperry had been making an alloy transistor and the departing employees set up shop to make roughly the same product, declaring that the Sperry management was incompetent, or words to that effect. It was an open challenge to Sperry.

About a year later, Sperry sued National and won. The Law showed up, padlocked the National building and enforced an order to destroy all of National's inventory. Somebody told me the courts forced the company to physically grind up all of their products. For all practical purposes, National Semiconductor was in receivership.

One of the National directors approached Peter Sprague, a member of the family that had done so well in passive electronic components. Peter was, at the time, a very young entrepreneur in his late 20s or early 30s. He was then, and still is, an extremely bright, articulate man. Sprague put up enough money for stock warrants to save the company and remained active well into the 1990s as chairman of the National board. In addition to his continuing involvement with National, Peter also participated in many other startup companies, including Wave Systems. One of Sprague's more interesting "saves" outside of the electronics industry was his acquisition of the Aston Martin automobile company, barely in time to save that British firm from bankruptcy.

National limped back into business, switched to silicon diffused-junction transistors and got into hybrid integrated circuits. The plant was located in Danbury, Connecticut.

Some time in 1965 or 1966, National bought a small Silicon Valley company named Molectro, which was a spinoff from the Fairchild R&D staff. Molectro was making a version of Micrologic, the RTL-based line of integrated circuits that had given Fairchild such headaches. Molectro was no more successful in RTL than Fairchild, Philco and GMe had been. The yields were low, the demand was low, and everyone lost money on RTL.

The total sales of National Semiconductor in 1967 were on the order of $7 million. That same year, Fairchild Semiconductor did more than $100 million.

Watching the Defections

I was general manager of Fairchild Semiconductor, reporting to group vice president Bob Noyce. I got along well with Noyce, I liked and admired him, and my growing desire to "run my own show" was not in any way a reflection on our relationship. But I had seen a lot of good people leave Fairchild to establish their own operations. Among other companies, Fairchild had spawned

- Signetics
- GMe
- Molectro

- Amelco
- Rheem

As far as I could determine, none of those companies was making a whole lot of money, but money was only a secondary consideration in my growing dissatisfaction at Fairchild. We were having difficulties with our East Coast corporate management and we felt that they did not really appreciate what it took for long-term success in semiconductors. So I was receptive to the general idea of doing something on my own, but I hadn't taken any action until Pierre Lamond came back from an overseas trip and told me about a chance meeting.

The Plessey Possibility

Pierre had run into a man who ran the semiconductor R&D operation at Plessey, the British electronics firm. The Plessey man said that his company had some good technology and needed a management team capable of exploiting the accomplishments. The Plessey man thought that his company needed "some U.S. management to break out."

Pierre concluded his report by saying that "something interesting might be arranged."

Accordingly, we approached Plessey and they indicated some interest in us. Sir John Clark, CEO of Plessey, came to the United States in mid-1966 to see if there was "anything that could be done here." We met at Rickey's and discovered that we had mutual interests. That started us talking seriously about how we might come to an agreement.

I began making frequent trips to England. I would catch a plane on Friday night, fly to London, have long meetings with Plessey people, and then fly home again on Sunday afternoons. Eventually we developed a plan.

The idea was to start a new U.S. company and make me CEO of all Plessey semiconductor operations. Plessey would provide all of the money. We would be free to manage as we saw fit, providing that we met our targets. We put the whole plan on paper and included Pierre Lamond, Fred Bialek and Roger Smullen in the management group. We "had it all together" and by the fall of 1966 we were enthusiastic about our futures with Plessey.

Clearly, some influential people within Plessey were not in favor of our ambitious plans. They had enough influence on the board of directors to force a "final review" of the contemplated expansion. Accordingly, a committee of four Plessey executives was formed and sent over to California to check us out.

A Deal-Killing Dinner

The four Plessey men, and the four of us (myself, plus Pierre, Fred and Roger,) met at a restaurant. We began with a lengthy cocktail session. The date was inconvenient for me, because it was a Friday evening and I had promised to take my family on a skiing holiday that weekend, but I delayed our departure long enough for the Plessey meeting.

We had barely finished dinner when one of the Plessey representatives leaned into the table and in all seriousness, asked, "Now what, exactly, is a semiconductor?"

Roger Smullen had the first reaction. He tossed his napkin on the table, got up from his chair and left the restaurant. I made my excuses about a family commitment, and Pierre and I left Fred Bialek to stay with the Plessey men. Fred had the stomach for such discussions. He could handle that sort of conversation a lot better than I could.

After reading an earlier draft of my version of the meeting, Fred sent me a note with his own recollection of that meeting. This is Fred's summary:

> "We actually finished the dinner. Then the four of us decided to
> bail out, and I was left with the task of telling the Plessey dele-
> gation that we weren't going to go ahead with the deal. I went

> to their hotel the next morning to tell them of our decision. They
> chased me down the hall in a panic, asking me to reconsider
> because they knew they had blown it and feared what would
> happen to them when they got home."

Whatever the exact chronology, I telephoned Sir John Clark, with
whom I had a genuinely good relationship, and told him that I didn't
think our planned venture would work. Thus ended the Plessey
opportunity.

A Better Prospect Closer to Home

Even though it didn't come to anything, the Plessey incident motivated
us. We really wanted to do *something*, and we all had our eyes open for
the right opportunity. We knew that if we were going to start something,
we would have to attack the market with better manufacturing efficiency. We might have been able to start a new company with a new
product line, but our choice was to exploit our manufacturing expertise.
Gradually, National Semiconductor came into focus.

During the prior year, Bob Widlar and Dave Talbert had left Fairchild
to join Molectro, the small I/C company owned by National. I knew
and admired Widlar and Talbert, and I felt they were important to
Fairchild's continued success. Later, I heard somebody suggest that the
Widlar/Talbert departure from Fairchild was part of some plot I had in
mind, but nothing could be farther from the truth. I did my best to dis-
suade them from leaving Fairchild and there was no connection
between their decision and mine. Their departure, however, drew my
attention to National.

An examination of the National balance sheet indicated that they
were, essentially, bankrupt. Their inventory was out of control. They had
far too many employees for their level of sales. Whether or not they
knew it, they were down for the count. But I knew that if we took over

management of the company we could make substantial improvements in a short period of time. And with Widlar and Talbert involved, National could carve out a good position in linear circuits.

I met with Dave Talbert and described my interest. He agreed that the company was in desperate need of "decent management" and he relayed my interest to Don Lucas, a member of the National Semiconductor board of directors who later became a very successful venture-capital entrepreneur in Silicon Valley. Lucas and I started having serious meetings in January of 1967. I proposed a plan wherein I would bring some competent people from Fairchild with me, and we wanted complete decision-making authority, along with a free rein to turn the company around. Lucas was favorably inclined and he presented the idea to other board members, including Peter Sprague.

Sprague was not enthusiastic about the recommendation at first, because he had been instrumental in bringing Jack Hegarty into the CEO slot. Eventually the board went along with the proposal and it was agreed that Pierre Lamond, Fred Bialek, Roger Smullen, Floyd Kvamme and a fellow from Hewlett Packard named Ken Moyle would join my new staff at National.

I told Bob Noyce of my decision to leave during a lunch meeting in February of 1967. Bob asked me if he could do anything to change my mind, but it was a done deal and my thoughts were already occupied with plans for National. Bob understood my desire to be my own boss, he had sympathy for our frustrations with the Fairchild corporate management, and indeed, he would soon turn in his own resignation to become one of the Intel founders.

Surveying Our New Domain

We joined National Semiconductor on a Friday. National was in the process of holding a sales meeting in the San Francisco Bay Area and the five of us went over to be present as the announcement was made.

There was quite a stir. National's stock had been selling for about $5 a share, and when news of new management was released, National's stock jumped to $11 that same day. We had been able to buy some stock with money we borrowed from the company, and of course we also had some options. In that first day on the job the value of our "deal" doubled! Eventually the original investors in National Semiconductor, including Don Weeden and Don Lucas, realized a 400-fold growth in the value of their original investments!

Don Weeden was another remarkable presence on the National scene. Son of the founder of Weeden & Company, an investment firm his father started in San Fran-

Peter Sprague and I pose for a photo in the late 1960s

cisco with an initial investment of $20,000, Weeden was one of the original investors in National Semiconductor in 1959. He remained active on the National board well into the late 1990s and strongly supported the company's growth. A feature article about Don Weeden in the June 1999 issue of *Greenwich* magazine reviewed his life and career and paid special attention to his role in overturning the traditional attitude of the New York Stock Exchange regarding competitive commission rates by member brokers. They called him a renegade at the time, but he insisted that freedom to discount commissions on stock trades would result in an overall greater volume of business for brokers. He won his battle on May 1, 1975, a day that old-line brokers called

Mayday. A "renegade" at first, Don Weeden is now respected as an enlightened and forward-thinking man. And I'm proud to call him one of my good friends.

Back to 1967. At the time, Molectro had something like 30 employees, and the main National plant in Danbury had about 600 workers. The weekend after we joined the company, Roger Smullen, Fred Bialek and I went to Danbury. We met with all of the managers and told them to come back in a few hours and tell us the absolute minimum number of employees they could retain and still operate effectively. Then we took their proposals and cut them dramatically. We said we would begin Monday morning with the pared-down work force.

By Monday night the Danbury plant had gone from 600 employees to 300. The result was instant profitability. We had rationalized the work force with the sales level. It was our strategy to squeeze the Danbury plant for the capital we needed to expand the IC operation at Molectro in Santa Clara. I put Fred Bialek in charge of the Danbury plant, where he did a great job.

There's a story about Fred at Danbury that reveals a lot about the clash of cultures that existed at first. Late one afternoon Fred wanted to have a meeting with the managers, but he couldn't find some of them. A little searching turned up the news that they were outside playing golf. Fred hadn't even noticed a putting green on the grounds, but there it was.

The following day Bialek called in a landscape service, had the golf course rototilled and sodded, and that was the end of golf on the company grounds.

Molectro had great potential. The little company had the first linear voltage regulator on the market (the LM100). We shut down the RTL (Micrologic) line and concentrated on linear ICs and launched a new line that turned out our version of the Texas Instruments version of TTL. Sylvania, Fairchild and TI all had TTL products, but the Texas Instruments approach had the best acceptance in the industry.

Another Look Overseas

As was true of other companies by the late 1960s, National was doing some assembly work in Southeast Asia. The facility National used was actually a subcontractor company established by John Yih, Fairchild's first engineering manager in Hong Kong, who by then had spun off from Fairchild to run his own outfit.

National had a unique plastic-encased transistor called the GEM. It employed a system of three metal leads, held in place by adhesive tape. The tape was fed into a positioning jig, then a bonding machine established a connection to the die, and the tape indexed to the next position of three leads. Once the process was complete, the tape was sheared off and a plastic case was molded around the chip.

It sounds clever but the system never quite worked as desired. There was always something a little bit off where the leads met the transistor die. And when we compared our costs with those of Fairchild, which we knew because we had just left Fairchild, we saw that the Hong Kong operation was out of line. We knew we had to establish our own assembly facility. We phased out the GEM transistor line.

I was in Taiwan when I got a telephone call from Chuck Woodward, a fellow Fairchild veteran who had been in charge of automation, and who was then working as a consultant. Woodward had tracked me down and called from Singapore. He had words of high praise for Singapore and asked me to have a look for myself. I flew over, liked what I saw, had fruitful discussions with the government and met a lot of very bright and talented people. Singapore had a very good engineering school and in addition, plenty of Western-educated technical people. The government was putting a lot of effort into training people for industrial careers and offered us an initial location on one of the floors of their industrial training institution.

My observations of the situation in Singapore convinced me to select that nation. I sent Fred Bialek to Singapore to finalize the details, and when we listed the advantages they included

- Freedom from taxation for a period of years
- Training grants
- No import duties
- Good availability of labor, engineering and supervisory personnel
- Very low overhead costs

When I joined National, the most recent annual sales amounted to $7 million. During the final six months of fiscal year 1967, (which were our first six months with the company,) we assembled enough products to result in total annual sales of $11 million. Our first full year of operations yielded sales of more than $20 million and we continued to grow. We committed to build our own factory in Singapore, we got a good deal on the land we needed and the government helped us with some capital. We were the first semiconductor facility in Singapore, and then TI came in shortly thereafter.

Building a Company

The building process at National was straightforward. We knew exactly what we wanted to do, and who could do it. And when we needed additional experienced personnel, we could reach into the Fairchild organization and take anyone we wanted. There finally came a time when Roger Borovoy, Fairchild's lawyer, told us to stop hiring people from Fairchild's technology areas or they would sue us. When people came to us and said they would rather be at National than at Fairchild, we told them to get a job somewhere else for a while and then come to us. It was our little "workaround" for the threat of legal action from Fairchild.

We caught up with Fairchild in total sales within seven or eight years, and then we really zoomed past them.

As early as our first year, we set up a test operation in Hong Kong. We picked Hong Kong for testing because we knew we could sell the fallout from testing (those transistors that didn't quite meet official specifications,) into the toy industry.

Here at home we established a TTL process line with the help of Jeff Kalb, who joined us from Texas Instruments, and we started "covering" the TI product line. Our three-pronged TTL strategy included

1. Re-engineering the TI product line
2. Launching unique TTL products, designed by Jeff Kalb, who was the co-inventor of Tri-State Logic
3. Attacking TI on price, which we could do because of our offshore cost advantages

For a time, TI matched us on price, but their volume was so high that price reductions really hurt them. In a single year, the per-gate price dropped from more than a dollar a gate to somewhere in the 10-to-15-cent range. TI finally stopped their policy of aggressively matching us on price, and the market got a lot more sensible.

Now many manufacturers caught on to the advantages of product assembly in Southeast Asia, and there was a race to find countries where all the resources were available. India, for example, had very low labor rates, a good technological infrastructure and plenty of well-educated people, but government restrictions made it too difficult for us to set up shop there. I remember running into an employee of Raytheon Semiconductor in the Wagon Wheel one evening. He had been building a factory in India and he had been sent home to recover from dysentery. It was a common affliction for Americans all over Southeast Asia.

The Animals of Silicon Valley

We grew rapidly in linear integrated circuits. We had an excellent reputation in linear and we captured many design contracts. We were establishing new fabrication facilities at home and rigid cost control was the order of the day. If we were going to base our growth on price and volume, we needed to keep a firm hand on overhead costs.

Once, during a period when cash was short, we decided not to spend any money on keeping up the landscape around our Santa Clara plant. The grass grew tall and Bob Widlar had one of his crazy inspirations. He bought a sheep and tethered it in front of the plant to eat the grass. Then he called the *San Jose Mercury* and tipped them off to the gag. The Merc ran a photo of the sheep along with a funny story. The picture caption was something like "Cost control at National Semiconductor."

Pierre Lamond, not normally given to frivolity, didn't think the sheep stunt was funny, and he managed to coax the sheep into Bob Widlar's Porsche.

Somehow we acquired the reputation of being "The Animals of Silicon Valley." We liked

That damn sheep

the tag and we exploited it. In later years I liked it less.

Bob Widlar's Adventures in Paris

Everyone who knew Bob Widlar had a story about his ability to turn the most ordinary situation into chaos. Bob knew he was a genius, and when he applied himself he was a tremendously prolific performer. He would work on a design project almost nonstop, and then when he finished the job he would go on a binge for weeks. He was as impressive a drinker as he was a designer. He had brought Fairchild to the No. 1 position in linear integrated circuits and then he brought National to the number one position.

Here's my story about Bob Widlar . . .

We were in Paris for an engineering seminar. There must have been at least 500 French engineers assembled to hear Bob Widlar, Floyd Kvamme and Dale Mrazek speak. Widlar was fine in the morning, and then there was an open bar just before lunch was served.

I kept an eye on Bob as he started drinking straight gin. When the lunch hour came to a close and the seminar was about to reconvene, I spotted Widlar weaving back to the head table with a tall glass full of straight gin. He sat down next to Peter Sprague. I knew we were headed toward a rocky afternoon. I went over to Peter and told him to get rid of Widlar's gin, and in one of the most heroic actions ever undertaken by a person in defense of a commercial enterprise, Sprague picked up the glass and drank all the gin.

The Wild One: Bob Widlar

When he was called on to speak, Bob reached for the glass, saw that it was empty, and in a loud, slurred voice, shouted out, "I'm not going on until this is refilled."

Somebody got another drink for Bob, and the afternoon was off to a running start. Widlar was stone drunk. He gave very rude answers to questions from the audience. His speech was slurred. Almost anyone else would have been humiliated. But the audience loved it! Widlar's brilliance was so obvious that his inebriation just added to the overall effect of his genius.

When the meeting was over, we took the Paris Metro back to our hotel, and while we were waiting for our train, Widlar stood at the very edge of the platform, weaving back and forth over the empty space. Here was one of my company's most valuable assets, only inches away from self-destruction. I couldn't decide whether to grab his belt and save his life or let him fall onto the tracks and fulfill his death wish. Fortunately, a train came along and we got aboard safely.

We went to a restaurant and Bob got into a rude exchange with some Belgians at the next table. I wondered if we were going to have to fight our way out of the restaurant.

It was finally late enough to put Bob to bed. We escorted him to his room and made sure he was safe for the night.

It had been a tough day and I went down to the hotel bar for one last quiet drink before retiring. I was looking out toward the lobby when I saw a familiar form move toward the hotel door. It was Widlar, up and dressed again and headed for more trouble.

I followed him down the Champs Elysee to an establishment that featured liquor, music and rent-a-ladies. Bob was already at the bar showing off with one of his favorite tricks, which was "How to have a drink without using my hands." The trick involved clutching the rim of the glass with his mouth and tilting his head so that the contents could run through his teeth and down his throat.

It might have been an impressive trick if he hadn't been so drunk, but in his enthusiasm to show off, Bob had bitten through the glass. His mouth was full of broken glass and he was bleeding. A couple of the girls took him off to the ladies' room to apply first aid, and eventually Bob came out more or less in one piece, and allowed me to escort him back to the hotel.

Considering his history, one might imagine some sort of creatively bizarre ending to Bob Widlar's life, but he actually succumbed to a heart attack, suffered while walking or jogging on a quiet beach.

Regis McKenna, who was in charge of all marketing services at National before he organized his own highly successful advertising, PR and consulting business, had some Widlar memories of his own to share.

"Bob and I became very close friends. He used to come to my office and we often had lunch. Up until actually a few months before he died we stayed close friends. I used to do his data sheets for him.

"It was an art working with Bob because he would do things his way, and to get him to change anything or do anything, you couldn't be direct because he wanted to manage his own life in his own way. I would spend a lot of time sitting talking with him

Bob Widlar, shortly before his death.

about lots of things. I remember him telling me once that he had figured me out and that I was getting my own way, so he told me he had a tree up in the hills with my name on it that he used to shoot at. He'd tell me that, and then I knew he was just giving me the message not to push too hard.

"I had a printer friend that I brought over one day, and I said, 'Bob, we gotta get the data sheet done.' And Bob had just returned from a long lunch and he was in good shape. I said, 'Bob, we need to have the data sheet ready, because the printer is here.' So, the printer is standing there, having heard stories about Bob Widlar, and Bob is fumbling, trying to get the staple out of a sheaf of papers. Finally he puts the data sheet on the desk and goes over and gets his axe and he comes over and chops the staple and the desk. The printer left, and I never saw him again.

"He believed that if you went beyond 25 years of age, you just lost it. There was no way you could design anything beyond the age of 25. So, I think a lot of it was his feeling of living hard and driving hard to a certain age, because beyond that, it was all gone.

"When he left National and was living down in Mexico, he would travel back and forth, and when he went across the border, the guards would always ask him where he worked, and he said, 'I don't work.' So, that really used to stop them and they would search his car and put him all through these kinds of things, because he said he didn't have a job. So he and I over lunch devised a business card, and the business card had a skull and crossbones on it and it was Morgan Associates (Morgan was a highwayman), and his title was 'Bob Widlar, Highwayman.' (I still have these business cards.) I had those printed for him and he would give them a card which said he was a robber, and they thought he fixed highways, so they used to let him go through.

"He also was a pretty good photographer. He had an enormous collection of Nikons, and used to loan them to me. I have some photos that he took of eclipses and other kinds of things.

Remember the big seminar in France?

Oh, well, trying to manage him! My job was to run those things. I bailed him out of jail in Holland or one of the Scandinavian countries because he threw a chair through a window, and they called the police, and took him off to jail. One night he was drinking heavily, and we had a seminar the next day, and I had everybody set their watches two hours ahead, and he says, "Jesus! It's midnight!" I said his watch must be wrong. So, we got him into bed two hours early. We had to do all kinds of things to manage him, and he used to like to keep a glass of gin on the podium.

"You know, when you think about what he did and what he contributed . . . But I used to go out a lot with Bob, and I don't know why he and I got along, but we did.

"You know, Charlie, I often think about people like Widlar because software engineers today you know, they have the long hair and they're artists and creative. But you know, there were the same sort of people in those days and there were fewer of them. But Widlar was one of them. Today, he would be one of these wild-ass software guys. So each generation has that sort of people, and I think it's really valuable to go back [and remember the past.]"

Marketing Against the Master Marketers

So many of us had come from Fairchild that we continued to view Fairchild as our arch competitor. Tom Bay had been put in charge of the semiconductor division when I left, and he "inherited" Don Valentine as marketing manager and Jerry Sanders as sales manager. I knew Tom would re-evaluate the situation and designate one of them to be his choice as overall marketing manager and I also knew that whoever wasn't picked would come over to National. I liked both men and when Tom picked Jerry Sanders I was pleased to hire Don Valentine.

One of the major factors in our early success was Don Valentine's strategy of taking full advantage of our distribution network. Don made the distributors feel like full partners in our marketing activities and paid more attention to them than was normally the case at that time.

National did not have a direct sales force at first. Because we used independent sales representatives, we were able to put more people on the street than we otherwise could have afforded at our level of sales. Another advantage we had was a team of field application engineers located in the field, the first in our industry. Not only did this give us a close relationship with our customers, but it also provided us with a source of developing management talent that we could draw upon as we grew.

We hired some very capable people from the Fairchild marketing organization, but it was not an easy pull because Jerry Sanders inspired strong loyalty from the folks he supervised.

Once, I remember, after there had been so many changes at Fairchild and Les Hogan was running things over there, our people put together a motivational film for our salesmen. It was loosely based on the movie "Patton," and it used old newsreel shots to draw a parallel between Fairchild's mounting difficulties and the last days of the German war effort in the mid-1940s. They referred to me as General Patton and made some humorous references to "Hogan's Heroes."

The Rain in Spain

Our rapid expansion at home and abroad ate up capital at an alarming rate. We were starving for money and we didn't have any corporate treasury to tap. One possible source of some money was a company called Piher Semiconductor, based in Barcelona, Spain. National had sold Piher the rights to assemble GEM transistors in Europe. We made the transistor dice and sent them over to Piher. When the opportunity presented itself, we sold the fabrication technology to Piher for $500,000 and sent Max Stanton over to Barcelona to help them set up a line. Max was very important to National Semiconductor over the years, first as a process/product engineer during our earliest days, and later as the manager of all of National's facilities in Southeast Asia.

Max would send his questions over to Roger Smullen and Smullen would provide the answers. I guess the back-and-forth of telegrams finally became a burden to Smullen, and one day he responded to a question by writing "The rain in Spain falls mainly on the plain." The general manager of the Piher facility saw the telegram and didn't think it was funny. Max found himself in hot water.

One consideration that had somehow escaped our notice was the Spanish law against taking pesetas out of Spain. We had overlooked the provision in our agreement that allowed Piher to pay us our money in Spain in an equivalent sum of Spanish pesetas. Which was a great inconvenience because we needed the money in Santa Clara. I guess we just assumed that we'd get checks in the mail from Spain. Every time one of us visited Barcelona, we would load up a suitcase with pesetas, fly to Paris and exchange them for U.S. dollars at the Bank of America office.

Still More Overseas Expansion

We never seemed to have enough factory capacity. We were going strong with TTL, linear circuits and transistors, and we were running out of assembly capacity in Singapore. Additionally, the Singapore government wanted us to do more than just assembly work. They urged us to add engineering, wafer fabrication and other operations.

We knew we had to expand again, and again we went looking.

I received another telephone call from Chuck Woodward, who had been instrumental in recommending Singapore, this time from Penang. He suggested we look into Malaysia as a plant site. At his urging, I went to Penang, surveyed the situation, and liked what I saw. We set up the first semiconductor operation in Malaysia to make molded DIP TTL products and over time it became, by far, our most successful offshore facility. Shortly after the Penang plant was running we set up another Malaysian plant in Malacca to assemble linear molded DIP products. Ernie Friburg was the engineer in charge of putting those facilities together.

Ernie Friburg was our project engineer in charge of all of our overseas facilities expansion. He was a legendary plant engineer, both at Fairchild, where he had put up the Hong Kong and Korean plants, and then at National, where he and his wife, Inez, literally roamed the world on our behalf.

Now we were running strong in Hong Kong, Singapore, Penang and Malacca. It wasn't enough.

The European Push

As we started an extensive market penetration campaign in Europe we ran into European pressure to manufacture over there. We needed more wafer fabrication capacity and we looked for a location.

Germany was our best customer, but Germany was fully industrialized and factory costs (as well as salaries and overhead,) were high. France expressed an interest in having us locate within that country, but the plain fact is that we did not trust the French government and the commitments they offered.

(Some years later, as our penetration of the French semiconductor market approached 10%, the French government hinted that our continued sales growth in that country would be stymied unless we established some sort of a French joint venture. It seemed like a good idea at the time, and we built a facility near Aix-en-Provence to produce CMOS silicon gate devices. National Semiconductor provided the technology and most of the money for the plant came from the French government through a partner company called St. Gobain-Pont-a-Mousson. The facility, near Marseilles in Southern France, was successful and productivity was excellent. We were ready to revise our opinion of doing business with the French government when, to our astonishment, the venture was "nationalized." In return for our investment of time, money, technology and the efforts of many of our talented people, the French venture gave National Semiconductor one dollar. The whole sorry business proved the wisdom of our earlier reluctance to do business with the French government.)

Our choice for the first European facility was Greenock, Scotland, on the Firth of Clyde just outside Glasgow. Once again Ernie Friburg built the plant, a wafer fabrication facility where we made TTL, linear products and MOS. Glasgow was a good choice, with all the suppliers we needed. Our American quartz fabricator put in a facility near our Greenock plant to support us, and we found good employees plus excellent technical people among the local population.

The Greenock plant was more than successful; the employees produced excellent wafers and we relied on them for many important products. When a fire did a great deal of damage to the plant we simply could not get along without the production. After a very rapid conference with the immigration authorities, we brought the Greenock workers over to a number of our U.S. facilities including Utah, Santa Clara and Danbury, where we ran around the clock with different crews for each shift. The tactic was successful, we had enough material for our needs, and at the end of the "emergency," a surprising number of our Scottish employees elected to stay in the U.S. I understand that more than a few marriages that had been shaky in their home country ended when wives on temporary duty in the U.S. concluded that they were happier without their spouses.

It surprised me that the prevailing thinking in the U.K. did not match our own enthusiasm for the people and their outstanding industrial capabilities. After we rebuilt the Greenock plant and things were back to normal, I went over there for a visit. We had an informal press conference in London and a number of the reporters asked me questions about the effectiveness of the workers and the general productivity of the plant. I said that the people were "great," and my response seemed to surprise the reporter. My reading may have been all wrong, but I sensed a lot of national self-doubt in those questions. That was years ago, and nowadays the U.K. no longer exhibits self-doubt. The U.K. is a very effective competitor in technology-based industries.

Some Thoughts About Our Presence in Southeast Asia

It has become fashionable in recent years to view the industrialization of Southeast Asia as some sort of sociological or ethnological disaster. Along with millions of other newspaper subscribers I have read stories about mistreated workers slaving away in shoe factories, earning pennies a day for making products that enrich absentee owners. If I had not been directly involved in the efforts of Fairchild and National to establish assembly plants in Southeast Asia, I might have some of those negative feelings myself.

The truth is, our pioneering work in places like Malaysia brought significant benefits to the local economy and to the people who came to work for us. Penang, for instance, was a completely nonindustrial society before we accepted the government invitation to establish a plant there.

Our employees were very good people and rapidly became excellent workers. But they came to us in a pre-industrial "condition" and we had to add a few unanticipated subjects to our training curriculum. One of the first issues we had to tackle was personal hygiene and sanitation. We literally had to teach our workers, especially the younger ones, basic skills in that category. We also set up formal classes in housekeeping and career advancement. The idea of "climbing the corporate ladder" was not part of the native culture.

Religion was another issue. We didn't pretend to understand every nuance of the religions we encountered, but we did our best to respect the local beliefs and to accommodate them. It wasn't unusual to hire a religious leader to help establish the exact placement of a building, and after it was completed, to go through a ritual of purification and dedication. We did our best to schedule around holidays and other special events where public participation was expected.

When we went into Southeast Asia, we found a 19th century view of life. After we—and other companies—had been operating our factories for a while, the people were dramatically better off. Compared to their counterparts in nonindustrialized areas, their financial situation was greatly improved, and they were far healthier. I know that some people cherish the idea of non-industrialized tribes living a peaceful, natural life in some faraway Shangri La, but that's not how it is. Those peaceful, natural lives are artificially shortened by poor health, poor sanitation and a lack of some basic amenities. There may be some shameful exploitation going on here and there, but I am satisfied that our employees were fairly treated.

A Short Experiment in the Caribbean

Puerto Rico is a beautiful place with unique laws as they apply to industrial activities. In one of our expansion periods we set up a test and shipping facility in Puerto Rico, with an assembly plant in Haiti.

Unlike our experience in Southeast Asia, we couldn't find technically trained people in the islands who were willing to function in a hands-on capacity. I don't think we ever arrived at an understanding of the labor hierarchy in the Caribbean. We just couldn't figure out how to get things done. And our management struggle was further complicated by the government of Haiti.

Haiti was a totalitarian dictatorship and totally corrupt. There was a price for every government approval or permit, and I absolutely forbade any of our employees from paying a single penny in bribery money. The Haiti plant was a failure and a fire in our Puerto Rico plant helped us decide to abandon our Caribbean experiment.

The trouble was, we knew we might have our hands full just getting out of Haiti. The militia was everywhere, and we feared that our people might get arrested if they were caught shutting down the plant. Fortunately, our manager in Haiti was able to arrange for a cargo ship to come in at night. He synchronized everything so that our equipment could be moved rapidly from the factory to the ship, and, still under cover of darkness, we loaded up and left Haiti.

Sidetracked by Consumer Products

It would be possible, by selective recall, to present a picture of National Semiconductor as an unfailing, always-right cruise down Easy Street. We did have long periods of satisfying growth and success. But we had some distractions along the way that provided good examples of what not to do.

We were in the electronic component business, making relatively inexpensive semiconductor devices that were sold to others for incorporation into much more expensive end products. Our business was cyclical with periodic demand fluctuations, and during our "down" times we were receptive to other ideas for growth. Our metal gate MOS product line was a good case in point.

Bob Johnson, one of the major design managers during the period of National's most dramatic growth, had an engineer in his group who came up with a totally integrated calculator chip. We started marketing the calculator chips and they sold very well. And then somebody within our company asked, "Why don't we make these calculators ourselves?"

It was a reasonable question. It seemed to us that the most complex part of a calculator, certainly the most critical, was the chip we manufactured. So Fred Bialek got the assignment of making a calculator. He shopped around for the various parts, found good, low-cost vendors, and came up with a calculator that could sell for a lot less than others on the market at that time. Our calculators sold like popcorn.

Within a short time, Texas Instruments and Fairchild also got into the business, and we branched out into much more complex products. We made money in our consumer products venture until Hong Kong and Japanese manufacturers came in with similar merchandise, and then the competition got brutal.

At one time we made chips for wrist watches. Modern timepieces are really just simple, special-purpose electronic circuits with a provision for a digital display or a driver unit for the analog "hands." First we made and sold the timekeeping units, then we escalated our participation from chips to complete modules that included the display, and eventually we were making finished watches. Overall, we eked out a piddly profit, but the amount of attention we had to pay to our little consumer ventures, and the amount of detail required was criminal. My discussion with Gordon Moore about the watch business, noted in an earlier section of this memoir, confirmed my conviction that the watch business, along with other consumer product ventures, is an entirely foreign enterprise to a semiconductor manufacturer.

I think the biggest mistake companies make is dilution of effort. We certainly made that mistake, along with others in our industry. One of the most important components of success is to understand the core products of a company and pursue that path, and avoid dilution of effort at all costs.

Checkout Scanners

We were working in the early 1970s on a contract from Brother, the Japanese company that was well known in this country for their sewing machines. The assignment called for a lot of complicated chips that had to work together in a high-end business machine, and the work was beyond the design capability we had at the time. It was really the same sort of assignment that started Intel on the road to microprocessors. But Intel solved it with a programmable controller designed by Ted Hoff. We didn't come up with a single-chip alternative, and we were never totally successful in making adequate deliveries of the multiple-chip set.

Then we were approached by a representative from Certified Grocers, a cooperative of independent supermarkets, asking for some point-of-sale equipment. The deal called for National to manufacture the equipment, and for Certified to do the selling and servicing. (It was another one of our "slow periods" when we temporarily abandoned our focus on core products.)

About the time when we began to turn out supermarket checkout scanner systems, it became obvious that Certified was not capable of selling them, nor could they handle the maintenance requirements. Without really intending to, we suddenly found ourselves manufacturing, selling and servicing POS systems. In spite of our unprofessional entry into the POS business, and under the management of Fred Bialek, we had an initial blush of success in this venture. We captured 35% or 40% of the market and grew the business to the point where it made some real money. Then the increased efforts of IBM and NCR amounted to more

competition than we felt comfortable with, and we sold the whole operation to ICL in 1987.

Mainframe Computers

We were in the DRAM business but memory didn't amount to a large
part of our total sales. IBM was the world's biggest user of DRAMs, but
IBM made their own for incorporation into the computers they produced. After-market add-on memory modules for IBM computers became
a huge business. IBM made and sold add-on memory, but their prices
were sky high. We, along with Intel and AMS, made equivalent modules
and priced them about 10% under the IBM price. At first, we all enjoyed
growth and profits in add-on memories.

Floyd Kvamme ran the memory business and one of his good customers was Itel, (not to be confused with Intel,) a marketing and service
company. One day Itel approached us with an interesting proposition.
According to Itel, there was a small company in San Diego that made
mainframe computers equivalent to the mid-range models of the IBM
370 series. Itel suggested that National buy the struggling company, make
the computers, and Itel would sell and service them.

We started making computers, we priced them lower than IBM
charged for similar computers, and Itel enjoyed very satisfactory sales. It
was an excellent business for quite a while until IBM took notice of our
competition and crashed their prices. Suddenly, our market collapsed.

Our contract with Itel forced them to take the machines, but Itel
couldn't sell them. The situation finally got to the point where the Itel
management told us, "You guys should buy us."

Our systems people were in favor of buying Itel, but there was a com-
plication. Itel also had a contract to sell high-end computers manufactured by Hitachi, and we were on record as being strongly against certain
Japanese business practices. We would, in effect, be selling products
made by a company we had branded as an industrial arch-enemy. I told

Floyd that I would buy Itel, but only if I could do it without spending any money. I wouldn't spend a dollar of up-front money, and I would only pay out as product was sold. I didn't want to short our semiconductor component operations.

We made that deal. We took over Itel, went in and repriced everything in inventory. We downsized the staff. We forced an immediate revision in the Itel life style, especially as it concerned expense accounts. We put Itel on an even keel and then faced up to the fact that we had to come to an agreement with Hitachi. Hitachi, after all, made the high-end machines we needed for a complete product line. We never could keep up with computer developments at IBM on our own.

As part of our diplomatic efforts, Floyd Kvamme had to go to Japan to meet with Hitachi. When Floyd arrived and called on Hitachi, they wouldn't even receive him. Not only was he a representative of a company that had been vocal in the fight against Japanese competition, but Floyd himself had been a highly visible spokesman for the cause, specifically targeting Hitachi.

It took some fancy maneuvering to make contact with Hitachi, but we finally resumed selling their products.

Now IBM got much more competitive with their computer pricing and made it a tougher business to be in. And then things took an ugly turn. Hitachi was trapped in a deal where they were accused by IBM of stealing trade secrets.

Floyd Kvamme was selling Hitachi computers to the Department of Justice while the DOJ was investigating Hitachi on the IBM trade secrets complaint! And IBM, which had suffered plenty of government investigations, really had the bit in their teeth. They aggressivly pursued the litigation. By the time it was over, Hitachi settled with IBM for $300 million, and Hitachi also paid all of our legal costs because National had been drawn into the case along with Hitachi.

I know this hasn't been easy to follow. We went from making semiconductor components to larger systems, and then to complete product lines, such as mainframe computers and point-of-sale systems. In each case we had some success but the complications of the "other" industries just ate up a lot of our time and attention. Now it was time to get back to doing what we really knew how to do.

We got into negotiations with Hitachi to sell them our advanced systems division, which included computers and the add-on memory business. The negotiations were delicate and quite secret. Hitachi felt that it was just a sales operation but we knew we had more than that. While we were still negotiating, Hitachi leaked a story to the Japanese business press that they had purchased the operation from us for $300 million. We said no, we wanted $400 million. (At the time, sales were in the neighborhood of $900 million.)

Gary Arnold hammered out the eventual deal with Hitachi. We would let Hitachi tell the world they got the business for $300 million, but they would actually pay us $400 million. It was one of those face-saving compromises that are important to Japanese companies.

Then we turned around and sold our P-O-S business to ICL for $100 million.

Getting Hosed in Memory Products

We put Bob Johnson in charge of memory products in 1983, following his excellent performance in device design. When I spoke with him recently, he had some vivid recollections of the chaos he faced.

> "By 1984 we were making 64K DRAMs and prices started sliding by about 25 cents per device per month. The market started out at $4 a unit, and eventually came down to $2. That would have been bad enough, but there was more misery to come.
>
> "In April of 1985, we all heard rumors that both DEC and IBM were sitting on huge inventories of 64K DRAMs. DEC supposedly had 40 million pieces that they had purchased at $4 each. DEC started dumping their memory inventory on the market, and

spot prices dropped immediately to a dollar each. Then 90 cents. Then 75 cents. This all took place in late 1985.

"Hitachi shipped 100,000 devices by mistake to Siemens. When Siemens informed Hitachi that they hadn't ordered any of the devices, Hitachi told Siemens to keep them for free!"

We, too, had an inventory of memory devices. Our cost basis had been something like $2 each, and we sold what we had for 25 cents each. Then we got out of the memory business.

I heard a joke that could have been inspired by the collective experience of American semiconductor manufacturers in the memory business in the mid-1980s: One day a man in the ladies ready-to-wear industry told his partner that a circus was folding, and was selling the elephants for $1,100 each. He suggested buying an elephant.

"You have to be crazy to buy an elephant," said the partner. "You can't just keep it in the back yard, you need expensive veterinary care, and it'll eat you out of house and home."

"Wait," replied the man, "You haven't heard the best part. They'll sell you two elephants for $1,500!"

"$1,500 for two elephants? Hey! Now you're talking business!"

Missing the Microprocessor Market

Even though we made a lot of very complex integrated circuits, we didn't have any product that we viewed as a central processing unit, or CPU. By the time Intel started selling microprocessors, we had a CPU design that we called the 16000 series. Our engineers said that it was technically superior to products from Intel and Motorola, but those two companies were already established in the market and had captured significant shares. We were later than Intel, later than Motorola, and just plain late.

Then IBM went with the Intel chip in 1975 and the ball game was over. It didn't really matter what our 16000 could do. Intel went into high-volume production.

I was on a skiing vacation with my family when I got a telephone call from Andy Grove at Intel. Andy said microprocessor sales were so strong that Intel needed a second source. I went back to the office, discussed the proposal with others and then told Andy we weren't interested. We were so enraptured with our own product that we couldn't see the value of cooperating with Intel.

We should have collapsed our in-house CPU effort and grabbed the Intel offer. It was a mistaken decision that Pierre Lamond and I made together. That's the deal that Intel made with AMD.

It wasn't the first time we turned down an opportunity to work with Intel. I can remember a time in the early 1970s, when Intel was going through a difficult period, especially in manufacturing. Bob Noyce came up with the idea of putting Intel and National together. Noyce thought that he could be chairman of the company and I could be CEO. At the time, National was a lot bigger than Intel and we weren't interested. It would have been tough to parcel out the responsibilities and I was enjoying being the boss at National.

Nothing significant ever came of our 16000 series. Bosch used some product in their CNC machine tool controllers, Siemens used some, and a Portland company put some in a special-purpose computer. But our CPU never went into a personal computer, where all the volume was.

A Note About Process Development

One of the recurring themes in my semiconductor career is the difficulty we encountered in developing new manufacturing processes. In the early days at Fairchild, the problem was one of technology transfer. R&D would deliver up a new process and expect the factory to read the instruction sheets and coast into high volume production. When things didn't work out, there was a lot of finger-pointing back and forth between R&D and the factory. We thought we had the problem solved at National when we insisted that new process development be pursued right in the factory, on factory equipment. Bob Johnson pointed out some collateral difficulties.

> "When we divided into separate product line organizations, we insisted that each product line subsidize its own process development funding. When you think about it, the product line that was most in need of something new was least able to afford the development cost.
>
> "The only way to rationalize this situation is to 'edict' that all product lines contribute equally to process development costs regardless of the beneficiary."

Johnson found another way around the dilemma when he made a deal with Oki of Japan, for some design and manufacturing cost assistance in return for a guaranteed pricing advantage. The normal Japanese practice would have been to conform to an existing fabrication process that was known to be 'manufacturable.' The design compromises that Oki made assured a continuation of 'manufacturability,' if there is such a word.

That's not how things were done in our industry. Our designers had the freedom to optimize device design at the expense of process. Bob Johnson's insight into the Oki approach helped us realize what we had been doing wrong. It is vital to consider manufacturing implications in new device development. We were a little slow to realize this at National, but eventually we learned and applied the lesson.

CHAPTER TWENTY-ONE

SPIN-IN: NATIONAL
ACQUIRES FAIRCHILD

While new companies were being formed in Silicon Valley and new technologies were emerging, Fairchild Semiconductor, the grandfather of so many firms, was limping downhill. In 1986, now owned by Schlumberger, Fairchild had sales of about $500 million and was losing money.

The Fairchild product line was broad, including linear integrated circuits, DTL and TTL logic elements, diodes, transistors and even a microprocessor called the "Clipper." The once-dominant R&D facility was still effective, and Fairchild had a good position in emitter-coupled logic, commonly called ECL. But with all of that, Fairchild seemed incapable of turning the corner to profitability.

Along came Fujitsu of Japan with an offer to purchase 80% of Fairchild for a figure that *Business Week* magazine, in the November 10, 1986 issue, described as "book value:" $225 million. Schlumberger had paid $425 million when they bought the company seven years previously.

The offer raised a storm of negative comments from many industrial and government organizations. In various ways, the Department of Commerce, the Department of Defense, the Justice Department and even the CIA went on record as objecting to the deal. An article in *The Washington Post* in November of 1986 identified Fairchild as "a major supplier to the Defense Department and the only maker of a computer chip that is the heart of the electronic guidance, sighting and firing systems of the F16 jet fighter."

Apparently, nobody was alarmed about Schlumberger's ownership, even though Schlumberger is a French company. The Post dismissed France as "not a major factor in high technology." But Japan was a different story.

Concluding that the deal with Fujitsu would take a long time to reconcile, Schlumberger abandoned the agreement and turned over the task of getting rid of Fairchild to their bankers, Lazard Freres. Now the sale was out of the hands of the technology experts and strictly a brokerage issue.

I was aware of the situation and it seemed to me that there was an opportunity to make a very advantageous purchase. I discussed the possibilities with Fred Bialek, a former National Semiconductor vice president and by then an independent counsultant, and Jim Smaha, vice president of general manager of National. Fred and Jim represented us and did very well.

We bought Fairchild Semiconductor, with all of that company's properties, for $122 million. As previously mentioned, we gradually sold off parts of Fairchild for more than $150 million, and then we sold the remains of the company to new owners for $500 million!

CHAPTER TWENTY-TWO

FACING THE CHALLENGE
OF JAPANESE COMPETITION

The history of my involvement in our industry's efforts to deal with Japanese competition is really a separate subject with its own chronology. If I had tried to weave it into the individual company stories presented earlier, it would have been disjointed and confusing. Here's how I remember the issue and the important events that were ultimately successful in dealing with a threat that could have spelled the end of the American semiconductor industry. (I am grateful to Daryl Hatano for his exhaustive help in getting the facts straight, materially assisted by his file copies of memos, documents and minutes of meetings.)

Many of us in management positions had come to the semiconductor industry from other branches of electronics, and we had seen some early results of the Japanese competitive onslaught. We had seen radio, television and other industries go to the Japanese and now there were indications that semiconductors could be just as vulnerable. By the mid-1970s our collective frame of mind was conducive to addressing the challenge of Japanese competition.

It is hard to imagine now that the U.S. semiconductor industry could have been so agitated by the Japanese semiconductor industry, but it was a fact. The Japanese were a very major threat to our future at the time, and every trend analysis indicated that the threat was growing.

I remember a 1973 meeting I had with some securities analysts in Los Angeles, where I warned that the Japanese had a protected domestic market for semiconductor devices and had launched a government-sponsored program to dominate the large scale integrated circuit industry. I said at the time that, "They (the Japanese,) are coming down the pike, aimed squarely at us."

Most of us belonged to the Western Electronic Industries Association (WEMA,) but WEMA included all electronics manufacturers, and there was only a diluted interest in semiconductor issues. (Later on, as more electronics companies from around the U.S. joined WEMA, it was renamed the American Electronics Association: AEA.) It was also true that many WEMA members were equipment manufacturers who were major buyers of semiconductor components, and they were not displeased that Japanese competition helped to keep semiconductor prices depressed.

While those of us in the semiconductor business worried about Japanese semiconductor competition within our domestic market, we also experienced frustration in selling into the very large Japanese market. American companies, collectively, accounted for about 60% of semiconductor sales in Europe, where both American and Japanese companies competed for business, but only about 10% of sales in Japan.

Japan had a centralized establishment that had great influence over manufacturing, trade and investment. The entity was known as MITI, the *Ministry of International Trade and Industry*. By the early 1970s, with the protection and assistance of MITI, Japan was making a strong move in semiconductors, as they had already done in the home entertainment electronics industry.

We would have had a much larger share of the Japanese market, consistent with our competitive performance in other parts of the world, without the artificial barriers of MITI. Our potential Japanese customers simply refused to buy from us, and Japanese government restrictions made it difficult for us to deliver products into that market. Japanese equipment manufacturers were using enormous numbers of semiconductors and we were significantly restricted in going after that business.

Birth of the Semiconductor Industry Association

WEMA collected and published sales statistics, and in theory, at least, could have developed some sort of response to the Japanese challenge, but no such response had emerged.

Many of us were concerned about the worsening situation and this concern prompted Wilf Corrigan, then CEO of Fairchild Semiconductor, to invite a few of us to discuss the issue. That first meeting included Jerry Sanders of AMD, Bob Noyce of Intel, and me, as CEO of National Semiconductor. The four of us agreed that we needed our own industrial trade organization, and it seemed natural to call it the *Semiconductor Industry Association* or SIA. We also decided that we needed the participation of as many American semiconductor manufacturers as possible. When we described our objectives to John Welty of Motorola, he joined us. Each of the five founding companies put up $10,000 to get the organization going, for an initial bankroll of $50,000.

Our first executive was Bernie Marren, an experienced semiconductor marketing executive who had a long and distinguished career at Fairchild, and who served as Fairchild's vice president of marketing after that company was sold to Schlumberger. Bernie was only with SIA for a short time before he joined Marshall Cox in the formation of a new company. Marshall Cox, another long-term Fairchild veteran, went on to be the founder and later the CEO of Intersil, a successful Silicon Valley semiconductor company. The business Cox established with Marren,

Western Micro, is a well-respected distributor of electronic components. Marren's replacement at SIA was Tom Hinkelman, who did an excellent job as CEO of the organization. Tom was so dedicated to the success of SIA that he drove a car with a personalized license plate reading "TDH SIA." Hinkelman, too, tried to recruit Texas Instruments, then the largest U.S. semiconductor company, without any success.

We all agreed that we were not pursuing a negative agenda. We had no intention of asking for protection of our domestic markets. We were focused on a quest for fair access to the Japanese market, within an over-all context of free trade. Our avoidance of any nuance of "protection" added to our credibility and played a part in our success.

Even so, those early days were not easy. Tom Hinkelman visited the assistant secretary of the Treasury in August 1977 during the Carter administration, to discuss SIA concerns about the Japanese government support for VLSI (very large scale integrated circuit) development. Our government official told Hinkelman that "It is not in the interest of the United States to save the American semiconductor industry at the expense of the strategic importance of Japan." By the time the SIA matured, however, our government recognized 'the strategic importance' of our own domestic industry.

We were quite certain that the Japanese thrust into our industry had potentially dire implications for the American defense industry. Modern military weapons are strongly based on electronics, and if a foreign power dominated the component business, American ability to meet an emergency could be threatened. When we brought our concerns to the Department of Defense, we found a sympathetic ear and a lot of support.

As our formative discussions about the SIA progressed, we dealt with the question of the so-called "captive" semiconductor companies. Outfits like IBM, AT&T and DEC had important semiconductor capability, but no significant outside sales. We wondered if they would be sufficiently independent of their parent corporations to play an active role, but our speculations were groundless. They and their corporations became strong supporters of SIA and their presence was a positive factor in our success.

Information published by the SIA included estimates on how much business each company was doing in each market sector. The various company identities were not revealed, except that a given member's own statistics were highlighted in the report sent to that particular member.

Anybody could buy statistical data from the SIA, and it so happened that a major bank in Dallas purchased one of the reports and then shared the information with Texas Instruments, which was not, at the time, a member of SIA.

We were aware of a negative experience that TI had with WEMA some time in the past. As we understood the incident, officials at TI felt that data they had given to WEMA in confidence had been leaked, and thus allowed their competitors to learn specifics of their activities in certain sensitive areas. They left WEMA and declined to join any other trade organizations. The message that came through was that TI was big enough to do without information about the semiconductor industry in general or about any other company in the business.

Now, however, it appeared that TI was interested in SIA data. When Tom Hinkelman found out about the incident, he telephoned Mark Shepherd, CEO of Texas Instruments, and argued, in effect that TI clearly needed that sort of information and might as well become a fully participating member. His representation was so convincing that Mark Shepherd agreed to join SIA in the course of that phone call. The presence of Texas Instruments lent considerable strength to our organization.

It is my strong feeling that the establishment of the Semiconductor Industry Association was the most effective step we took to meet the Japanese challenge. Without the SIA, we could have lost the battle.

The Specifics of Our Concerns: Dumping

What was it, exactly, that triggered our collective action? Beginning in the mid 1970s and continuing into the 1980s, the Japanese steadily increased their participation in the market for dynamic random access memory (DRAM) devices. This was a period of explosive growth for computers of all sizes, and memory products were the hottest semiconductor market segment.

The core strategy of the Japanese semiconductor industry was to add manufacturing capacity at a pace unrelated to their market share. We knew how much capacity existed in Japan because the companies would publicize new plant construction and if any of us visited Japan, we were given escorted tours through the new facilities. It didn't take much detective work to evaluate Japanese capacity. The SIA studied and clipped all professional and business publications, including those published in Japan.

Normal entrepreneurial behavior calls for selling a product at some combination of manufacturing costs plus a reasonable profit margin. But the Japanese were determined to capture a market, and they ignored their actual costs. They simply priced their products at whatever number would undersell their American competitors. The common term for this tactic is "dumping."

Japan's aggressive attack on the marketplace caused havoc within American companies. DRAM profits disappeared and companies with major interests in DRAM products were forced into huge loss positions.

At the time, memory products represented a major percentage of the semiconductor industry—perhaps as much as 50% of the total market! Even today, memory products account for about 25% of the market.

One example of the aggressive Japanese approach to the memory market was provided by Hitachi.

Hitachi issued a memo to their field sales representatives instructing them to bid a price on memory chips 10% lower than the lowest bid by any American company. If the 10% price reduction didn't get the order, they were directed to drop the price by another 10%, and to keep discounting the price until they were successful. The practice of artificially reducing a price, regardless of actual manufacturing costs, is a classic example of "dumping," and there were (and still are) existing trade laws in this country against such behavior.

The SIA obtained a copy of the Hitachi memo and used it in representations to our government. Government trade officials investigated the situation and agreed that Japanese companies were, indeed, dumping product on the U.S. market. According to established law and conventional trade practices, increased tariffs could be levied against the products, adjusted specifically to individual companies.

However, if the United States imposed antidumping duties on Japanese imports, prices in the United States would increase while prices outside the country remained low. Consequently, in July of 1986, the United States agreed that it would not impose antidumping duties and the Japanese companies agreed that they would cease dumping both in the U.S. market and in other markets outside Japan. As described later, the Japanese firms also agreed that they would open their market.

And then there was a negative reaction from some American manufacturers of electronic systems who were not in favor of higher prices. The reaction caused problems within the SIA, and some members expressed dissatisfaction with this approach.

Japan stopped dumping in the U.S. market, but dumping continued outside the United States. Also, there was little progress in gaining access to Japanese markets.

President Reagan decided to impose sanctions on Japan in 1987, the first time there had been such a move since World War II. The economic sanctions took the form of 100% duties which effectively barred the product from the U.S. market. Rather than impose those sanctions against Japanese semiconductor imports, which might have harmed U.S. purchasers of chips, it was decided that the sanctions would be imposed against systems manufactured in Japan by sister divisions of the semiconductor companies that were dumping. In other words, if a Japanese corporation made both semiconductors and TV receivers, we wanted import sanctions against the TVs as a penalty for dumping semiconductor components. This idea won the support of most members and the U.S. government agreed. It proved effective in the long run.

There was a great irony for me, and the company I headed, in that 1987 decision: One of the items on the proposed sanctions list was mainframe computers. The Hitachi computers that National Semiconductor imported from Japan were one of our few profitable lines at the time. I found myself in the uncomfortable position of publicly supporting the sanctions while working behind the scene to get mainframe computers exempted from the sanctions!

It is only fair to mention that that success of the Japanese companies in their attack on the DRAM market was not totally due to their artificially aggressive pricing. The quality of their products was excellent and they had developed outstanding manufacturing efficiencies. Some unit within Hewlett Packard had done a formal evaluation of all DRAM products on the market, and had come out with a declaration that the quality of Japanese memory devices was superior to that available from American companies. Unfortunately for us, the statement was fairly accurate and it did not help our efforts to respond to Japanese competition.

That H-P quality study also included an evaluation of TTL components, and it gave high marks to the TTL products of Fujitsu. Ironic, because National Semiconductor was supplying TTL dice to Fujitsu.

Here's a fascinating note on that era: Professional bicycle racing was a popular activity in Japan, as was betting on the outcome of the races. I understand that some of the profits from bicycle race betting were plowed into Japanese LSI development projects. Imagine what we could have done with a piece of the Las Vegas action on NFL wagering!

We developed some excellent U.S. government contacts in the course of our early SIA activities, which stood us in good stead when we tackled the issue of cracking the closed markets inside Japan. We met with the secretary of commerce and with many senators and U.S. representatives. Several members of the SIA set up political action committees (PACs) to back up our positions with campaign contributions. We traveled to Washington, had luncheons and cocktail parties, visited members of Congress in their offices, and hammered away at our concerns that the

Japanese were unfairly shutting us out of a market that had great importance to our economic future.

Our First Meeting with Japanese Industrial Leaders

At some point in the period 1981–1982, we had meeting at Rickey's in Palo Alto with some high-level people from Japan, including executives from Hitachi. The Japanese companies called the meeting and showed up with exhibits purporting to explain how and why they had succeeded in each competitive area. They had released their presentation to the press prior to the meeting, generating a certain amount of negative opinion regarding American companies. Even before the meeting started we were ready for an energetic confrontation.

One of the Japanese executives, comparing American and Japanese manufacturing strengths, described U.S. firms as "boutique semiconductor companies." I remember that the comment, among others, inspired Bob Noyce to get into a shouting match with a representative from NEC about the question of Japanese government support for Japanese semiconductor companies. There was clearly a lot of emotion at work on both sides.

The meeting was open to the press and I made some strong statements. I said that the Zaibatsus are back. (Zaibatsus were very strong industrial trusts in prewar Japan, which were replaced after the war by Keiretsu industrial families.) My remarks were not cordial and I must have looked like the Devil Incarnate to the Japanese attendees. I said that the Japanese had been caught carrying on a number of unfair practices and that they were not "normal" participants in free trade.

An Unfortunate Memory Loss

By 1982, when Tom Hinkelman approached IBM about joining SIA, Erich Block, who later became the director of the National Science

Foundation, characterized our organization as "The most effective trade organization in Washington." IBM joined us.

Our success in slowing the trend of Japanese semiconductor penetration into the American marketplace made us proud, but by the time the dust had settled, we were, for all practical purposes, out of the memory business. At one time, Texas Instrument, Micron Technology, Motorola, National, Fairchild, Intel and Mostek, to name just a few, were all making and selling DRAMs. Prices dropped. Operating losses were huge. For example, in one year, prices for the most popular memory chips went from around $6 a unit to less than a dollar. By 1985, only TI and Micron, of all the American companies, were still in the memory business. The others had all been knocked out by fierce price competition.

Both Andy Grove and Gordon Moore told me of a conversation regarding the fading prospects for memory products at Intel. Moore was reluctant to throw in the towel on a business segment that had been Intel's early bread and butter, but Grove pressed the issue. "If you were just coming into the company, and we presented you with profit and loss figures for each of our product lines, and the relative investments involved," argued Grove, "What would you do?" Moore reluctantly conceded the point. Intel, too, caved in to Japanese memory strength in 1985.

Memory products were particularly suited to the Japanese industrial capability, which was manufacturing-strong but had only modest design strength. It was no great challenge to predict the demand for memory capacity a year or two into the future, and the Japanese could tool up accordingly.

The whole episode, however, triggered some intense soul-searching on our part. How much better were the Japanese memory yields? Why were the Japanese doing better than we were? With our political efforts bearing fruit, we turned to practical concerns within our own industry. Most of us got out of the DRAM memory business and concentrated on design-rich products, where we had clear superiority over the Japanese.

Our collective efforts to deal with the issue of Japanese memory products inspired all of us to be more cooperative within the envelope of the SIA. Andy Procassini, who had held responsible positions at Motorola and Fairchild before taking over the executive leadership, and who had some prior experience in Japan, had a very strong team at SIA. Daryl Hatano was a particularly effective SIA executive, as was Warren Davis. Alan Wolff, who had been a deputy U.S. trade representative in the Carter administration, was the SIA counsel in Washington.

The SIA also became a forum for issues that were not directly related to Japanese trade. We were concerned that government expenditures for R&D programs in colleges and universities were declining. Fewer basic research programs resulted in fewer graduate students capable of undertaking advanced R&D programs in our industry.

Historically, the Bell Labs research capability within AT&T had been enormously influential in semiconductor development. When the government broke up AT&T, the premier device development laboratory in the world was affected. There was an overall reduction in funding for semiconductor research and development work.

Industrial Funding for University Programs

Out of our concern for basic research, we formed an independent, nonprofit organization in 1982 called the Semiconductor Research Corporation. It would be the mission of SRC to sponsor graduate work in semiconductor R&D at American universities. Larry Sumney was put in charge of the SRC, contributions from member companies funded the research grants, and an office was established in Research Triangle Park in North Carolina. The U.S. government participated in the SRC as a member. Before long, we were sponsoring programs at institutions such as MIT, Cornell, Carnegie-Mellon, Stanford, Harvard, Georgia Tech, the University of California at Berkeley, etc. Today the SRC provides more than $25 million a year for semiconductor related research work in universities.

Moving Toward Face-to-Face Confrontations with Japan

Andy Procassini reminded me of the complications that the Japanese semiconductor industry faced by 1985:

1. The Japanese were being sued by Intel, AMD and National for dumping memory products.
2. Micron Technololgy was suing them for dumping 64K DRAMs.
3. The U.S. government was pursuing the Japanese for dumping 256K and larger DRAMs.
4. The SIA was pressing Japan for market access.

Up and Down in Okinawa

The Japanese market remained formally closed for many years. U.S. firms could not even put a factory in Japan. The power—and intransigence—of MITI was perfectly illustrated when National Semiconductor made an attempt to set up a factory in Japan. Fred Bialek made an appointment to see an official of MITI and showed up on time. He sat outside the man's office all day, the following day, and part of the third day without ever being shown the courtesy of that prearranged meeting.

In 1969, Fairchild learned that the U.S. was about to return the World War II prize of the island of Okinawa to Japan. George Scalise, who is now president of SIA, was with Fairchild at the time and he put an assembly plant on Okinawa so that it would be in place when the island was returned. The factory was put up in less than a week, with the equipment quickly shipped and installed. The Japanese government learned of the ploy and threatened to close the factory after Okinawa reverted back to Japan. The Fairchild factory became a snag in U.S./Japan Okinawa negotiations and the result was that Fairchild agreed to close the facility. In exchange, Japan agreed to allow Fairchild to do business in Japan through a joint venture with TDK, a Japanese firm.

Mr. Morita's Overture

The Japanese finally became convinced that they needed to reach some sort of an accommodation with U.S. semiconductor manufacturers. Akio Morita, CEO of Sony Corporation, telephoned Bob Galvin of Motorola and suggested some joint efforts toward resolution of the issues. Jerry Sanders remembers the exact details of the Morita overture somewhat differently than I do, but the important thing is that we all agreed to meet.

The meeting took place in a Los Angeles hotel, and the physical arrangements resembled a high-level United Nations conference. There were two long tables with a space between them. The Japanese at one table faced the Americans at the other. It was supposed to be a conference of semiconductor company officials, but there were other people I didn't recognize, and who were not introduced. The Japanese party included a senior official from MITI, but no representative was present from our own government. Mindful of antitrust considerations, we had asked for some government presence but nobody showed up. Our desire to avoid any antitrust complications prompted us to have our lawyers at the meeting. The unofficial attendees just kind of hovered off to the sides of the tables.

Galvin and Morita, as ad-hoc co-chairmen, opened the meeting with statements. Galvin said the Japanese were dumping products and that American companies had only 10% of the Japanese market because of Japanese government restrictions, while the American share of the European market, where trade was more nearly free, amounted to some 60% of that market.

Morita said the Japanese companies were not dumping, that American companies were not designing products Japanese manufacturers needed, and that American quality was inferior to that of the Japanese. But Morita also said that the Japanese wanted to resolve the conflict and were present to work on a solution.

The Americans and the Japanese traded comments back and forth for a while, and then Morita posed a key question. He asked, "What would make you happy?" This prompted us to call a recess.

There followed a private conference of American manufacturers out in the hallway, at which it was determined that we would ask for 30% of the Japanese market. We based our figure on our experience in Europe, where, collectively, we had about 60% of the market. We thought that half of that penetration in Japan would be about right.

When we reconvened and presented our demand, the Japanese were incredulous. They couldn't believe our request. They said they didn't control all of the companies in Japan, and there was no way they could guarantee us such a high percentage of their domestic market.

We repeated our request and said that, with their help, we could compete fairly for business in Japan.

To our surprise—and delight—the Japanese countered with an offer to allow American semiconductor companies 20% of their domestic market. The meeting ended with a Japanese promise and handshakes all around.

Another Version of the Same Meeting

I mentioned that Jerry Sanders had a lively recollection of that meeting. He captured the drama as well as the essence of that pivotal day . . .

> "Yes, I do remember that meeting. First of all it was at the Beverly Wilshire Regent, which was a delight as far as I was concerned because I'm an L.A. guy, you know, that's my principal residence. What I remember was being incredibly, incredibly flattered and honored by a phone call from Akio Morita. He asked me if I would ask you and Bob Noyce to attend such a meeting. He had been told that the U.S. semiconductor industry executives weren't interested in having such a meeting, and that they had spurned all of the overtures from the Japanese. Whether that's true or not, I don't know—but he called me and

said he heard that I was a man of reason and 'what harm could it do?' My view was, 'What harm could it do?'

"Of course, I didn't realize that the U.S. State Department and our government were going to put us where we could have been in jeopardy because they wouldn't send representatives to ensure that we wouldn't have some antitrust problem."

Jerry Sanders cites the State Department's absence at the meeting, but the real culprits were the Department of Commerce and the U.S. Trade Representative's office. What Sanders remembered, but didn't mention directly here, is that the Federal Trade Commission actually opened an investigation on the meeting. The FTC didn't back off until the USTR and the Department of Commerce both verified that they had been informed of the meeting and that it was not a violation of antitrust laws.

Daryl Hatano sent me a copy of the letter that Robert W. Galvin, chairman of Motorola, sent to U.S. Ambassador Clayton K. Yuetter on March 20, 1986, with a very detailed, six-page report on the meeting and the agreements that were reached. It is the closest thing to "minutes" of the meeting that has come to my attention. As were all of us, Galvin was alert to the hazards of an antitrust accusation.

Jerry Sanders goes on with his recollection . . .

"But I called you, and you were amenable to it. I called Bob [Noyce] and he was amenable to it. I even may have called somebody else, and we all convened down there.

"There was somebody there from TI and from Motorola, too. Bob Galvin came as the sort-of co-chairman with Morita. (I later learned) it was Bob Galvin who told Morita to call me because they skied together and had been friends for years.

"Anyway, Galvin called Morita, and told Morita he wasn't getting much success with the Silicon Valley guys. Call

Sanders. And he did. We set it up. Galvin, of course, in my view, was the real key player in the Los Angeles negotiations. Not who he was being hurt as much as some of us were, but he was the guy who had a better understanding [of the situation] and had more ongoing negotiations with the Japanese. What I remember most about that meeting was that he said 'We should ask for 30%.' I mean, Galvin said, 'We should really go for a big number.' Of course, the reaction of all of us, as I recall was, 'Wow. Even 20% sounded like an incredible thing!'

"I remember that Galvin played a key role. What was good about the meeting was the solidarity of the U.S. industry. We weren't trying to gain any advantage against each other; we just wanted to have a level playing field and the ability to compete for their market and to have them cease their dumping. What I then remember was that immediately afterwards, they signed all this stuff and they continued to dump. They paid no attention to it.

"But they made the mistake of misreading the U.S. government. If it wouldn't have been Reagan as president, it might have been a very different story, because Reagan looked over to Baldrige, and the story is (whether it's accurate, I believe it is)—'a deal is a deal' is what carried the day. That's such an American thing. The Japanese just came back with 'No, a deal's not a deal. A deal's a deal until it's not a deal.' So the cultural thing to the Americans was just, you know, like Gila Monsters lock onto their prey.

"But I remember that meeting very well. It was a very formal meeting, and a classic Japanese arrangement of them sitting on one side and all of us sitting on the opposite side.

"Then we went into this other room off to the side, and Bob Galvin was pretty much the chair of that discussion, and it was a watershed event, not only in international trade, but also I think in the way we looked upon one another."

A Failure to Communicate

As later events were to prove, we and the Japanese had two different things in mind when we discussed market percentages. The American assumption was that 20% of the market—or any percentage under discussion—was a percentage of total semiconductor sales within Japan.

In the minds of the Japanese executives at the meeting, however, references to percentages applied only to the Top Ten Japanese corporations by size that manufactured both semiconductor components *and* electronic products. In other words, a company such as Hitachi might be bound by the agreement to purchase 20% of the semiconductors they needed to build radios, TVs and computers from American firms, because they also manufactured semiconductors. But some smaller Japanese company with no semiconductor capability would not be bound by the agreement.

That is my interpretation of the misperception floating around the room, and it was confirmed when I spoke with Andy Procassini for this interview project. Andy was in Japan years later and met with a high-level executive at Toshiba who told him that "We never meant 20% of the total Japanese market; we meant 20% of the purchases by the ten major Japanese manufacturers." I should mention that Bob Galvin's memo to Ambassador Yuetter can be interpreted to confirm that Galvin, at least, did understand what the Japanese were saying and promising. But it wasn't that clear to me at the time.

The Secret Letter of Agreement

If there was a misunderstanding, it was not picked up by either side during the meeting. And it so happened that a representative from the U.S. Department of Commerce met shortly thereafter with MITI in Japan. Detailed negotiations continued, and eventually the two parties drafted a letter of agreement outlining the 20% concession in language that was unequivocal. Foreign semiconductor manufacturers were to be allowed a 20% share of the Japanese market.

The letter was supposed to be a secret, and our government did not circulate a copy to any American company. Nobody was supposed to know that the letter existed. But we all knew about it and we knew exactly what was in it.

Some time later the Japanese denied that they had agreed to the 20% deal, but copies of the letter from MITI floated around and the issue was settled. We all added sales reps in Japan, MITI eased the way for us to enter the market, and our sales did, indeed, grow to 20% of the very lucrative Japanese market.

There is an interesting sidebar on this complicated issue, one that I hadn't remembered until Daryl Hatano read over an early draft of this chapter and sent me a comment. Here is what he wrote . . .

The final deal was reached in the 59th minute of the 11th hour. By law, SIA's 301 case had to be concluded within one year of its initiation, which put a time limit on negotiations. In the end, Japan agreed to the deal because they became convinced that President Reagan would hammer them if they did not. Part of President Reagan's calculus was that he had to be firm on opening foreign markets in order to convince Congress not to override his veto of a protectionist textile bill. Coincidentally, the textile override vote was set for the week following the conclusion of our 301 case, and the Reagan administration was concerned that if the textile bill was overridden, the Democratic Congress would be emboldened to try to override his veto on a bill related to opposing Communists in Nicaragua, which was an administration priority. So he had to be tough on chips in Japan to save his Nicaragua policy.

In all fairness, I must add that not everyone was pleased with the accomplishments of the SIA. The European semiconductor manufacturers, in particular, were incensed. They were convinced that we had struck an agreement with the Japanese to split up the Japanese market and shut out the Europeans. In retrospect, I think we should have found a way to involve European manufacturers in the agreement.

As a result of the 1986 trade agreement and President Reagan's imposition of sanctions against Japan in April 1987, Japan finally stopped dumping by the end of 1987. The trade agreement and sanctions also catalyzed a major change in the behavior of major Japanese electronic companies and encouraged U.S. companies to open one new sales office or design center in Japan every month during the five years of the 1986 agreement. Foreign market share in Japan eventually climbed to the agreed-upon "20%" level at the end of 1992 and was greater than 30% by the mid-1990s.

An Unexpected Benefit

Considering all of the difficulties—on both sides—in negotiating a resolution to a highly emotional trade disagreement, I think it is important to recognize at least one of the unexpected benefits that came from our willingness to talk over common interests.

In July of 1993, a Sumitomo chemical plant was destroyed by fire. This plant made 60% of the world supply of a key resin used in the packaging of semiconductor chips. Much of the remaining resin capacity was held by other Japanese chemical firms. Given the pervasiveness of chips in computers, cars, etc., the potential impact on the world economy could have been serious. Had it not been for the U.S./Japan agreement, American companies would have feared that Japan was unfairly allocating the scarce resin in favor of Japanese chip makers. But now there was a level of trust that led to a number of cooperative activities, such as shared information on resin inventory levels. This helped reduce panic buying and allowed new resin capacity to come on line before serious shortages developed.

CHAPTER TWENTY-THREE

THE BIRTH OF SEMATECH

In 1986 we had a meeting of the SIA board at the Hyatt Regency Hotel in Boston. All of the company representatives were present, and we discussed the "Japanese Problem" in general. I remember that I spoke up with some strongly held thoughts.

"We have the SIA and the SRC," I said, "but are we doing all we can?" I said that I didn't want to be sitting around with my grandchildren some day bemoaning the fact that they couldn't find work in the electronic industry because the Japanese controlled all manufacturing. It was important to me (and to others at the meeting) that we find ways to improve our competitive position against Japanese manufacturing.

The Japanese still had a significant manufacturing advantage over most American companies in large scale integrated (LSI) circuits. We were very concerned, and some respected observers were predicting the fall of the American semiconductor industry.

As a sidebar to history, an MIT professor named Charlie Ferguson predicted that only IBM and Intel would still be in business after the passage of another decade. Ferguson might have been right if we hadn't found a way to cooperate in our battle against the massive competitive push of the Japanese semiconductor industry.

Clearly, the problem was one of manufacturing. We had a strong advantage in product design and in marketing, but the Japanese, with a great deal of help from their government, were far ahead of us in their factories. What could we do about manufacturing?

The SIA budgeted $100,000 to investigate the possibilities. Because I had brought up the subject, I was assigned to pursue it. I spent the better part of many months talking to CEOs of semiconductor and equipment manufacturers to see if we could come up with a program approach to address the issue.

What to Do?

Early in the program there was a suggestion that we create an American consortium in the memory business and use it as a vehicle to improve manufacturing effectiveness. It was even suggested that the consortium could sell memory products on the open market. This idea wasn't pursued because TI and Micron were still in the memory business. Most of us, however, agreed that we needed to concentrate on the manufacturing technology side of our industry, that we needed some government participation, and we could use some government money. We felt that we needed a minimum of $200 million a year and it seemed reasonable to ask the government for half of that sum.

IBM and AT&T were initially opposed to any government participation. AT&T had been broken up by the government and IBM had been sued by the government. Both companies were gun shy when it came to any involvement with government agencies. Fortunately, their fears were unfounded. The deal we made with the government called for them to refrain from exercising undue influence or trying to micromanage the project. Ultimately IBM and AT&T became major supporters.

We formed a committee to determine what programs we would pursue and how we would function, and we got the American equipment manufacturer's trade association involved. We developed a formula for contributions from the various companies based on their sales volume and then dealt with the concerns of Intel and AMD, that IBM, with its huge sales volume, would be too dominant in Sematech. That issue was solved by putting a limit of $15 million per year on contributions.

Our "membership taxation" plan would generate around $100 million a year. We needed an equal amount from the government and we soon learned that only the Pentagon had that kind of money plus the power to spend it.

At one point I addressed a congressional committee and used a chart to dramatize the growth of the Japanese semiconductor penetration in

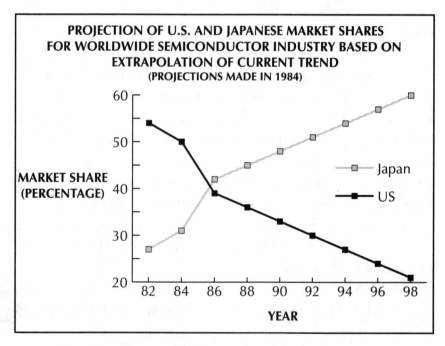

For 1999, Sematech estimates of the worldwide semiconductor market indicate that the U.S. has a 51% share, Japan has a 29% share, and all others have 20%.

American markets and the effect this growth would have on our domestic industry. I still have that chart and I still think that simple visual aids are the most effective way to get an idea across to elected officials.

Congress was with us. There was no real opposition to the concept and some of our people, most notably Larry Sumney and Sonny Maynard, had experience dealing with the Department of Defense. It came down to a need for a congressional bill to participate in the funding of Sematech for a period of five years, at a level of $100 million a year. The bill passed.

As Sematech became an operating reality, some members expressed a fear that we would be overly supervised by our Department of Defense co-sponsors. Our official interface was the Defense Advanced Research Projects Administration (DARPA) and we never had any problems with them. Under terms of the congressional act that granted us $100 million per year, the sponsorship would run out after five years. Congress extended the grant somewhat, and ultimately we found ways to support ourselves without government funds. Today Sematech operates independent of any government handout.

The only obstacle to quick passage of the bill was some intense competition for the location of the Sematech facility. Everyone involved in the congressional process wanted the operation in his home state. Texas offered the best package of incentives and we settled on Austin as the site of the facility. The other states, reluctantly, went along with our decision.

An Ideal 'Volunteer'

Then we faced the complicated task of organizing Sematech. A committee of representatives from IBM, Texas Instruments and AMD took on that task and recruited people from each company to provide staffing. Sandy Kane from IBM, George Schneer from AMD and Jim Peterman from Texas Instruments served jointly as "The office of the CEO." I was elected chairman of the Sematech board and launched a search for a permanent president of Sematech.

Bob Noyce and I had been in Austin on Sematech business and were flying back to Silicon Valley. I think Bob was chairman of the executive search committee, and he had reviewed the qualifications of many candidates. As we flew along we discussed various possibilities for the position of Sematech president. We brought up several names and then, to my great surprise, Bob said "You know, I'm really the right person for that job." My immediate response was "You've got it!"

Many of his friends were a bit surprised by Noyce's willingness to take on the Sematech responsibility, but I think I understand his situation at the time. Bob had gone through the exciting years of running and building Fairchild Semiconductor, and then had repeated his success even more impressively at Intel. But he was no longer active at Intel. At the age of 59 he was still a comparatively young man and he was spending most of his time giving talks. I think he was bored. Some of his colleagues speculated that he had aspirations to get into government at a high level, and viewed the Sematech position as a springboard. If that is true, he never shared the thought with me. Whatever his reasons, there could not have been a better person in the world to run Sematech than "Mister Semiconductor."

I found myself in the unusual position of negotiating a salary with Bob Noyce. It had been almost 30 years since Bob was my boss at Fairchild and I had always viewed him with great respect. Now I was his "boss," but only in an official, organizational way. We came to an easy compensation agreement, Bob bought a house in Austin and moved his family there, and acquitted himself with great distinction until the day he died unexpectedly some three years later.

An Impressive List of Achievements

The achievements of Sematech continue to benefit the entire American semiconductor industry. Even in the early days, there were a number of significant accomplishments:

1. Sematech created an environment wherein arch-competitors could cooperate in areas where they did not compete. This unusual degree of cooperation developed gradually and came from a mutual acceptance that all participants were behaving with integrity and dealing honestly with each other.

2. Sematech generated significant inputs to the equipment industry. For the first time, there was a body of objective comment and criticism of their products. Sematech also funded quite a bit of development work related to fabrication and manufacturing equipment.

3. The organization convinced semiconductor manufacturers to be more cooperative with the entire equipment industry, including the suppliers of chemicals and other support products and services. Intel, more than any other member of Sematech, developed profitable relationships with suppliers as a result of this emphasis.

4. For the first time, there were agreements regarding future trends in technology. Reasonable timetables were established for 8-inch wafers, ¼ micron geometry, x-ray beam lithography and copper conductors.

The stated purpose of Sematech was to reverse the trend of slipping worldwide market share. We said that American semiconductor companies could be No. 1 in sales within five years, and we made good on that goal. But it would be less than accurate to credit the rebound totally to Sematech. There were other important factors:

- Our 20% market share agreement with the Japanese allowed us to sell more product while the Japanese sales, as a percentage of the total, declined.

- Most of us were forced to drop out of the unprofitable memory business, leaving only TI and Micron Technology. (Motorola left the memory business as well, but re-entered the field a short time later.) Once we were finished with that unprofitable sector, we were free to focus our attention on design-rich products.

- The real strength of the American semiconductor industry was an ability to determine what the market needed, and to design and build products suitable to customer requirements. Because most leading-edge PC and network companies are in the United States, our working relationships with those firms and our design capabilities resulted in great growth.

- Finally, the new emphasis on design-rich products had an enormous impact on total U.S. semiconductor sales volume. With sales of approximately $30 billion a year, almost all in microprocessors, Intel stood head and shoulders above whatever the Japanese competition might have sold. The exponential growth of Intel in microprocessors was a major contributor to the market share gain of U.S. manufacturers.

Sematech was thriving under the leadership of Bob Noyce. He knew the industry inside and out, and all members respected his expertise and objectivity. When he reached outside of the industry to deal with governmental or educational organizations, his reputation as a great scientist and his informal, friendly way of getting along with people made for effective contacts.

It was a terrible blow when Bob Noyce died in 1990. He was only 63 years old, he seemed to be in excellent shape, and he led an active life. He was brought down by a massive heart attack.

To replace Bob, I recruited Bill Spencer, formerly head of the Xerox R&D facility in Palo Alto, to take over the presidency of Sematech. Bill was a very effective leader who really brought maturity to Sematech. He deserves a lot of credit for its ongoing success, just as Bob Noyce is credited with the initial success of Sematech. When Spencer retired, Mark Miller Smith from AT&T became president and continued the accomplishments of the organization.

Nowadays Sematech has some European members, and even a few based in Southeast Asia. True to the original purpose, there are no Japanese members. The organization is totally funded by member companies and there is no longer any financial support from the government.

As far as I know, Sematech represents the only totally successful, full-scale industrial consortium. It was created to address the Japanese practice of protecting a domestic market by providing major government funding and, if necessary, buying into a target foreign market. The American semiconductor industry was the first to stop the Japanese and reverse the trend of Japanese dominance.

T his book began as an effort to interview as many influential participants in the development of Silicon Valley as possible. My original idea
was to transcribe all of those interviews and publish them just as I
recorded them during our discussions. As I mentioned in the introduction, I spoke with more than 50 individuals and some of the discussions
lasted two hours or more. I have all of those interviews on tape.

Unedited transcripts, I soon realized, would not make for a readable
book. There was a great deal of repetition from one conversation to
another, some of the asides and parenthetical comments were not germane to the subject, and at least a few of the spontaneous remarks were
intended for private conversation, not meant to be published for a wider
audience. But the material presented herein as direct quotations is,
indeed, accurate.

The process of selecting and weeding out material was a painful
one for me. Many people who made important contributions to our

industry took the time to speak with me and will be disappointed to note that their input is not cited by specific reference. An even larger number of scientists, engineers and managers will doubtless feel that I missed an opportunity to present the whole story because I never contacted them.

The criticisms will be fair. Even as we were putting the finishing touches on this manuscript, I thought of many more individuals I should have interviewed, and additional chapters I should have included. But I have reluctantly concluded that a book has this in common with every engineering project I've ever undertaken: There comes a time when you have to stop fussing with it and send it to the factory. Or to the printer. I apologize to those I failed to name, I regret the omissions and I cringe at the unintentional inaccuracies herein. At the same time, I sincerely feel that this book provides unique insights into the development of Silicon Valley. Perhaps, if I receive enough detailed comments from disappointed readers, I'll attempt a revised and expanded edition.

Why Here?

Why here? Why did the companies of Silicon Valley become such a dominant factor in the semiconductor industry? Well-financed semiconductor companies all over the United States were established and running before the first transistor or diode was produced on California's San Francisco Peninsula. The list of early manufacturers is impressive and includes at least these well-known names:

AT&T	Hughes	Raytheon
CBS	ITT	RCA
Delco	Motorola	Sylvania
General Electric	Philco	Texas Instruments

Even so, within a very short span of years Silicon Valley went from a cold start to world dominance. Most of my colleagues agree that there were four major attributes, made many times more powerful by the fact that all four qualities were present—and evolving—at the same time.

Technical Excellence

The pioneers of Silicon Valley were men with outstanding academic backgrounds and a unique grasp of the physics, chemistry and electronics of semiconductor devices. There may have been others just as capable at some of the older companies in other places, but no other region had quite the concentration of technical expertise. Bill Shockley hand-picked his employees according to his own uncompromising high standards, and later, as spinoff companies were organized, the charisma of leaders like Bob Noyce, Gordon Moore and others attracted the finest technical people in the world.

Management Informality

The informal atmosphere of the new California companies was significantly different from the protocol-driven, strictly hierarchical management atmosphere that prevailed in old-line corporations of East Coast America. Age differences between supervisors and subordinates in California were narrow. Middle- and top-management people roamed the halls, laboratories and factory floors, engaging everyone in conversations and doing their best to answer questions. Everyone was addressed by first name. All employees felt they had the freedom to stop by an executive's office and deliver an informal progress report or even discuss a personal issue. (In most companies, there were no doors in the executive suite, and the offices were literally open.) In some companies there was a beer-and-conversation session every Friday afternoon, where everyone, regardless of position, came together to gauge progress, discuss problems and take on personal goals for the week ahead.

A Focus on Innovation

Companies that had never before existed were manufacturing devices that had never before existed, using technology that had never before been mastered. In such an environment, innovation was the order of the day and an embrace of innovation carried over into all aspects of company activity. One of the most important innovations was the use of stock options to reward good performance and to keep good people from looking elsewhere for career advancement. A good idea, or a good suggestion, was never ignored for lack of precedent, or because it went against established company policy. Innovation was not encouraged in the older, more conventional corporations where approvals had to be obtained up and down the chain of command.

The Absence of Labor Unions

I would hate to be an assembly worker at the only factory in town, subject to the cruel whims of an exploitative taskmaster. That's what unions were invented to address. But unions have a way of evolving into extremely stubborn obstacles to innovation. We were constantly changing our processes, trying out new tools and equipment, and shifting assignments around to make best use of individual talents and skills. It would have been impossible to move ahead with the rapidly developing technology of semiconductors in an organization hampered by union formalities. Obviously, our ad-hoc approach to our industry was just as exciting for our assembly workers as it was for us, because no semiconductor facility in Silicon Valley was ever unionized.

In addition to the four major points, several other factors set Silicon Valley apart as a unique industrial region.

Most of us knew each other and, at one time or another, had worked together. We competed against each other, we tried to hire good people away from each other, and once in a while we sued each other. But just about all of the people who started in Silicon Valley remained in Silicon

Valley for a lifetime. If we met in restaurants and theaters, we were genuinely cordial to each other. We knew we were moving toward a huge
worldwide market and we knew there was room for everyone. Yes, there
was a tremendous competitive spirit in our behavior, but we found it possible to work together when our industry was threatened by foreign competition. Organizations such as the SIA and Sematech proved that we all
had a feeling for "our Silicon Valley."

The ultimate innovation was the spinoff. A given semiconductor
company could do a good job of pushing technology and building new
markets, but there came a time in every company when collective efforts
had to be more narrowly focused on a set of formal company goals.
Inevitably, it would become necessary to tell some creative individual
that his pet project simply could not be accommodated within the current company resources. That's when some of the most entrepreneurial
people would quit and start yet another new company. People left for a
variety of reasons, some to pursue a goal of being the big frog in a small
pond, some to "make it big," and some just to get out from under a developing corporate environment. Whatever the reason, people did leave,
and Silicon Valley became the epicenter of the spinoff movement.

A good idea is only half of the recipe. Money is the other half, and
money, in the form of venture capital, was readily available. The old
model, of borrowing limited sums from a bank, or cashing in one's life
insurance, gave way to the new idea of packaging a good idea and selling
shares to outsiders as growth investments. Many semiconductor company
executives graduated into the venture capital field and made large sums
of money for their investors and for themselves as the new companies
they funded grew and prospered.

Silicon Valley: Still Viable, Still Growing

The semiconductor industry in Silicon Valley seemed destined to enjoy
perpetual growth and a steady stream of good earnings from the late

1950s until the beginning of the 1980s. And then we all blinked our eyes in wonder as we recognized the threat from Japanese competition.

Alone among the nations of the world, Japan had dissolved the separation between so-called private industry and official government behavior. Through a combination of easy financing, protective tariffs, government control over all international sale and purchase transactions, and other, more subtle measures, the Japanese government had become a driving force in international industrial competition.

Japanese industrial strategy destroyed the American personal entertainment industry. There were no American-made radios, TVs or tape recorders. Japanese automobiles were giving Detroit fits. Japanese cameras and Japanese film threatened to wipe out our domestic photography industry. By the early 1980s, the American semiconductor industry was under heavy Japanese pressure.

As I said, during the time we were beginning to think about the Semiconductor Industry Association, I didn't want my grandchildren to be deprived of an opportunity to participate in an industry that had given me so much excitement, and so much in the way of material rewards.

Now that the 21st century has arrived, I am pleased that one of my sons and three of my nephews are employed in the semiconductor industry. Thanks to the SIA, Sematech and the enlightened cooperation of my colleagues and competitors, it seems safe to predict that my grandchildren, too, will have no difficulty finding a career in semiconductors, if, indeed, that is what they want to do.

CHARLES E. SPORCK
SILICON VALLEY, CALIFORNIA, USA

A Lot of Help from My Friends

As mentioned elsewhere, some 50 individuals who played important roles in the development of California's Silicon Valley were patient enough to sit with me and share what they knew and remembered. To my "subjects" I express my gratitude. Whether or not you are directly quoted, or even mentioned, please know that your contribution was important.

Most of the tapes from those interview sessions were transcribed by Nadia Korths, who did a magnificent job of converting the spoken word to hard copy. She dealt with countless names that were unfamiliar to her, technical terms that she had never before encountered, and a lot of imperfect recordings that included extraneous noise and the inevitable dropped voice, incomplete sentence or disconnected phrase.

If I were to attempt a formal credit for each person who helped me with facts and details, I know I would leave out someone who spent time and effort to make this narrative more accurate and informative. Nevertheless, there were a few who went the extra mile with me . . .

Daryl Hatano of the Semiconductor Industry Association read several drafts of the manuscript, dug out names, dates and official records, and caught a few errors in the spelling of names.

Fred Bialek, Floyd Kvamme, Jay Last, Jerry Sanders, Peter Sprague and Don Weeden all went through the manuscript and made important editing suggestions.

George Rostky, editor emeritus of *EE Times*, was a most helpful source of details for many of the early historical segments. Even today, after so many decades, George can still get in touch with virtually everyone in the industry who is still alive and active. George read several drafts and found numerous ways to improve the narrative.

The photos are unattributed because they came to me from many archival files. Even so, it should be noted that much of the early photographic documentation of Fairchild Semiconductor people and products was the work of Richard Steinheimer. I'm not sure which photos he shot, but he took literally thousands of pictures at Fairchild. Steve Allen was a photographer who recorded much of our work at National. Don Shapero is another photographer who was active in Silicon Valley, and I'm sure his work, too, is represented herein.

Some of the key figures quoted here were kind enough to read the segments they sourced. In every case, I am pleased to say, their corrections were minor matters of dates or spellings. All of them allowed their original comments to stand as they are on my tapes.

In the end, however, reality is a personal experience.

This is what I remember. This is what I lived.

CHARLES E. SPORCK
JULY, 2000

RICHARD L. MOLAY

Dick Molay began a long career in the semiconductor industry when he was hired as a technical writer for Hoffman Semiconductor in Evanston, Illinois, in 1959. By 1964 he was director of public relations for Hoffman Electronics Corporation, at the time a New York Stock Exchange-listed company based in Los Angeles. He joined Fairchild Semiconductor in 1964 as director of public relations, a position he occupied for three years until he left Fairchild to join ITT Semiconductor in West Palm Beach, Florida. He returned to Silicon Valley in 1971 to manage marketing services for Teledyne Semiconductor. During his years in the semiconductor industry he met most of the people mentioned in this book and developed friendships with many of them.

Molay then spent the years between 1973 and 1983 as an advertising agency creative director, specializing in industrial and technology-based accounts. He left the agency business in 1983 to pursue his present career as a free-lance writer. He works in a home office near Tampa, Florida.

There was a brief period, in the mid-1960s, when Molay's PR responsibilities at Fairchild Semiconductor coincided with Charlie Sporck's time as general manager of the company, but there had been no contact between the two until a mutual friend put them together in 1997.

Dick Molay's contribution to this project was largely editorial. As he describes it, "Charlie knew what he wanted to do, he knew what he wanted to say, and he conducted all of the interviews. Charlie wrote this book just as he built production lines, factories and entire companies. He laid out the plans, he established the specific objectives and he monitored every detail of the work as it progressed. Just as he employed carpenters, plumbers and engineers to build what he wanted, he assigned me to build sentences and paragraphs. The result is Charlie's book, and whatever I did was strictly trim-and-finish work."

During the two years that this book was in preparation, Molay and Sporck had a unique opportunity to develop a friendship. "We met many times in different parts of the country and we spent countless hours discussing everything that came to mind—this book, current events, social and political trends in the United States and the world at large, the personalities and achievements of other high achievers, and his love for the unspoiled territory of the Adirondack Mountain region of New York.

"Charlie Sporck is more than a key figure in the development of the semiconductor industry," observes Molay. "More than any other executive I have ever met, he is a whole person. Now that I've worked with him in telling the story he wanted to share, I look forward to sharing a story of my own—the unique and pleasant experience of getting to know a man who personifies the very best in American industrial management."

INDEX